Through the Day, through the Night

Through the Day, through the Night

A Flemish Belgian Boyhood and World War II

Jan Vansina

The University of Wisconsin Press

The University of Wisconsin Press
1930 Monroe Street, 3rd Floor
Madison, Wisconsin 53711-2059
uwpress.wisc.edu

3 Henrietta Street
London WC2E 8LU, England
eurospanbookstore.com

Printed in the United States of America

Library of Congress Cataloging-in-Publication Data

Vansina, Jan, author.
Through the day, through the night: a Flemish Belgian boyhood and
World War II / Jan Vansina.
pages   cm
Includes bibliographical references.
ISBN 978-0-299-29994-1 (pbk.: alk. paper)
ISBN 978-0-299-29993-4 (e-book)
1. Vansina, Jan.   2. Flemings—Belgium—Biography.
3. Belgians—Biography.   4. Historians—United States—Biography.
5. Belgium—History—German occupation, 1940–1945—Biography.
I. Title.
DH689.V36A3   2014
949.304′2092—dc23
[B]
2013033115

Riding, riding, riding, through the day, through the night, through the day.
Riding, riding, riding.
And one's courage has grown so tired, and one's longing so great.

Rainer Maria Rilke, "The Lay of the Love and Death of Cornet Christoph Rilke" (1906)

Contents

Preface

I love stories, especially stories that really happened. I like to listen to them, I like to tell them, and I have heard a great many more or less true stories about the past as I studied oral history and oral tradition. In the last few years alone, my work has led me to the manuscript record of the oral memoirs of an African prince as well as those of a Dutch trader in the Congo. Each such account unfolds the story of another time, as remembered by an individual who experienced it from a distinctly personal point of view. So it was perhaps inevitable that even a casual suggestion made in a swimming pool would lead me to write this story of my own past in a tumultuous and now-distant time.

Given my professional reflexes, it is also natural that this tale about my boyhood long ago and in a foreign country, addressed mostly to listeners in another age and of a different culture, emphasizes its historical and ethnographic dimensions. I grew up during the most turbulent years of the twentieth century, in Flanders, the northern half of Belgium, a small country in western Europe, and in telling my story I have in mind an audience with no direct experience of the events I describe. In a modest way the story aims therefore to contribute to the ethnography of Flemish culture in those days.

I have also taken great pains to ensure that it fully rests on evidence, so that it becomes itself an oral history backed to some extent by written data. I want to add something to the existing historical literature, namely, an account of those times as seen through the eyes of a child, and especially a boy's experience of World War II. In reconstructing the chronology of the period I have often checked my memory against the relevant documents, be they concerned with momentous events such as the death of a king or the start of a war, or with more private happenings such as births, deaths, school reports, and family matters. Nevertheless, the core of this account stems directly from my own reminiscences. I am fully aware of the fragility of this kind of evidence, and I have been as diligent as I can to crosscheck my own memory against that of my surviving siblings, without asking leading questions. But I also have been fortunate in that three of them, at my prompting but without further suggestions, wrote down substantial accounts of their reminiscences, while three others contributed some memories about specific events. Hopefully the resulting book will provide a new and more concrete dimension to that period and correct at least some of the distortions caused by wartime propaganda that still haunt most popular accounts of the period today. In particular, I would be pleased if readers came to question the pernicious stereotypes that abound in such accounts and, more broadly, to question any statement about any group of people that treats it as if it were a single person with uniform values, motivations, and actions.

Yes, ethnography, history, historiography . . . the story of my growing up may well contain a bit of all of these, but first and foremost it is just a story about growing up, a tale to be enjoyed. May its readers do so.

Is the child really the father of the man, as the well-known adage has it? Many among us believe this to be true, at least to a certain extent, so that when a child grows up and the proverbial "man" happens to be a scholar, other scholars may well wonder how much that child's experiences influenced the adult scholarship that emerged. I happen to be a case in point, because in the end I turned into a historian of Africa. Hence some former colleagues or students will no doubt search this story for telltale clues about distinctive patterns in my later scholarship. Until now I have written virtually nothing about my boyhood, and even those most familiar with my work do not realize how different the culture of Flanders at the time was from that of the United States now, nor have they any inkling about the impact the turbulence of the times had on me. What, if anything, did my childhood have to do with my later views about the notion of culture, for instance? How about my convictions concerning the importance of language as an expression of culture and a source of history? Did my later notions of tradition and my sensitivity to oral history have any precursors in my younger years? Did youthful experiences prepare me especially for encounters with foreign cultures, and how did I acquire the self-reliance necessary to thrive in unfamiliar surroundings and to adopt the patterns that rural life fieldwork imposes, including its lack of many amenities and commodities, or its relative absence of medical assistance?

Those who know my work well will soon figure out for themselves exactly how my childhood shaped my later personality and scholarship, even though I do not dwell much on such issues anywhere in this story, for I do not want to suggest that I was somehow predestined to spend my adult life as an Africanist. After all, the same tale might just as well have led to a wholly different outcome, and in these early years of my life the world still offered infinite paths I might have taken through innumerable landscapes. Still, at the end of my story, in the epilogue, I do provide a list of clues for those who delight in such sleuthing. Happy hunting!

Acknowledgments

This book would never have been written without the input of Dr. Gwen Walker, acquisition editor for the University of Wisconsin Press. Initially, a remark by a sociologist acquaintance suggested the idea of an autobiography to me and led me to send a vague query to Dr. Walker about the feasibility of such a venture. Once I had told her the whole story orally she strongly encouraged me to forge ahead with it. But this was not the genre of book I was used to, and I rather doubted whether I possessed even the minimum literary skill required to write an autobiography. But as I wrote one sample chapter after another she kept reassuring me and encouraged me to persevere. At first she only made an occasional suggestion for the improvement of the literary presentation of some chapters, but those proved to be essential for the way the narrative developed. Later she graciously offered to edit the whole book herself in spite of her considerable workload, and in doing so she greatly improved it. Faced with so much generosity I can only say: Thank you, Gwen!

Moreover, this book could not have been written as it is without the approval and the input of my many surviving siblings. All of them first approved of the idea in principle, and then nearly every one among them helped me along as best they could. Veva and Chris separately systematically recorded almost one hundred pages of their own reminiscences for this period in writing, while Guido, Rina, Bea, and Suze contributed some of their remembrances in writing as well. Some of these texts are included as such in the book because they are so revealing about the period, and whenever I do so their source is mentioned. Later nearly everyone also provided illustrations for the text, especially Suze, Guido, and Mietje: indeed Mietje by herself came up with well over twenty photographs of good quality. All of this put more and better data at my disposal and allowed me to write this story with far greater assurance than would have been the case otherwise. So I am also full of appreciation for the care, the enthusiasm, and the work my siblings contributed to this endeavor.

Besides these major inputs I am grateful to Dr. Jos Van den Nieuwenhuizen, my friend at Louvain and the former archivist of the city of Antwerp, who provided such documents as the programs of various Christmas parties and photographs of our years together at Louvain. In addition he read and approved a large part of chapter 7 in which he appears. I also thank the various archivists I contacted in search of information for illustrations, especially those of Mr. Omer Timmerman, the archivist in charge of the papers of the Abdij van St. Andries Zevenkerken, who waded through some eight hundred illustrations in an ultimately fruitless effort to find what was wanted.

The unusually large number of readers to whom I sent the whole manuscript at various stages of its redaction is itself a sign of my initial insecurity about writing this project. The first of these were Mrs. Anne Gilbert Curtin, Professor Renée C. Fox, and Dr. David Henige. They as well as my siblings Veva, Guido, and Bea provided sometimes quite detailed comments on the first draft. At a later stage Dr. Beatrix Heintze, Professor Bruce Fetter, Professor Florence Bernault, and Professor Victoria Coifman also read the whole work and reassured me from their various perspectives that the work had some value. So did two anonymous readers for the University of Wisconsin Press. Suggestions made by all these readers have further helped to improve this biography, and I am grateful to them all. Very grateful indeed, but that does not mean that I have adopted all their suggestions nor that any of the ones I adopted have altered the story of my early life in any way, although they improved the telling of it. In a nutshell one can say that the book exists thanks to Dr. Walker, that much of its confidence and documentary strength is due to my siblings, and that the lucidity of its exposition owes much to my readers, but that none of them can be blamed for any part of its content.

A Note on Spelling Conventions

Place names in this book are cited in standard English, as they appear in the *Oxford Atlas of World History*, and not in Dutch. Thus we write Bruges rather than Brugge, Courtrai rather than Kortrijk, Louvain rather than Leuven, and Lys rather than Leie not because they are French but because they are standard English spellings and therefore consistent with Antwerp, Brussels, Ghent, and Mechlin (as in Mechlin lace).

Through the Day, through the Night

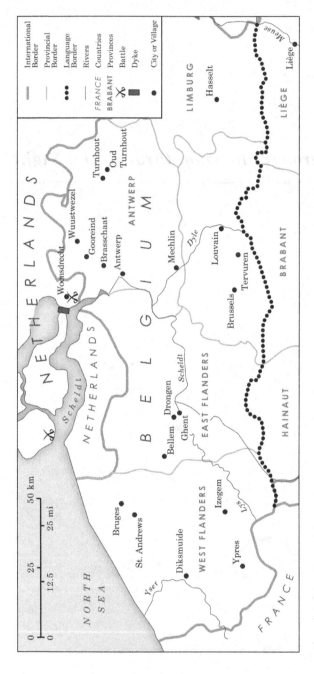

Flemish Belgium, 1933–1951

1

First Discoveries

1929 to 1933

Magic. I look happily up at a flood of sunlight filtered by some material streaming toward me from high above. Two shadowy blobs, one to the right, one to the left, are hovering over me, the one to the left twinkling from time to time with light.

This is perhaps my first memory as I stepped into my life, or rather, as I step into the memories of that life in its youth. And like all memories of my early youth, it is a record of discovery. These first memories are often mere flashes of images and feelings, like impressionist paintings or lyric poems devoid of plot. Later, though, some of my memories become more complex—such as this one:

I am scrambling up high marble steps on a staircase in a castle with two adult women talking to each other about me. One is saying that such a young child should not be allowed to witness death, while the other disagrees. Next we are in a large bedroom with a still pale figure with a peculiar smell lying in bed. This was the mother of my mother, my *bomama*, I am told, and she has left us forever to go to heaven to be with someone called Deezeke ("little Jesus" in dialect) and his angels, and where they eat rice pudding and brown sugar with golden spoons. Strangely enough, they seem to think this is sad, but surely it is a good thing. This is a memory I can date. My grandmother died on May 6, 1933, when I was three years old. In this reminiscence—two successive snapshots in my mind—there is a hint of movement and of a story, but it is only in my next memory that death first appears to affect me with its weighty permanence.

Desolation. I am standing next to nanny at a high window looking out—alone, it seems, because the older children in my family are at school. The sky is a dirty white-gray, at once opaque and seemingly endless. It is peeling, and flakes are slowly falling down from it. Nanny has just told me that our king has fallen from a rock and is no more. The world is falling to pieces. What will happen now? For this person called *king* was extremely powerful. He had protected us from evil things like this falling snow, and now he is gone. What now? King Albert I of the Belgians died in a mountain climbing accident on Saturday, February 17, 1934. This memory is therefore almost a year more recent than the previous one, and even though it is much more focused on a single image, the understanding it contains is becoming somewhat more complex.

As the memories increase in number and complexity, they begin cumulatively to define me as a person, self-aware of who I am. It would seem, therefore, that my life, hitherto merely in bud, unfolded during the mid-1930s.

I was born on September 14, 1929, in a large house dating to 1567, in the city of Antwerp, Belgium, as the seventh living child and the second living son of Dirk Vansina and Suzanne Verellen. No doubt my older siblings witnessed an unusual commotion in the household that day, just as I in turn would later see a similar upheaval surrounding the birth of some of my younger siblings. Nervous maids would be running up and down the stairs endlessly bringing basins of warm water or fresh linen to my parents' bedroom where the family cradle stood next to the bedstead, and nobody paid any attention to the children as long as they were not underfoot.

That same day my father, Dirk Vansina, registered the birth at the imposing sixteenth-century town hall, where the certificate was signed by no less a personality than Frans Van Cauwelaert, a leading figure in the Flemish movement as well as the founder and eventually head of the Flemish wing of the Catholic People's Party, the largest party in the country. During the 1930s he alternated as mayor of Antwerp with the equally impressive socialist Camille Huysmans, who is best known outside Belgium as leader of the Second International.

Meanwhile Juffrouw Maria, the governess, no doubt told her charges that a little brother had joined them. The next day I was brought to a baptistery at the entrance on the left side of the baroque church of Carolus to be christened with water and salt. Pretty ribboned little paper cones (blue for a girl, pink for a boy) containing a few colored oval sugar plums were handed out to every child, while every adult involved received a quarter-pound box each, as well as elegant little cards destined as markers for people's prayer books or missals. In addition a printed announcement without religious connotations went out by mail to all and sundry acquaintances. In reply, family and friends sent my parents visiting cards with congratulations. Among these there was one from Miss M. E. Belpaire, another eminent figure in the Flemish movement. Her wish: "May he become a man." None of this was exceptional; this was the way Catholic bourgeois families in Antwerp handled births in those days. Nevertheless it was quite a welcome into life and a clear statement as to what was expected from this child: to be a devout Catholic, a staunch Fleming, and a straightforward man.

Places

What sort of place was it in which I was born? Antwerp, an old city on the right bank at the very head of the estuary of the river Scheldt, was already a settlement in Gallo-Roman times and has experienced a long series of ups and downs since then. It was a medieval city of some importance, as attested by its Cathedral of Our Lady, the largest church in the Netherlands and the emblem of the city. However, Antwerp's heyday occurred between 1500 and 1650, when it was the second largest city of western Europe and the economic capital of the Low Countries at least until 1585. That year a Spanish army conquered it, and many of the inhabitants emigrated to various other cities in the Netherlands, especially to Haarlem and Amsterdam, but Antwerp recovered to emerge again as an economic center and a cultural and artistic pivot of the Counter-Reformation. A profusion of monuments and paintings from those centuries survive in the city today, in addition to four major churches, half a dozen chapels, and some civic buildings that date to the Middle Ages. Today it is still largely unacknowledged as a tourist center.

Between the two world wars Antwerp was the second most important city of Belgium and the largest in Flanders. It counted some 750,000 inhabitants in its urban agglomeration, of whom 450,000 lived in the city proper, including around 35,000 Jews. That was not much less than the capital of Belgium, Brussels, at the time. Antwerp's relevance, however, went far beyond Belgium, for it was one of the major harbors on the continent and in the world, vying with Rotterdam in the Netherlands for first place. As a result the city was cosmopolitan. It contained consulates of countries of all sizes, from the United States to Haiti, and people of about a hundred different nationalities were registered as residents. Antwerp dominated the diamond trade, albeit in symbiosis with London and Amsterdam. It was the foremost center in the world for diamond sales and diamond cutting, an industry that was four centuries old here and that had recently received a boost after the discovery of diamonds at Kimberley in South Africa and a little later lesser discoveries in the Belgian Congo and Angola. Income from this source as well as from the harbor and its associated industries allowed Antwerp to remain an independent financial center even in the 1930s, despite constant pressure to centralize all financial activity in Brussels to the detriment of the autonomy and wealth of other cities. Jewish financiers played a significant role in the diamond industry, and a large number of Hasidic Jews from eastern Europe in Antwerp were diamond cutters.

As to its social makeup, a majority of the city's inhabitants were blue-collar laborers such as dockers, diamond cutters, or workers in various factories, some of which were connected to the harbor, but there also was a sizeable white-collar middle class of artisans, shopkeepers, and civil servants. The fishermen, barge-shippers, and sailors formed a separate class. Most of them were not well off and lived in their own compact quarter around their church. The Jewish population was concentrated around several synagogues in two different parts of the city but without forming a complete ghetto because some of them lived among the general blue-collar population. A bourgeoisie of lawyers, physicians, and merchants such as my father's people constituted a governing elite, surpassed only by a handful of quite wealthy ship owners and industrialists. The Great Depression hit the population hardest in the early 1930s and reached its zenith of unemployment and misery in 1934, when half of the labor force in the diamond industry was laid off. But even during those dark years shipping was not affected very much, and a sharp recovery in the diamond business took off in 1937 as a result of the impending war, which caused the demand for diamonds to rise sharply because of their capacity as portable wealth.

The local political landscape was dominated by four parties. The two major ones, always vying for first place, were the Catholic party (later Christian democrats), or *japneuzen* (yellow noses) in popular parlance, and the socialists ("reds"). The liberals ("blues") were much weaker but usually partnered with one of the major parties to form conservative or anticlerical city governments. In addition there were Flemish nationalists, most of whom worked within the established Catholic party, but a minority among them had formed the VNV (Vlaams National Verbond), a party striving at that time for Flemish autonomy within Belgium.

Flanked by the Netherlands and France, the North Sea and Germany, Belgium is a small country, only a little larger than Maryland, but it is densely populated. At the time of my birth it counted around eight million people and boasted the highest population density in the world and the densest network of railways and waterways. It was and remains for the most part a country of cities, yet there were only two large metropolitan areas, Brussels and Antwerp, barely twenty-five miles apart from each other. This situation resulted in large part from the presence of a network of public transport by train, tramway (light rail), and bus of such efficiency that huge numbers of people easily commuted daily from most of the countryside into the major cities or into the two main industrial areas. Some regions of the country were highly industrialized while others remained primarily agricultural. In 1929 the country was still held to be the tenth richest in the world despite its small size, and it was often deemed to be the most capitalist one because most of its economy was concentrated in the hands of two or three holding companies whose leaders more or less ran the country behind the scenes. Wealth itself was quite unevenly distributed by region and by social class. The generally recognized major social classes were the nobility, the bourgeoisie, a white-collar middle class, a blue-collar class, and farmers, but there was much acknowledged gradation within each of these groups. As to religion, up to four-fifths of the inhabitants were nominally Catholic although in some industrial or metropolitan areas not much more than half of them practiced their religion. Most other people were free thinkers, although the country also sheltered a small number of protestants (Lutheran and Calvinist) and an equally small number of the Jewish faith. At the time only a few hundred Muslims at most lived in the country.

Although Belgium was divided in nine provinces, its administration was nevertheless strongly centralized in Brussels, where a strong current of financial centralization at the expense of other cities was proceeding apace ever since the onset of the Depression. Yet despite all of this, at the time the country was split over its whole length into two major ethnic units: in the north were ethnic Flemish speaking Dutch dialects and in the south were ethnic Walloons speaking either French or Wallon. There were even two small German-speaking cantons in the east. Brussels lay in the Dutch-speaking area, but almost four-fifths of its inhabitants were francophone or bilingual, while most of the social elite in all the major Flemish cities was also bilingual. Even more importantly, the whole educated political elite used only French as its medium of communication at the time.

Politically the country was, as it is now, a constitutional monarchy and a parliamentary democracy, but it was a unitary state, not a federal one as it is now. However, compared to others of its sort this state displayed two special features. The first, *pillarization*, means that its main parties—Catholic, socialist, and liberal (free-thinking)—were not merely parties but also social movements whose ideologies shaped the "pillars" of Belgian society. The Catholics ran their own schools; they as well as the socialists had their own youth movements, their own trade unions, their own mutual insurance companies for health care and pensions, their own associations by occupation or class, their own "homes" for relaxation, and even their own "harmonies" or brass bands, to which the Catholics added their parishes and their church. The free-thinking liberal party, by then a much smaller component of society, rested on a more restricted variety of such associations.

The second special feature of the Belgian system was the extent of royal power. The king was the supreme commander of its army and not just an honorary one. This allowed Leopold III, who acceded to the throne in 1934, to overrule his government and parliament in 1936 when he backed a policy of strict neutrality for the country and again in 1940 when he took command of the army, disregarded his government, and surrendered the army to the Germans.

Within this overall framework, politics in Belgium was in the hands of three traditional parties and three or four smaller parties. Parliament was dominated by the Catholics and socialists so that one of these two was always leading a government of coalition, usually with the liberals. But these "old" parties were challenged by the communists; by the francophone group known as the Rexists, who dramatically broke through on the parliamentary scene in 1936 to fall back again in 1939; and by two Flemish nationalist separatist parties, the main one of which advanced steadily onward from one election to the next starting in 1929. Most political power definitely lay in the hands of the parliament at large, not in the government and not in the parties, a situation that resulted in an almost constant crisis in the executive and in the general perception that the political system could no longer cope with the dire economic and international situations of the 1930s.

The two main political issues in the country during that decade were the lure of strong leadership as an alternative to a parliamentary democracy that had obviously failed to overcome the Depression, and the so-called linguistic question when Flemish nationalists wanted to have Dutch declared as the sole official language in their part of the country and equal to French at the national level and in Brussels. The Rexists addressed the first problem, attacking the parliamentary system whenever possible and extolling fascism. Most members of the Flemish movement were Catholics and, led by Frans Van Cauwelaert, formed a wing within that party in 1936, but a smaller portion of Flemish were seduced by separatists who after 1935 also became more and more fascist as time went by.

Home

In 1567 Lodovico Guicciardini, a well-known Florentine historian, published his celebrated description of the Low Countries. During the same year he also moved into a large, brand-new house at 14 Markgrave-straat in Antwerp, a house built on a plot already occupied in part by two fifteenth-century dwellings. The front part of these was demolished to make room for the new house, and the rooms at the back were incorporated into it. That incorporation explains why the plans of the new house are too complex to be detailed here. Yet its overall layout is clear and similar to that of other late sixteenth- and seventeenth-century houses in the city. It consisted of three wings around three sides of a rectangular internal courtyard closed off on its fourth side by a wide arcaded corridor or loggia. That was the house in which I was born 362 years later.

My earliest childhood there was a time of magical discoveries of places and of people, first of this home, its household, and the immediate neighborhood, somewhat later of kinship and family. The house was one of a small number along a narrow cross street between two larger thoroughfares with tramlines. Given its ancestry it was registered as a historical monument, which meant that nothing could be altered in it without official permission. The house still stands to this day.

If home is a house with personal memories, then that house was my home, and it must therefore be described as I remember it, including at least some of the memories that cling to it in my memory like barnacles to their hull. Its front door, made of heavy varnished blond oak with a carved jamb of a fisherman carrying a huge fish, stood in a very early baroque blue ashlar surround above two heavily worn stone steps far to the left side of a long façade enlivened by three tall and undecorated rectangular windows. Along the street the building was three tall stories high, crowned by a wide gutter, above which rose a fourth floor consisting of a penthouse of recent vintage with a terrace behind it. Out of sight, the back wing of the house included yet another floor, a mezzanine.

On entering the house one stood on the dark blue and white flag-stone pavement of a short hall and the arcaded loggia beyond. Although its arcades had been glassed in, one still saw the inner court paved with cobblestones and a forlorn-looking streaky statue of Cleopatra on a high pedestal on the side of the front wing. During the depths of the Depression it was in the hallway that, as a tiny tot, I was allowed to give a big round loaf of bread to each of several sad-looking and despondent men in turn as they silently waited in a short line. Much later I learned that they were more or less destitute unemployed workmen. In this and similar ways I learned that most people had a hard time making a living, but I did not understand that this was the result of the Depression.

From the front door one saw part of the side of a monumental wooden staircase along the back of the house. The kitchen walls were

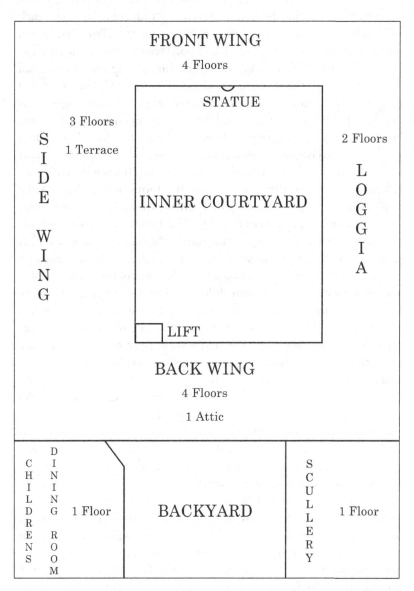

FRONT WING

4 Floors

STATUE

3 Floors

1 Terrace

S
I
D
E

W
I
N
G

INNER COURTYARD

2 Floors

L
O
G
G
I
A

LIFT

BACK WING

4 Floors

1 Attic

CHILDRENS
DINING ROOM

1 Floor

BACKYARD

SCULLERY

1 Floor

Sketch plan of Markgravestraat 14

covered with sixteenth-century illustrated tiles made in Antwerp and known as *plateel*. Like the better-known Delft tiles of a later date, each tile displayed a miniature painting, mainly in green, yellow, and brown colors on a white background. These portrayed various scenes such as anglers, willows next to a brook, windmills, fishing cutters, and tall ships. The side of the staircase was also covered in similar tiles rendered in brown and white but of much later vintage, probably eighteenth century. Behind the kitchen and beyond the main back wall of the house a one-story scullery with tiles like the kitchen jutted out into a modest cobbled backyard, while on the opposite side of the yard another one-story rectangular room stuck out in the yard. That was the children's refectory. We were allowed to reach that room only by way of the scullery and through the backyard. There we sat down four times a day to eat and drink at benches at a long table. Eating or drinking outside of the hours set aside for breakfast, lunch, the four o'clock snack after school, and dinner was an absolute no-no. Indeed I can still visualize the box of Quaker Oats at breakfast and the slices of bread on the table and hear the chattering of high childish voices. I still feel us hankering for the inevitable yellow pudding out of the mold shaped like a fish. I still remember the wait for a look at the line of comics in the newspaper after my older siblings were through with it. Even before I could read properly, I could hardly wait to see the latest exploits of Popeye the sailor or Mickey Mouse (I never thought much of Minnie). One day a large white, shiny metal box appeared in a corner of the room. My older siblings warned me that it was taboo to open this, because it was a magic box called a refrigerator. As proof a much older sister opened the door and took out an ice cube. "Look at this stone," she said, "and see how it turns into water when you hold it in your hand. Such is the magic of this box, that it turns water into stone!"

Along the back wing of the main courtyard and along the tiled side of the staircase ran a glassed-in corridor at right angles to the main loggia. It led to the stairs themselves, to two doors giving access to the formal dining room in the corner of the house, and to a large office along the third side of the quadrangle. Both of these rooms were out of bounds to children, as was a small elevator in that corner of the inner courtyard. That elevator gave access to the floors above, all the way up to the roof terrace. Most of the time only my mother used it, but it never failed to attract us if only because it always seemed to contain a big tin full of De Beukelaere biscuits.

Rarely did we enter that formal dining room. Only one child at a time was allowed to dine there with our parents. Hence, among the pool of older children, it would be Annie, the oldest sister, the first week of a new series; next it was Mietje, who was second oldest; the following week it would be the next one by age, and so on. Moreover, year after year, as one child after another grew to be old enough to be included among the elect, she or he would join the pool. However, diners there followed the golden rule that "Children must be seen but never heard," and every time our parents wanted to discuss something at the dinner table that was not intended for young ears they would switch to French. My turn to join that table finally came only a year or two before the end of our stay in the house. The room was intimidating, with a renaissance style table and six chairs under a large crystal chandelier in the middle. On one side there was a chimney with a marble mantelpiece ornamented with blue and white Ming vases, next to a large painting depicting a snowy landscape in Flanders, while on the opposite one stood an elegant sideboard in chocolate-colored wood, carved with garlands of flowers and fruit, with a marble top, under an even larger sixteenth-century church painting depicting a biblical scene that also showed a table groaning with foodstuffs of all kinds.

The huge study and sitting room was perhaps the most impressive room. Its interior was illuminated by tall windows on the inner court-yard that always threw a gently filtered light on its interior through a multitude of ancient yellowish-brown leaded rectangular panes. Its wallpaper was nineteenth century, it displayed tall shelves along some of its walls loaded with books of all kinds, and its massive writing desk next to a window exuded authority. One year when the wallpaper had to be renewed, it was found that it had been glued onto so many earlier layers of paper that the whole had to be removed. The first surprise that followed was that all of it rested on a foundation of newspapers from the time of empress Maria Theresa in the mid-eighteenth century. The two pages I received as a souvenir regulate the prices and kinds of bread. But the real discovery came behind that. Under the newspapers the walls were covered with square blocks of tooled Cordovan leather, decorated with exotic birds and mysterious flowers. That probably was their original cover both here and in the dining room.

Beyond the office lay a drawing room that stretched most of the way along the front wing of the house between its façade and the last side of the quadrangle court. From its ceiling hung two great glittering, tinkling crystal chandeliers. Its thick wooden floor was laid out in an ancient parquetry pattern, and its tall windows on the two long sides of the rooms were framed with darkish velvet drapes. As to the furniture I cannot state what it looked like, because most of the time nearly all of it was swathed in white dust sheets, like lurking ghosts to us when we managed to steal a peek into the drawing room, for entering it was absolutely out of the question. From what I learned later, its main pieces of furniture, besides a sideboard surmounted by copper statuettes, a clock, and a standing statue, were a heavily gilded wavy Louis XVIth showpiece chest and its original rococo chairs, so delicate that one of them once broke down under the weight of one of my aunts, to the great delight of some of my older sisters, whom she was always criticizing. At the far end of the room a floor-to-ceiling brown curtain divided it from its anteroom, which was itself accessible from the small hall behind the front door to the house. This usually served as Mother's boudoir. Besides her writing desk her upright piano stood here, and here we received piano lessons from a Miss Landwaard. Once a year she advertised by organizing a great recital of all her pupils in a hall called Beethovenzaal. There we were supposed to show our skills dressed in fitting outfits— mine not unlike that of a little Lord Fauntleroy. The year my turn came, my piece was to be a Haydn sonata I liked very much, but halfway through the performance, I became muddled and fled the podium in panic. No more piano for me after that, but Haydn remained my favorite composer all my life. Somewhat later my older sister Rina and I began to learn to play the violin, but only for a few months or so before we left Antwerp.

Going up one flight of stairs to the mezzanine, one arrived at the corner of the house next to a room for music practice above the kitchen. A second-floor loggia, also glassed along the quadrangle, ran atop of the first one from the staircase toward the façade of the house. Along its buckling external party wall it displayed a much-carved gold-brown wooden minstrels' gallery with a little staircase on the side. In bygone times that no doubt was used on festive occasions to play music for people milling in the quadrangle below. That mezzanine loggia led to a short staircase that gave access to the second floor of the front wing of the house. This contained a succession of three rooms. The first one was large and was apparently reserved when necessary for any child—including me—suffering from a communicable disease such as measles. The next two were small. When I was five or six, the last one became my bedroom. It was so exiguous that it basically contained only a child-sized bed, a tiny table, and a huge "antique" wardrobe. Although it was strictly forbidden, my younger brother Guido and I often managed to climb on top of this to play parachutist and jump from there onto the bed.

At the back wing of the courtyard a second flight of stairs led from the loggia to a landing with no fewer than four doors, one for the lift, two to rooms in the north wing, and one to a large room in the back wing. The first one opened into a large room that was the most meaningful for us children and was called the classroom. It was positioned around the back of the house and had an unexpected extension invisible from the outside. This space contained a chapel complete with an apse that stuck out in the inner courtyard on top of the upper loggia, an apse in which stood a small altar with candlesticks and a sizeable oil painting framed by a baroque edifice with Solomonic columns behind it, with a miniature communion bank in front of the apse, all contemporary with the house.

The adjacent room, called the classroom, was the place where we grew up when we were not at school. Here we did our homework at a few children's desks and played on the floor. Here, too, we learned to read, pasted images found inside chocolate bars—Martougin, or was it Jacques?—into appropriate albums, started stamp collections, and looked at the pictures in the weekly newsmagazine *Ons volk ontwaakt* [Our people wakes up].

One of the two other doors facing the staircase on the landing led to a set of bedrooms in the corner of the house, one of which was large enough to be ideal for laying out the track of a model railway, and the other door led to a very large master bedroom in the side wing of the house. This was where I and all my younger siblings were born. The family cradle with its tent of tulle stood next to the parental bed, and my first memory—the flood of sunlight through filmy fabric—probably refers to the view from that. After our first year we children entered that room only when we were sick and had to be checked by the family doctor, for in those days physicians still made house calls. In my mind's eye I still see a huge bald-pated Dr. Swerts looming over me as I waited for what was certain to be his unpleasant verdict.

From the landing with all those doors a narrow, steep spiral staircase also led to the next floor and beyond as far as a tiny platform on the roof. This was the remnant of what had been one of those lookout towers, called *pagaddertorens*, that were once quite common in Antwerp. From up there one espied the traffic on the river Scheldt so that when a ship in which one was interested sailed into harbor one could either announce its arrival or more likely try to turn that information into profit on the commodity exchange nearby. In our time we merely used the staircase to reach the next floor up where there were bedrooms for my elder siblings and for the governess, as well as a studio for my father along the street and in the side wing. But because the younger children were not supposed to go up there, I remember little about it all. My strongest memory of that floor concerns an image on the cocoa tin (Droste) in the room of the governess. It represented a lady in Dutch folkloric costume holding a tin in her hand ornamented with the same image of the same lady on it holding a tin with the same image . . . and so on. I squinted and squinted but could not find out whether this succession of ever smaller ladies went on and on forever into infinity or whether it stopped at some point. On the same floor in the back wing of the house next to two bedrooms for maids and just under the roof lay the bathroom where I was regularly washed by the governess. That is, oddly enough, the place where I seem to have learned my basic prayers by rote, or perhaps I merely had to recite them there as proof that I knew them.

Then on top of the house over the side wing lay a roof terrace. Six-foot-high railings separated it from the void of the inner courtyard and a six-foot-high wall topped with barbed wire bordered it along the party wall with our neighbor. The terrace space was closed on the front wing side by a penthouse with an anteroom and a painting studio for my mother next to it. Its windows on the street side disclosed the massive late medieval tower of St. Jacobs (St. James), rising as a rock above endless waves of restless roofs, a sight that Mother never tired of painting. All the furniture there, one table excepted, was crafted out of exotic varnished bamboo and stood on what looked like a bamboo floor mat. It is here that I spent countless hours practicing calligraphy while Mother painted until she eventually determined that I could write legibly, if not elegantly. On the back wing the terrace bordered on the gable of an attic one could enter by a little door. Apples for the winter as well as potatoes were stored there so that the attic always seemed to be perfumed with their mixed scent. Again this place was out of bounds to the extent that I never managed to roam around there. It was here under the roof hidden in the straw insulation above the bathroom that father once found a tin chalice and several engraved tin dishes hidden in 1798 or shortly thereafter in the context of the *boerenkrijg*, a short guerilla war fought "for altar and hearth" against the godless French revolutionaries who were occupying the country. They were used no doubt for clandestine masses in the house chapel below.

When the weather was mild the terrace that we entered by way of the spiral staircase became our outside playground—always under adult supervision. For us it was the most enchanting part of home, and we often longed to be there, but it was well guarded, and we never managed to sneak up there by ourselves. Here one could look up at the infinite sky and its traveling sun. On one side the well over three-hundred-foot-tall spire of Antwerp's cathedral rose into the sky above the then brand-new squat skyscraper, the Boerentoren (farmer's tower), which we were told was the first tall building in Europe and an expression of the financial power of the Flemish farmers' league (*boerenbond*). Here too we often enjoyed the captivating dances and airs of the carillon during the warm months but rarely the solemn call of the grand bell named Carolus after Charlemagne, which had been a gift of emperor Charles V. It was on this roof that one day there suddenly appeared an undreamed splendor, a regal gift from our uncle Theo, the one who was always far away in legendary countries such as Persia. It was a shiny red car to be pedaled all around that playground by each of us in turn.

But the roof terrace was not the most mysterious place at all. That honor belonged to the cellars under the main staircase, a place that I had been told erroneously was the abode of long departed inhabitants of the house. The cellars were strictly out of bounds, and as a child I very rarely was allowed down there. But later as a gullible adolescent I did go down—and found what I thought were several ceiling-high bulky sarcophaguses occupying the whole center of the cellar space, which I assumed contained the coffins of seventeenth-century masters of our home. In fact, there were none. There were only cellars under the three wings of the house, and what I had taken as the filled-up center of the cellar space was simply the unexcavated soil below the inner courtyard and the loggia space!

All of this, then, was our home, except during the summers. For as long as I can remember a bus would halt in front of our door one day around mid-July and swallow us all—children, governess, a maid or two, and parents—as well as mountains of bales and packages. Once everyone was settled in, off we went for a trip of almost an hour traveling about thirteen miles or so along a crowded highway to a cottage called Meezennestje, "the little titmice nest," that was our vacation home for the next six weeks or so. The place lay near one end of the main street of a village called Gooreind, almost directly opposite the smithy and close to the church that faced the end of the main street. There was nothing exceptional about this at the time. By the 1930s the proposition that periodical returns to nature and to the great open air were absolutely necessary for children's health had become accepted dogma, especially in large, often polluted cities such as Antwerp.

Indeed I also remember seeing long city trams crammed with children's faces in every window streaming by toward official playgrounds in the countryside—thanks, we were told, to the initiative of our aunt Torty (Hortense). Actually this and related initiatives were the product of charitable institutions such as the city's public assistance program or the Catholic charity Caritas Catholica, in both of which our Torty played a prominent role. We were not told, however, how closely linked such programs were to the general Depression. Nor could adults then, even our aunt Torty, realize that such charitable initiatives heralded the creation of the welfare state after the war.

Whatever the reason for being there, we greatly enjoyed that cottage. Some years we spent the Easter holiday there as well, and I still see myself as a three- or four-year-old tot high on a swing in the backyard on a Holy Saturday looking out in the deep sky for the bells of the church returning from Rome laden with Easter eggs for us, according to the tradition. And then suddenly there came this great noise from the church as its bells joyously began to clamor and ring all around. Finding eggs would not be long now. Even today the magic of that cottage is still there. Whole galleries of mental images still spring to mind when the cottage is mentioned: in the kitchen the cook Veronica's gay Hungarian ribbons fluttering in the wind, as she was pouring out glasses of lemonade from a large bottle with a colorful marble as a stopper, or giving us a taste of green paprika while babbling all the while in an utterly incomprehensible language; a huddle of children at night around a lantern during a raging thunderstorm; the smithy, where sparks were flying around the men with leather aprons who shoed a great ungainly horse as the burning smell of hooves filled the shed; the small church with its gaudy plaster saints, especially that of martial black St. Maurice in Roman uniform standing against a pillar in the back; and a mighty tree rending the sky in its fall as a great cry rang out when it crushed one of the lumberjacks. Then there were the first revelations of nature untamed: flaming gorse on a miniature dune; iridescent beetles; ants endlessly scurrying stuff around; arrogant flowers flaunting their bees and powerful scents; a juniper berry bush and its velvety berries that could be made into a magic adult drink, called *jenever* or gin. There I learned to ride a bicycle in the back yard, as well as learning the tragic story of Humpty Dumpty of the little brick wall that bordered it.

Family and Household

Families are important. But families are not always of the same importance everywhere. Their importance in a society varies by status, social class, and prosperity. Hence the notion of family has its own history. In Belgium between the wars family was still of great importance, especially for the nobility, but also among farmers and among the middle class, rural or urban. It meant less, however, to many poorer blue-collar workers. The estimated strength and reputation of a family was the outcome of many variables, among which demographic size, territorial dispersion, wealth, religion, and reputation were perhaps the most important ones. In the public domain Belgian laws and Roman canon law defined an informal ranking of family ties in the context of name, inheritance, marriage, and degree of aristocracy.

In daily life the complexity of kinship and family already appears in the names that labeled a newborn's identity. I was officially Jan Maria Jozef Emiel Vansina, in which Vansina referred to all kin linked through my father's line. Jozef and Emiel referred to family members in my mother's paternal line, a line named Verellen. The first was the name of my godfather and a cousin of my mother, and the other commemorated a long-since-deceased mother's brother. There were no names available on my father's line because his effective family was small, and the available names had already been used for my older siblings. My first name, Jan, one of the most common names in the Netherlands, referred vaguely to more distant members of both sides of the family, but it was in reality my parents' own choice, independently of the family, just as had been the case for the first names of all but my three oldest siblings. As to the first middle name, Maria, that was a pious addition made by my mother, who consecrated all her children to the Virgin Mary.

One's family is not just an institution. It is also the outcome of a long process of learning as a young child meets more and more of his or her relatives. I recognized my *mama* from the start and soon afterwards my *papa* as attested by the remembrance of his twinkling glasses above me as seen from my cradle. That was well before I understood their place on the genealogical tree and even longer before I knew who they were in terms of the outside world and then much longer before I began to sense who they "really" were. Many decades of my life would pass before I achieved that kind of insight.

Among the first things the infant Jan had to learn were distinctions between the members of the household who interacted with him daily. Were they family or not? Did they exercise authority? Were they more or less equals? Julie the cook was the absolute despot of the kitchen, but she was not family, nor was her aide, the daily, nor were the two upstairs maids with whom I had very little contact. Even the children's governess, Miss Maria, the foremost figure in our early life, was not family. Yet she exercised authority over us, at least in all routine matters, but then her authority was only delegated by Mother, the quintessence of family. Miss Maria was a niece of the parish priest in Bertem, a rural village near Louvain. As overseer of all the children she also acted as a nanny for the younger ones like me. My elder sisters chafed under her despotic rule, dubbed her "the dragon," and often complained about her. We, the younger children, knew only that she was strict, and we soon learned not to count on her for any consolation or sympathy, but most of the time she was fair. So as long as we did what she wanted, she was satisfied.

But eventually in early 1937 Miss Maria overstepped the boundaries of her authority and was dismissed for mercilessly beating the youngest baby, Veerle, who was just twenty months old. She only ceased when Mietje, the oldest child around at the time, attacked her. She was replaced by Eva Krysiak, a lively seventeen-year-old, barely a year older than my oldest sibling Annie. I soon learned that she was Polish—her red and white ribbons were different from those of Veronika—but unlike my older sisters I never learned anything about her past. She was the illegiti-mate child of a Polish count and had been raised in a convent until a year before she joined our household. She loved to tell us stories, mostly about her country, its colorful folk dances, its special saints, some of its folk tales and so on, and she captivated us. She had a special devotion to the image of the Child Christ of Prague as ruler of the world. This was a waxen figure under a glass bell dressed in the richest and stiffest brocades, wearing a huge golden crown with many points, and holding a globe and a marshal's staff in its hands. True, she taught us far less by rote than Miss Maria had, but she was fascinating and we all enjoyed ourselves much more.

Siblings were different. Among them I first learned to recognize my equals, that is, those who were closest to me in age and with whom I played. It took somewhat longer to recognize the older ones, and it was especially difficult to acknowledge my two oldest sisters as siblings. They were misses, six and eight years older than I, and we smaller children did not often see them. It would be only much later that I became well acquainted with them. Nevertheless, just as Miss Maria coached us to recite our daily prayers until we knew them back and forth, she drilled us to rattle off the names off all the living children in order of birth on the fingers of both hands: Annie, Mietje, Veva, Bea, Chris, Rina, Jan, Guido, Nico, Suze. Beyond ten fingers I had become old enough to add Veerle and Marleen to the list, when they came on board, especially as I was Veerle's godfather. But the notion of family first really entered my head as the result of a quarrel when I was five or six. Chris, my older brother, belligerently proclaimed one day that as the oldest of the boys he was "the head of all the children" and not my oldest sister Annie. The older girls just ignored him, but I was furious about this question of precedence: Why would seniority make him more privileged than any other child? Miss Maria explained that he carried the family name and according to her would be responsible for the family's reputation in the future. No one but Chris believed her, but the notion of family stuck.

The whole household, family or not, was ruled over decisively by my mother Suzanne Verellen (1895–1990). She was a small, well-proportioned, beautiful lady with the most wonderful blonde hair. What struck me most about her was a boundless energy, a sometimes surprising generosity, flights of optimism and enthusiasm tempered with prudence and common sense, and, once her mind was made up, an unexpected firmness in carrying out her decisions.

Born in a street nearby our home as the eldest daughter of a very wealthy industrialist, she was placed after primary school in a fashionable French-speaking boarding establishment in Brussels, run by the inevitable nuns. There she was to be educated as a charmingly mannered lady ready to take a worthy place in high society. However, she was not well suited by temperament, and she was also far too intelligent to be content with that kind of future. So once back home her father sent her in 1913 to a school in Wales for a year to become fluent in English. He planned to follow this up with another year in Germany, but World War I intervened. Meanwhile she had developed a deep interest in literature and the arts, especially the visual arts, and she resolved to become a proper painter. Her parents allowed her first to enroll at the academy of fine arts in Antwerp and then at its counterpart in Amsterdam. Thus she became a talented painter in the line of the north German expressionists, especially Nolde. Yet she chose not to pursue a painting career and exhibited her work only once or twice. Mother first met Father several years before the war when they were both taking dancing lessons, and after the war was over they married. They went on a honeymoon to Italy and spent two and a half months in what was then a prerevolutionary country, going from city to city and from museum to museum studying art. As a result they both became thoroughly knowledgeable about Italian art, while Mother also acquired a solid reading knowledge in the language. After their return they settled down, and soon she was absorbed in babies and running a family. Of course, as a small child I knew nothing about any of this. I only knew that I adored her. It would only be as time went by that I gradually began to discover more and more who Mother actually was.

Even as young children we were well aware that Father was a public figure in Flemish literary and artistic circles, because his portrait in a soldier's uniform was one of the set of *Vlaamse koppen* or Flemish Thinkers (literally *kop* means "head"), a celebrated collection of picture cards of writers that had already been popular well before World War I. Soon after 1920 Dirk Vansina, in his capacity as the foremost poet of World War I, was added to the set of images. The original publication and the success of the venture in the twenties is best understood in the light of the fact that all advanced schooling at the time was still in French. Yet the writers in that set of cards showed that Dutch was just as efficient as French to express complex thought or poetry and that intellectuals could express themselves in Dutch despite the handicap of a French education. Nevertheless the success of the series betrayed a lingering inferiority complex among its customers. In 1929 and 1930 two enlarged new editions of the photo portraits followed. By the time we were in the third or fourth grade we had learned to declare proudly to anyone who asked that our father was a writer. It would, however, take many years before we became aware of why he was so well known, especially among Flemish Catholics.

The poet, essayist, and painter Dirk Vansina (1894–1967) was born in Antwerp, again, only a street or so away from our later home. He was the only son of parents whose unusual and then flourishing business— almost unique in the country—was to produce artistic flags and banners. These were flags embroidered with the figures of saints, scenery, slogans, and emblems, all according to the patron's wishes. Although they were ordered by all sorts of civic groups, including the descendants of the old guilds or the main brass bands linked to more modern associations, the main customers were churches and their confraternities. Hence the business also produced rich church vestments and altar linen. It was flourishing, and his parents firmly intended him to take it over. Hence, after high school at St. Jan's Berchmans College, they agreed to let him attend the academy of fine arts, mainly because it made good business sense. It was out of the question that he might enroll at any university. In any case in those days a secondary education with French as the language of instruction was generally considered to be more than enough. The argument that Father was a "natural" intellectual was irrelevant. So after high school he became a lifelong autodidact. In any case World War I soon intervened. He volunteered and spent most of the war in the foremost trenches laying telephone lines for his mortar unit, often in no-man's land.

The war marked him forever. The outrageous behavior of Francophone officers toward their Flemish troops turned him into an ardent Flemish nationalist, the suffering and the dying he witnessed turned him into an ardent Catholic, and he sublimated the whole experience into poetry. By war's end he was acknowledged as its foremost Flemish poet. After 1918 he first helped revive *Dietsche Warande en Belfort*, Flanders' leading literary journal, joined the Pelgrim (Pilgrim) movement practically from its foundation in 1925, and became the editor of its journal of the same name. The Pelgrim was a movement of influential Flemish writers and artists who wanted to promote a modern Catholic-Flemish art and to give it the place that they felt it deserved in Belgium's overall cultural life. In practice the group fought for a more meaningful Catholicism against the then ubiquitous and officially sanctioned devotional sentimentality, for a decisive break with the tyranny of the official neogothic, and for an intellectual emancipation of Flemish culture from French dominance. The movement inspired Father's paintings, most of which dealt with religious themes, and it absorbed many of his literary endeavors as well.

Those were the activities that had made him one of the "Flemish Thinkers." But in addition he was also associated with an activity of a more political nature called the IJzerbedevaart (pilgrimage to the Yser River). Started by a committee of Flemish veterans in 1920, it soon became one of the major manifestations of the whole Flemish movement and was violently opposed at all times by Belgian chauvinists of all stripes. The IJzerbedevaart was an annual pilgrimage to the trenches organized to commemorate the fallen Flemish soldiers in World War I. Its slogan was "Never again war, autonomy and God's Peace" and the motto was "All for Flanders, Flanders for Christ." As a prominent war veteran he was involved from the inception of the movement long before the inauguration of a commemorative tower, in the shape of a cross at Kaaskerke in 1930, but he was only marginally engaged because he stood aloof from involvement in any political party or movement.

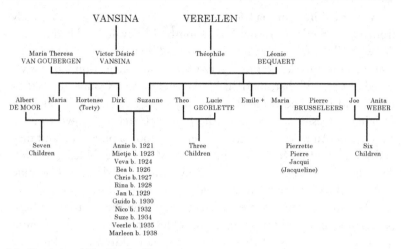

VANSINA				VERELLEN			

Maria Theresa VAN GOUBERGEN	Victor Désiré VANSINA			Théophile	Léonie BEQUAERT		

Albert DE MOOR	Maria	Hortense (Torty)	Dirk	Suzanne	Theo	Lucie GEORLETTE	Emile +	Maria	Pierre BRUSSELEERS	Joe	Anita WEBER

| Seven Children | | Annie b. 1921 Mietje b. 1923 Veva b. 1924 Bea b. 1926 Chris b. 1927 Rina b. 1928 Jan b. 1929 Guido b. 1930 Nico b. 1932 Suze b. 1934 Veerle b. 1935 Marleen b. 1938 | | Three Children | | Pierrette Pierre Jacqui (Jacqueline) | | Six Children |

The Vansina and Verellen families

For his parents his literary and artistic endeavors were just a sideshow, and he duly took over the shop in 1930, just when the Depression began to ruin the business. The demand for artistic flags or vestments dwindled to a trickle as women in religious orders began to produce most of what was required for the religious in cheap materials adorned with simple stitched motifs, while flags and the like for lay associations were now often crafted out of plain cotton cloth and decorated in stenciled appliqué by ladies among the members. Despite various attempts at diversification the shop did less and less well as time went by, and Father also began to sell art books and a variety of devotional items.

It is interesting to observe that while both my parents were born in Antwerp, only one of my grandparents was, an observation that corroborates general figures about the high levels of immigration into the city toward the close of the nineteenth century. Perhaps as a consequence of their departure from the settlements of their close kin, both of my grandfathers became founders of new branches of their families. As far as I was concerned, at least, they were true mythical founding figures. I never met my mother's father or my father's mother, I only saw my mother's mother on her deathbed, and while I only dimly remember meeting my paternal grandfather once, it is only his funeral that springs vividly to mind. As a result, for me meaningful family has been defined as the sum of their descendants only, and even so not all of them.

Victor Désiré Vansina (1862–1937), my grandfather, came originally from a large family in Kessel-Lo, a suburb of Louvain, and had broken ties with all the family groups—we may call them lineages—of his relatives in Louvain. So we knew very little about them. Bonpapa, as we called our grandfather, married Maria Theresa Van Goubergen (1862–1937), and they had three children: my aunt Maria, my father Dirk (originally Désiré after Grandfather), and Hortense, known to us as aunt Torty. Aunt Maria married Albert de Moor, a physician, and they had seven children (Piet, Jan, Françoise, Mia, Jackie, Noella, André). They lived only two streets or so away from us, and hence I became acquainted with them at an early age.

I became suddenly aware of their existence on the occasion of Bonpapa's funeral when I was seven. As the oldest of his three children, aunt Maria de Moor insisted that all the Vansina children of walking age should attend the funeral and should all wear full mourning, that is, specially made black outfits that would later be useless for anything else. Despite my mother's entreaties, Father, the male head of the family, gave in to his elder sister. Mother was furious. She had to bring us to be measured by a tailor near the parish church who specialized in funerals, and twenty-four hours later she had to bring us all back again to try on the clothes. All the while she kept muttering, "*Ils l'ont voulu*" (They wanted it), so that, French or not, I learned the phrase and its implication: "Let them deal with the consequences." For the funeral we went to the church, where I stood in line, along the coffin, as a very young Vansina of the direct line of descent, to shake hands with everyone in a seemingly endless procession of serious men murmuring their condolences. When we finally left the church an unforgettable sight awaited us: two large horses clothed in huge black and silver covers and wearing a bunch of tall ibis feathers on their heads impatiently pawing the ground in front of a black and silver hearse. On that occasion I learned all at once what the word *family* could imply, and that the de Moors were family.

Théophile Verellen (1844–1916), my mother's father, was a baker's son from Wuustwezel, a village at the Dutch border some twenty miles north of Antwerp. He went to the city in 1868 and eventually made a fortune as a major manufacturer of cigars. His wife, Léonie Bequaert (1869–1933), came from Dessel, a village in the same Kempen region as

Wuustwezel but at the opposite end of the province Antwerpen. Among their children the families of Theo and Maria remained French speaking, while we, Suzanne's children, were Dutch speaking, and the children of the youngest child, Joe, were wholly bilingual. Since none of them lived close to home we only discovered those cousins years later. But later we became close to our aunt Maria Brusseleers-Verellen and her three children, Pierrette, Pierre, and Jacqueline. Some time after that we also came more frequently in contact with our uncle Joe and aunt Anita, my godmother—although I suspect that she often forgot it—and their six children, Jean-Pierre, Miel, Jo, Paul, Anita, and Jacques.

Interestingly enough, I never remember meeting my uncle Theo, who lived abroad in faraway countries, nor his wife Lucie, who lived in Brussels. I was aware of uncle Theo, because from time to time truly wonderful gifts would appear to which his name was attached. After the red push-pedal car, his greatest exploit later on was to have Suske the donkey, a true Arabian donkey, brought over from Saudi Arabia on an oil tanker. Along with Suske came a splendid half-size traveling carriage with upholstered benches that he pulled to take us children for rides. The whole equipage, however, was a gift of *bomama* Verellen. Uncle Theo's children, whom I never met, remained unknown, and I have therefore never counted them or their relatives as family, although some of my elder sisters did. In the same way, some of my elder sisters kept up the contacts mother had with her own Verellen cousins and their off-spring in Wuustwezel and elsewhere, although most of the other children ignored them.

Such situations strikingly illustrate the difference between a conception of family that may be called "virtual," which includes any relative by kinship, and a conception of family restricted to what I will call "actual," which only includes those relatives who recognize each other as such, who maintain at least sporadic contact, and whose relationship is based on feelings of mutual solidarity. When one speaks about the tyranny of the family, it is the "actual" family one speaks about. For the "actual" family expects its members in good standing to at least attend all family funerals and preferably other gatherings, from births to marriages, to eventual reunions, or even to the birthday celebrations of the family's most senior members. In the case of large actual families, such events could be very frequent and the attendant obligations quite onerous. On the other hand, such families offered more security because everyone was expected to help everyone else as necessary, either by warning fellow members about any lurking social dangers or by exerting backstairs influence to further their careers. Any family member who was influential enough to assist in the promotion of a career was honored as a *kruiwagen* (wheelbarrow), and in this context nepotism was definitely a virtue. In practice, though, my parents did not hold truck with that notion, and Father never requested any such assistance in his career, but Mother was not always wholly averse to using the influence her family provided her.

One may well wonder how my family affected my own development. I was an extrovert child, and hence I never thought much about such topics, but in hindsight it is evident that both family and home influenced me very strongly. First and foremost this particular family set up an unusually radical distinction between inside and outside. Inside matters dealing with parents and siblings were the only really important ones, and no outsider needed to know what they were, not even cousins, although they were in limbo between the two universes. Moreover, because of the very size of the group of siblings, it served as our own reference group, rather than relying on any peer group outside the family. Hence I almost totally identified myself with parents and siblings. That included a strong inclination to cooperate and to conform, rather than to compete, and a desire not to stand out. However, this milieu of siblings, while recognizing and allowing for small differences in personality, did nothing to encourage individualism. Hence my personality developed later, and then more through outside stimuli than inside ones.

There is more to say about how my environment stamped the development of my own identity and personality by the time we left Antwerp, but only after the discussion of my upbringing and education in the next chapter, because these factors are inextricably intertwined with those of family and home in making my own self. Yet there is one topic, history, on which only family and home had a decisive effect: they and only they shaped the particular sense of history that was to affect my whole career. First, living in an old house and an old city made me very comfortable with the notion that the past is still part of the present and not just a distant legacy. More importantly, the situation fostered an awareness of two completely different kinds of histories, corresponding to the world outside and to the family, respectively. Outside history was one of monuments, kings, and glory, best exemplified by my idea at the time of "our" emperor, Charles V, ruler of the Holy Roman Empire and born in Flanders in 1500. That kind of history was quite old and ended with Napoleon just before the time inside family history even started. Indeed, that history began early in Napoleonic times both in my father's father's family and in my mother's father's family, and it consisted in the deeds of illustrious (to us) ancestors: illustrious because of their daring or their economic success. Outside history did not include such themes at all, and therefore, with the exception of tales about the heroic conduct of ancestors in wars against French and Dutch enemies, inside history never overlapped with the outside history. That dichotomy was so strong that it has been my strongest concern as a professional historian: to reconcile family and social history with general history and show how the latter grows out of the former.

2

A Carefree Beginning

1933 to 1939

Once when I was three or just four I received a fascinating tiny little vase painted with delicate blue flowers on a white background, and while admiring it in the company of Mother and two of my sisters I accidentally dropped it. When it broke in two I picked up the pieces and asked Mother to make the vase whole again. "Impossible," she said. "Once broken, nothing can ever be made whole again. The pieces can be glued together, but the vase will never be as it was before." On hearing this I threw a rare tantrum and rolled about on the floor, but no one picked me up to console me or help me to grapple with the existential discovery I had made. For it was in this instant that I first understood, with a shock, the irreversible direction of time, the meaning of wholeness, and the awesome finality of death as brokenness.

Luckily moments like these were very rare, however, in my young life. Indeed, the most striking facet of my growth from infancy to boyhood is that usually it was so carefree. Looking back on myself from my present perspective, I see a child without worries. Here was a happy-go-lucky infant and later a schoolboy without much foresight, a child who took the world as it came, with only the occasional fugitive moment of intense drama as in the tragedy of the broken vase. For quite a while I remained mostly unaware that I was growing up at all. I suppose that I first became vaguely aware of it when I was taken to the barbershop for the first time "like a big boy." Trailing behind Father, I went the usual way to our parish church, but once on the church square Father pushed open the gold-lettered glass door of a shop nearby, and we went inside. There I was, perched high on a regular chair watching as the barber spread a Santa-like beard of soap on the face of the white-cloaked person he was shaving. Then he produced a huge straight razor, scintillating in the harsh light of the work station, and in a few strokes wiped everything away. When my turn came I sat very still, though this time the fearsome razor did not appear; on me he used only scissors. Later a number of other recurring events, insignificant in themselves but telling as a sequence, fostered my self-awareness of growth, such as measuring my height against the wall or growing out of my clothes, until at last I began to attend school. From then onward I was constantly reminded of my place on the ladder to adulthood.

In contrast to myself, my parents were well aware of the process of growing up and of their responsibilities in that regard. From the beginning of each child's life they left little to chance. All of us were carefully brought up according to clear pedagogical rules and a strict timetable. As the seventh living child, my development followed a well-worn groove blazed by my seniors, and progress was measured year after year by a string of achievements that by this time my parents took in stride. By the end of the first year the cradle was swapped for a small bed. By the end of the second year the child was beginning to talk and walk, and his or her first hair had been cut and kept as a souvenir. And so on. Two weeks before I turned four I was sent to kindergarten, and after that further progress was measured by scholastic reports.

Some of my parents' core pedagogical principles differed significantly from those that are now usual in the United States. Outbursts of temper were ignored. A child who threw a tantrum was left alone, with the consequence that very few tantrums were thrown. Displays or expressions of emotions of any kind were frowned upon as "sentimental" and signs of bad taste, if not also of a lack of courage. Feelings could be expressed, but only in restrained fashion, in a tasteful way, and only at appropriate times. Another rule was that children should have a chance to be children and should not be exposed to situations or questions beyond their understanding. We were to be shielded as much as possible from any unpleasantness in the outside world, including current events. That also meant that we were not taught anything about "the value of money," and whatever our age, we did not receive any allowance.

With regard to health, my parents' maxims were new then but commonplace now. "A sound mind in a sound body" stressed the need to allow children enough time to play and to play outside as much as possible. Gymnastics was much encouraged, and every child learned to swim as soon as feasible. The maxim also applied to food: food was provided only at set mealtimes, snacks were outlawed, meals were nutritious (including perhaps cookies at tea time), and a child who refused to eat the meal simply left the table hungry.

Above all the mantra that sticks in my mind is: "Do not spoil the child." Corporal punishment was acceptable, usually, but not always, limited to a slap or a pulled ear. In any event, spoiling was apparently the greatest danger facing us, and constant vigilance was required to ward it off. Perhaps inspired by the Great Depression, our governess Miss Maria never tired of reminding us that we had been born with a silver spoon in our mouths and that this made it that much harder than usual to save us from spoilage. With that many children in the house it was easy to stress the virtues of sharing ("everyone in turn"), especially with toys. Hence most toys—dolls and teddy bears excepted—were not considered to be really one's own. Indeed, many were collective, such as a model railroad, a Meccano construction kit, or a doll's house. Although a boy in the family might receive a toy railway car, or a girl might be given part of a tea service for dolls, all of these gifts were destined to be used together for a common railroad or dollhouse. Nevertheless, from time to time a child was given a small toy of his or her own, such as the tiny luxury spring-driven car that became Guido's pride and joy.

The Rounds of Time

Daily life was regulated by the schedule of the schools, even for those of us who were still too young to attend school. That schedule dictated the hours of waking, breakfast, lunch, and tea time. Indirectly it also set the time to eat supper and when to put the children to bed. While the older children were at school, the younger ones were kept busy by Miss Maria. Part of the time she taught us by showing pictures and by telling stories. In this fashion we learned to count, to recognize letters, to color images, and a little later to read some captions. In between she patiently taught us some songs and basic prayers by rote. Part of the time she let us play with instructive toys such as wooden building blocks or puzzles. All my sisters had a doll or two, and the little boys had such things as a toy animal on wheels or a wooden locomotive to be pulled by a string, but military toys were absolutely forbidden. After the older children returned from school the classroom became much livelier. First the budding scholars, sitting at a few desks in front of Miss Maria's large table, did their homework, while the preschoolers, now unsupervised, ran around and played behind them on one of the two rocking horses or in a large sandbox at the very back of the room.

If there was time after homework and piano practice were done, we all played together. Often a group of us started a make-believe tale, usually patterned after what we supposed to be real life, and then developed it as we went along. It was great fun, while we also learned a lot from each other. Sometimes, though, such plays led to some unfortunate results, as for instance the day we played emergency room surgery. That ended when our Rina ran sobbingly to Miss Maria with her decapitated doll. Still we loved these kinds of games to the point that many years later, well into adolescence, we were still playing "Old Belgians," based on those delightful if reprehensible heathen ancestors who, according to a well-known school text, spent their time carousing, wassailing (with weak "war tea"), shooting dice, and taking part in similar unspecified mischief.

On Wednesday (for boys) or Thursday (for girls) afternoons we were free. It was apparently unthinkable that boys and girls in Catholic schools would have the same half-day off during the week, although on Saturday that was all right because the scholastic weekend started Saturday at noon. Such half-days called for a different routine. First the students did their homework, and then, weather permitting, all those who were old enough to walk went on an outing under adult supervision. That included activities such as going to the swimming pool, visiting the zoo, or watching the ever-changing marine life at the river Scheldt. Sometimes one or two of us were also allowed to accompany an adult to the great department stores. Such excursions were always the highlights of the week and the source for much discussion at home.

Sundays were wholly different. Then Mother would take all of us who could walk to St. Carolus Borromaeus, our parish church. This weekly trip was a genuine learning experience that left me with a bundle of memories. The trip ended on a large peaceful square, a space that particularly illustrates what I mean by "learning experience." On entering this square, often alive with strutting pigeons, one's eye was drawn to a fountain before the statue of a seated man in front of the city library, a seventeenth-century building of neoclassical style that occupied the whole opposite and left sides of the square to its entrance. The seated man was Hendrik Conscience, and a legend underneath proclaimed, "He taught his people to read." That was perfectly true. He was the first and the most beloved nineteenth-century novelist in the southern Netherlands, and his stories were a strong incentive for many to learn to read. His most celebrated work is *The Lion of Flanders*, a historical romance about Flemish resistance to the French in medieval times, and it resonates with nationalistic sentiments. Although written in a quaint and artificial Dutch idiom, its appeal was such that my three little sisters, for instance, reread that book so many times that they were able to converse in its bombastic and funny idiom and to pepper their remarks with hilarious quotations from it.

On the near side to the left as one entered the square, and opposite the statue of Conscience, rose the wide baroque façade of St. Carolus Borromaeus, with its majestic gesticulating saints and busy architectural decor around a prominent IHS in the center. In former times St. Carolus Borromaeus had been the church of the Jesuits, and IHS was their mark. The founder of the Society of Jesus, better known as the Jesuit Order, adopted these three letters, a Greek monogram for "Jesus," as its seal. The façade, allegedly designed by the great painter Rubens himself, gave entrance to a basilica with a wide vaulted nave, flanked by a smaller aisle surmounted by a gallery on each side. On entering the sanctuary attention is drawn to a colossal triumphal baroque structure in the apse opposite the entrance. It rises behind the main altar, bristling with architectural features including twisted columns, animated statues, and a large central painting depicting the raising of the cross, all surmounted by a great IHS seal in the vault. Below a profusion of glittering gold and candlelight focuses one's gaze on the main altar.

In front of this holy cliff we watched in awe as the sacred theater of High Mass on Sundays unfolded itself in a whirl of incense, rich vestments, and incantation, even though as small children we could only follow its progress through the chinks between the bodies of the worshippers seated in front of us. Yet we used to sit in the first rows, usually just in front of the monumental pulpit. Carried by a huge wooden lady representing the church triumphant and surrounded by various symbols, the pulpit was surmounted by an even higher soundboard rife with trumpets and rioting angels. When the sermon was preached a cascade of words fell on us from those heights, boring us to tears because it was completely beyond our ken. So we became restless and looked for distractions around us. One Sunday I managed to push my head out between the rungs at the back of my chair, but when I wanted to retract it, I could not do so and set up a howl. It took my blushing mother pulling on one side and an older sibling pushing on the other to get that head back out, albeit at the cost of chafing my ears to a beet-red hue.

Beyond the Sundays there were the truly memorable days, the succession of which made us first aware of the passage of time. For us children the year was ushered in by the return to school around September 1. It was an exciting day for those of us who went to school with fresh clothes, new books and pencils, a new classroom, and sometimes a new school altogether, while for the tots it only signaled a return to winter routine.

By then we already were looking forward to December 6, the feast of St. Nicholas, the children's friend. We knew all sorts of things about him and had never heard about any Santa Claus. Our St. Nicholas was a regular saint. He was the patron of sailors as well as of children, and not far from our home he had his own medieval chapel next to his secluded little square around a pump and a column on which his statue sat throned, sheltering two little children with his cloak. There was even a puppet theater on that very square. During the night of December 5 and 6 he brought sweets and toys to all the good children and nothing at all—or worse, a birch stick—to the bad ones. A few days earlier he could be seen in some streets accompanied by his helper Black Pete, who was the one with the birches. No one knew why Pete was black, but we thought it had something to do with his job. Was he not covered with soot like a chimney sweep as he traveled up and down the chimneys to deliver the goods? On some days the good saint would also be seated in one or another of the great department stores to greet good children and their mothers while Black Pete kept order. As a small child I did find him impressive, all right, but still something was not quite right about him. St. Nicholas brought us special sweets, among which the most celebrated were his own countenance or that of others in gingerbread reliefs that could be two feet high, as well as fruit in colored marzipan, and especially oranges. Oranges were his particular fruit for he was believed to come from Spain. Usually the great gingerbread bishop or man was for all of us, and after discussing where to begin we would each in turn break off a little bit to eat, but the figure had to last for several days. He also brought a single toy per child as well perhaps as another one to be shared by all of us.

The next day preparations for Christmas began. There were some Christmas trees, but the main decoration was the Christmas crib. In our house it was customary to prepare all of this in the parental dining room out of sight of the children. Then on Christmas Eve the door was thrown open for us to admire a large altar-size seventeenth-century painted nativity, a crib with foot-high personages around it, and an ox and donkey behind it with a decorated Christmas tree on the side. No gifts lay there yet. Then even the youngest child of walking age could stay up until we all went, around midnight, to the three masses at the medieval chapel of St. Anna, next to our grandfather Vansina's house only two little streets away. St. Annas was the chapel of the so-called White Fathers, a missionary order active in North Africa where their costume came from, as well as in various other parts of Africa including Belgium's colony, the Congo. None of that mattered a jot on that night. We were enthralled by the walk to the church. Sometimes a multitude of stars were twinkling above us—the only time as children that we ever saw stars—and sometimes romantic snowflakes surrounded us. That chapel had a deep blue vaulted ceiling strewn with stars echoing the sky outside, and not long after we arrived we little ones gently fell asleep under its protection. Once back home after the service, we all received a tiny measure of wine—the only time during the whole endless year when that happened—and then went to bed. The next morning we would find plenty of sweets and some gifts under the tree, such as a doll, a teddy bear, a coloring book, a board game, or a puzzle.

The most important feast of the year was Easter, and as school-age children we were all well aware of it. When in Antwerp we followed the special foot-washing ritual starting on Maundy Thursday. We experienced the desolation, the fasting, the stations of the cross on Good Friday. And we rejoiced when the Easter bells returned from Rome on Saturday . . . and brought the Easter eggs. Because at that age time passes so slowly, the sequence of Holy Week impressed us all the more. Easter was also the end of the second trimester at school and signaled a short but intense spring break often spent at the Meezennestje, our vacation home in Gooreind.

After Easter was over, it was spring, we could play more often outside, and we began to hanker for the middle of July, which was the end of the school year and the beginning of our summer in Gooreind. There was, however, one more last great feast during the summer, a feast to celebrate the family, "the birthday of all the children," which took place on the occasion of Mother's name day (August 1). That day there were flowers everywhere as each child presented Mother with a bouquet. The children organized a spectacle, usually a short play of their own invention. There were "big gifts for everyone," such as a bicycle, a soccer ball, a croquet set, a round game, or a picnic wagon. And the day ended with a first-rate celebratory meal featuring our favorite foods and drinks (lemonade for us). This celebration was the apex of our summer and the harbinger of the end of the festive year.

Some readers may wonder whether the omission of birthdays or of the national holiday (July 21) on my list of major feast days is an oversight. It is not. At the time such days were rather unimportant and uneventful. The national holiday was only of interest to politicians, the military on parade, and veterans. We felt that it had no more to do with us than the First of May, a holiday of labor celebrated by the socialist unions with parades and brass bands. As to the Flemish national day (July 11), that was not a recognized holiday at all. Apart from the collective birthday celebration, we usually acknowledged each other's birthdays with an appropriate chant but without any further ado, and sometimes they were completely forgotten. That happened to me even on my twenty-first birthday, which I only remembered a week or two after the event.

In addition to these major holidays there were other spectacles that returned each year. The Antwerp fair around Pentecost was perhaps the acme of these events, even though we were far too young for quite a number of stands or attractions, such as the tunnel of horrors or gypsies reading the future. The fair was always a huge success with its merry-go-rounds, its shooting galleries, its strong man tests, its crashing electric cars venue, its delicious waffles, and everywhere the lively tunes of its noisy barrel organ and harmonicas.

In the spring came the parades of various associations or guilds led by their banners, flags, brass bands, and drummers, and then the religious processions. Every year two of these were really impressive as the streets and most of the houses along their routes were festooned with bunting. The processions opened with young girl-angels strewing rose petals on the roadway followed by strapping young men carrying the statues of the saints amid tall lighted tapers, and once a year the crowned and bejeweled Madonna from the cathedral also made an appearance, as likely as not in its voluminous damask dress embroidered with roses and made by our own grandmother. Then came the officiating clergy clad in rich vestments, after which pious parishioners closed the cortege. The mother of all processions occurred on May 4, 1936, when the Belgian schoolship *Mercator* brought back the remains of the saintly missionary Father Damiaan de Veuster from the leper island of Molokai in Hawaii. Stationed at a window on the second floor of Father's shop on the Melkmarkt, we watched as an impressive flow of bands, military, scouts, and civilian civic associations streamed by. Though I was still too young to recognize them, King Leopold III, Cardinal Van Roey, and other dignitaries followed as an organ point by a triumphant catafalque sailed high above the crowd.

Early Schooling

Beyond the cyclical return of special days during the year, the progress of growing up was also highlighted from time to time by memorable moments of transition when major milestones were reached and a novel segment of growth was embarked on. The first and most important of these was the first day of attending kindergarten. For me that day came in 1933 when I was not yet four. Its first intimation came one evening after my bath when Miss Maria unexpectedly displayed a blue sailor uniform with white facings decorated with a little wooden whistle on a braided cord, short pants, and a little sailor hat. I had never seen such splendor before. Then she had me try it on; the clothing fit, and I was informed that this suit was intended for me. I was overwhelmed. In wintertime these clothes were the equivalent of school uniforms (after Easter and in the summer the suits were white with blue facings), so that besides me the older children also received sailor suits that day. The girls' suits were of the same style, but with skirts instead of pants, and without a whistle. When Rina complained about that oversight she was told, as if it was a fact of nature, that "boys have whistles and girls don't."

It was probably also on that day when I learned that I was finally allowed to attend school, provided I overcame a last hurdle, namely, to learn my names and our address by heart. In reciting the names I was to begin with the surname, because that was the family name that identified a person. I had to memorize our address in case I got lost. That street name was certainly a challenge for a three-year-old. But on the critical first day of school, when I was led through the role-playing exercise and asked once more, "Who are you, little lost boy?" there came the flawless reply: "My name is Vansina Jan. My address is Markgravestraat 14"— whereupon the door opened, and I was on the street with all my other siblings, on our way to the school of the "Ladies of the Christian Instruction."

That "Christian instruction" referred to the Catholic school system, for in Belgium there existed and still exist two parallel networks of schools: an official network of "state education" and a private network of "free schools," almost all of which were Catholic. As its name indicated, the kindergarten toward which I was walking in September 1933 was part of the Catholic network. Both networks were ubiquitous, ranging all the way from grade school to university, and they had roughly comparable enrollment figures, although at the time the Catholic network exceeded the enrollment of the other one. Unlike state education, Catholic schools were segregated by gender from the third grade all through high school. To defray its costs the state paid a controversial subsidy per "paper child," that is, for every child listed in the system. Parliament and the Ministry of Education laid down the curriculum at all levels and revised it fairly often. When I went to grade school it included the following subjects: the mother tongue, Dutch, because all Flemings speak Dutch dialects; French, but somewhat less intensive; handwriting and care of copybooks; drawing; arithmetic; geography alternating with national history; natural history and hygiene in the upper grades; and gymnastics. The subject called "song" was optional, I believe. At any rate, the Ladies did not teach the subject.

To this curriculum the Catholic schools added religion and "sacred history," that is, scripture. The chancery of Belgium's cardinal primate determined the curriculum for religious instruction for the whole country, although each of its six dioceses published is own catechism based on the text of the Catechism of Mechlin (Malines) seat of Cardinal Van Roey, primate of the church in Belgium. That explains why it was theoretically easy to switch from one Catholic school to another anywhere in Flanders.

Education has always been an issue of the first order in Belgium and a live rail in politics, not only with regard to control over its content but just as much with regard to the language of instruction. On the one hand, during the interbellum years the conflict between state and church about the confessional schools remained quiescent while during 1920s and early 1930s one of the main political battlefields became what was known as the "language struggle" (*taalstrijd*). After a decade of agitation and vacillation, the language of instruction at the state university of Ghent became Dutch in 1930, and two years later the Belgian parliament passed the main language laws whereby Dutch became the official language of instruction in all schools in Flanders and the sole language to be used by administrations there at all levels. The teaching establishments abided by the laws, so that the very year I first attended kindergarten was also the first one in which schools, and especially high schools, actually began to teach in Dutch.

Given the standardization of the curriculum, the teaching hours, and the academic schedule for the whole year, one would expect that one school in the Catholic network would be very much like another, but that was not the case: every school had its own personality and ideology. The Ladies were a female counterpart to the Jesuit order and espoused their attitude toward education, although the only indication of Jesuit leanings I remember was a huge wall painting along a corridor on one side of a courtyard. It showed a large hilly landscape clad in exuberant tropical trees and vines under glowering skies towering over a sandy beach at the bottom. Looking more closely the eye would find there a few tiny gesticulating figures, most of which seemed to be dancing. This, we learned, was a representation of South American jungles in which some admirable Jesuit missionaries and martyrs were tormented by "deluded savages." All of this impressed us no end, although it was actually that desirable exotic landscape, rather than the devotional figures, that left its mark of wonder on my memory. Nevertheless, for me it was that painting, rather than the stately yet comfortable buildings surrounding the inner courtyard, that defined the school's essence.

Kindergarten was a Froebel school, which meant that it used playthings to teach basic principles of number, to recognize forms of life such as images of rabbits, guinea pigs, or even guardian angels, and to discover beauty as in symmetry or color associations. But the class was also kept busy by practicing the principles of stitching, weaving, and origami, all on paper and cardboard. The best results were posted along the wall of the room, but my efforts were never singled out. In fact, to my great shame, I flunked kindergarten and had to do it over again. I did not realize then that I was still a year too young to be admitted to grade school. The second year of kindergarten was far more successful. I even earned a good conduct card, and a few of my efforts graced the wall of the classroom. At graduation in July, I was given a large album in which my best productions were displayed, interspersed with religious images—the largest one of which naturally was an innocent child under the eye of a huge guardian angel. Today that very same album reveals to me how relentlessly that kindergarten indoctrinated little girls in the basics of domestic skills, and to what extent the boys were merely tolerated there as fellow passengers.

The Ladies, like their Jesuit counterparts, were rumored to be strict disciplinarians. In kindergarten I never noticed such strictness, although my older sisters kept insisting on it. By the onset of the second grade, however, this feature became painfully evident. Christmas was near, and a crib with the holy infant and its entourage surrounded by the sheep of the visiting shepherds was set up in class. One day I apparently became rather too restless for the teacher, so she scolded me in front of the class, and to show where we stood, she produced a black sheep that was placed at the very edge of the holy scene. I was furious and vowed revenge, so that same afternoon, before our teacher appeared, I put that black sheep right next to the crib in front of every other animal and person. Fury overcame her when she saw this, and she dragged me out of the room and threw me into the pitch-dark coal cellar. As it happens, however, I was not afraid of darkness, so rather than uttering howls of distress as she expected, I settled down, played a little with all that temptingly glittering greasy anthracite, and fell asleep. Due to my silence the teacher forgot all about me until well after school was over. When she finally did remember she rushed over, obviously embarrassed, and tried to clean my seriously soiled suit somewhat before sending me home.

But school was not everything. Leisure time remained just as important to us. Reading and looking at illustrated books or magazines remained the main recreation among children in this age before TV and for all practical purposes before radio. Strangely enough, though, I am at a loss to remember a single book I read at the time, with the exception of a passage about Siamese kittens in a newspaper serial. But I do remember pictures of all sorts, including those of cycling heroes or soccer matches. Formal diversions for children, however, remained rather scarce. Starting in 1935, a puppet theater offered performances in a cellar on the little St. Nicholas square not far from home, but I was allowed to attend it only once, because the plays were performed in a raw local dialect rather than in the polished Dutch (*Algemeen Beschaafd Nederlands*) that we were supposed to speak, and the atmosphere was rowdy. When the villain threatened to do his worst, the audience booed, hissed, cursed, and occasionally hurled things at the offending puppet. Nor were there many films fit for children. The first one I attended was *Snow White* when it was shown by fashionable Cinema Rex in 1937 or 1938. *Snow White* was at that time the epitome of an American cultural "globalization" that had begun years earlier with the cartoons of my favorite Popeye the sailor and Mickey Mouse.

Leisure time also included learning three skills that were not taught at school: playing an instrument, swimming, and dancing. We were tutored in piano or later violin lessons at home, and the older girls spent much of their free time practicing or attending music school—where they did encounter some truly raw dialect.

During winter Mother herself took us every so often to the pool for swimming lessons. The older children swam in the deep end beyond the rope while the toddlers played in the shallows. I must have been very young when I was first taken there, because I remember slipping under the rope and venturing into the deep end, swallowing huge amounts of water, and scrambling not to drown. But I loved it. So the instructor would take out a big hoop at the end of a long pole. He then let me jump in at the deepest end, caught me like a fish in the hoop, and told me what to do. In this fashion I quickly learned to swim although not really in style. As he told Mother, "He is more under water than above it, but he gets there!" We were all crazy about swimming and especially diving, so that going to the pool was one of the most appreciated treats, even more so because after the exercise we all received a reward in the shape of one or another variant of creampuff. As to dancing, on a few occasions I accompanied some of my sisters to children's dance classes. There I learned the rudiments of dancing to music as well as some elementary steps of ballet before the whole endeavor was abandoned.

Another memorable moment of transition was the day of my first communion in 1935. In Belgium and France the first communion celebration marked the moment when a young child had attained "the age of reason" and was allowed to take the sacrament of the holy Eucharist after adequate instruction about its significance and that of the sacrament of confession that preceded it. This classical rite of passage clearly duplicated and prefigured the one whereby adolescents were inducted into adulthood by the sacrament of confirmation in the faith. The minimum requirement for first communion was to be able to recite one's basic prayers fluently and to know the answers to some questions of the elementary catechism. Usually first communion was organized as a collective ceremony during early summer in the parish church. All the communicants were dressed in white, and the girls wore a veil. A joyous family reunion followed the church service. However, because we were not in Antwerp but at the Meezennestje at the time set for our parish, my first communion occurred during a special mass celebrated by a Dominican friend of my father's at the church in Gooreind. I have just three fragmentary memories of that day. First there were the white clothes I wore, just as white as the habit worn by the impressive monk who had officiated, clothes that had to remain absolutely spotless and thus inhibited my every move. Later, after pictures were taken, I was placed at the far end of the table for adults during the subsequent feast where I ate a small doughnut-shaped slice of a delicious fruit called pineapple. Then I was excused from the further proceedings and immensely relieved to surrender my clothes more or less unscathed.

It is usually taken for granted that children of this age are easily indoctrinated, and that was true of my family to a certain extent. As small children we were still used to discovering regularly all sorts of astonishing new things in our surroundings, so that miracles seemed just another discovery to us. We were often shown portraits of holy personages, and we took them to be photographs in color. Even transubstantiation, the invisible transformation of the host into Christ, seemed easily conceivable to us. Indeed, when we were told to confess to the confessor, who would listen to us as a stand-in for God, I took this to mean that the confessor was also transformed momentarily into God. When Miss Eva, our Polish governess, realized this heresy, she told us all about how St. John Nepomucene was thrown into the river from a bridge in Prague and died rather than reveal the secret of confession, and to back up this story she had a nice picture showing the saint on a somber bridge being thrown in the river and already wearing a starry crown.

A Contented Schoolboy

A third memorable moment of transition occurred in September 1937 when I first attended the school for big boys, St. Lievens College, to start third grade. The most immediate benefit of that world came from the interesting sights as we trudged along the streets and the ever-changing spectacle of their traffic. The long way from home to St. Lievens was perhaps my earliest experience of that phenomenon. The first interesting place one came to on that trip was close to home at the end of a short street giving access to the stock market, a large building with entrances leading to streets on each of its four sides. At its heart lay a covered and sunken central square surrounded on all sides by a corridor that served as a shortcut between the streets. On the far side that corridor was bordered by glass-fronted offices bristling with papers, calculating machines, huge, forbidding-looking typewriters, and ticker tapes. Most of the time the brokers were in their offices, but from time to time the market was in session when we walked by the building. Then one saw a large throng of people standing in the central square gesticulating with little slips of paper in their hands as they were buying and selling and thereby, we were told, making or losing money. So at the tender age of seven I "knew" what the stock exchange was and had learned that the colorful pieces of paper called stocks or bonds were money, but money as impermanent as snow.

Emerging from there into another street one soon reached a crossing at the widest part of the Meir, the large artery that ran through the smartest and most expensive shopping district of the city. There was always something to be seen there, whether it be in the shop windows, among the motley crowd of pedestrians of every kind from shabby beggar to snobby grand lady hurrying along the very broad sidewalks, or in the dense traffic streaming by as tramways, taxis, trucks (not bigger then than an SUV today), some horse wagons, and a few saloon cars all ran pell-mell to a single crossing point where a single police officer in the middle of the bedlam orchestrated the flow of traffic in all directions from a little three-step podium.

Once safely across and into the next street, we came to the greatest attraction of all, the poshest toy shop in the whole city, adorned with two panoramic shop windows. In the fall its attraction grew by leaps and bounds as St. Nicolas and then Christmas grew nearer. Its doll-houses with tea services, dolls, plush teddy bears, and other animals held the girls spellbound while the boys were mesmerized by a huge exhibit of model railroads running through some sort of Switzerland in papier-mâché with signal lights of various colors reflected in tinsel snow banks along valleys with little Christmas trees and cottages toward one or more stations where tiny travelers with and without skis waited. Then the railroad ran straight through one or several tunnels bored through lofty mountains with rocky flanks and glistening glaciers that swallowed or suddenly ejected all sorts of trains. At other times of the year the exhibits were somewhat less grand, but there was always something to see for children and adults alike.

Next came a long street where the main feature was the entrance to a hospital in front of which often stood a huge beer wagon whose two monumental horses were either quietly munching their oats in drab nosebags or shuffling impatiently under the anxious eye of a driver fumbling with their reins. Once we arrived near the end of that street to turn into another one, an old house jutted out into the street, a house with a single window that sported a sailing boat built within a large bottle. But it was not always the same bottle or the same ship. From that point to St. Lievens, one only met minor attractions along the way, including the entrance to a girls' school and, near our own school, tucked in among some boring stores offering schools supplies of various sorts, a tempting small shop that sold sweets.

Not that there was much of a difference in teaching: the classes looked similar to those at the Ladies, the relatively small number of pupils per class (twenty to twenty-five) was similar, and most of the curriculum was a continuation of what it had been at the Ladies. Yet to us it was completely different. First, unlike the Ladies, it was far from home, and going to school was usually fun because there was always something interesting to see along the way. Then, too, it was a school for boys only, and upon entering the premises one saw on the playground all sorts of potential playmates. And last, the buildings were more modern and seemed to be larger. That school also had it own personality. It was a diocesan establishment for primary and secondary education run by regular priests, although the grade school was staffed by teachers who were laymen. Unlike other secondary schools in the city, including another older diocesan college, this one had a militant Flemish nationalist inclination and advocated the use of the motto of the then brand-new Flemish wing of the Catholic party and of its newspaper, *De Standaard*, as a heading on all reports, letters, or homework. This motto consisted in a set of letters arranged in the shape of a cross. The horizontal bar read AvV, *Alles voor Vlaanderen* (Everything for Flanders), and the vertical one VvK, *Vlaanderen voor Christus* (Flanders for Christ), with the small *v* at the crossing point. This motto stems from World War I when it was an inscription on the crosses marking the tombs of some Flemish soldiers. Its meaning, we learned, was that God, who created everything, had created Flanders as well and hence it behooved us to honor Flanders.

Essentially the curriculum here was a continuation of what it had been at the Ladies, except that French does not seem to have been taught until the fifth or sixth grade. So at home Mother gave me children's stories to read in French to keep up the knowledge of the language I already had acquired. Among the other subjects proficiency in Dutch was the most stressed. What we were taught was known as ABN, *Algemeen Beschaafd Nederlands* (polished Dutch), the denomination then given to the official standard Dutch. The perniciousness of dialects, which so divided Flemings among themselves, was constantly stressed, and "raw Antwerpian" was more than frowned upon. Dutch was also stressed because "language is the soul of the people." Finally, I had to do my best for Dutch because my father was the only father of our class who was a writer, and hence it was expected that I also should be proficient in the language. It was not surprising, then, that I ranked from third to first in the various examinations related to Dutch. My pronunciation became excellent, and apparently I developed a gift for story telling. One day I was asked to tell the story of Noah's ark in class and developed the theme with such gusto that it almost took the whole period, and my audience was spellbound. The performance was so well received that I had to repeat it sometime later before the same class but with the addition of a whole bevy of teachers. After that I was expected always to do exceptionally well on both recitation and storytelling.

On the whole I was an honorable but not exceptional student until the fourth grade. Then our teacher, believing apparently that there was more talent in this pupil than was evident, took an interest in me and thereby inspired me to work much harder. First of all he attacked my deplorable handwriting, so that I was set to remedy this deficiency by a plethora of homework exercises on the roof terrace under Mother's vigilant eye. Then he encouraged me to do better and better wherever I could. So I did, and surviving school reports indicate that my results improved from trimester to trimester until I wound up with seven first places in the first trimester of the fifth grade, after which we left Antwerp.

Most of what we were taught had to be learned by rote almost as strictly as the catechism. At the same time, though, most teachers explained the subjects carefully and always tried to use examples that would attract our interest. The overall effect was that while we accepted the authority of what was learned by rote without question, at the same time some interpretations struck our fancy and set us thinking. I still remember, for instance, my fascination with the never recurring numerals after the decimal point of little e, which we encountered in a discussion of compound interest. Geography was especially attractive because of the cosmopolitan character of the city. Our textbook told us there were five "races." There was no question about the "white," "yellow," or "black" races because we were familiar with such people. But what about the "red" and "brown"? None of us had ever seen either of them. "Red" we could more or less accept from stories about American

Indians, but "brown" remained doubtful. Knowledge of geography also became concrete by finding the nationalities of the ships we saw in the harbors, and by the stamps we collected.

Natural history and hygiene was another attractive class. A topic such as the human heart and the circulation of the blood, or the liver as a factory of chemicals, were memorable because they dealt with one's body, and in this case the teaching happened to coincide (on purpose?) with a great exhibition about the human body that featured a life-size human model in glass, displayed so that one could see all the major organs, muscles, and nerves and follow the circulation of the blood. That was especially fascinating because children were not allowed to attend the exhibition and because it was organized under the auspices of the provincial service of hygiene, which our own uncle Albert de Moor directed. We also learned about how the metacenter of a ship's keel is built so as to right the vessel's equilibrium after each rolling wave, or the three main components of artificial fertilizer . . . but not a word about natural selection or evolution.

The most memorable thing about history was that it ended with the First World War. Current affairs and their immediate antecedents were just as taboo as evolution. Despite the example of my parents and my own best efforts, drawing was among my weakest subjects. Only one of my drawings ever received high marks, and that was a soccer ball drawn with a compass and colored in a variety of reddish-brown shades. I had no luck with landscapes or Cézanne-like still lifes, but in the end poster-like drawings of an ocean liner and a sailing ship, made according to a standard formula, saved the day for me. As to the subject labeled "song," I only remember all the pupils turning round and round on a scene and singing a militant Dutch song referring to the golden age of their navy. It was about admiral Piet Hein, who captured the Spanish silver fleet on its return from the Americas in the 1620s, an achievement that the immortal lyrics summed up with the words, "Piet Hein, his name is small [short] but his deeds are great; he has won, won the silver fleet!"

I was still too young to take part in many school activities outside of class. Anyway, when class was over Victor, the middle-aged messenger of the Melkmarkt business, was nearly always waiting at the gate to bring us back home. Hence I did not participate in any after-school events except for the annual competition between classes to achieve the best results in fundraising for the missions by gathering the tinfoil from chocolate bars or by gathering canceled stamps. This was an exciting event, because every day during such a drive the results were posted in bar graph form, and we could see how our class was winning or losing against others—even though we confused the bars with thermometers. These missions could be anywhere. In the Americas, I thought, missionaries wore black garments, but in Asia and Africa they had pith helmets and wore white. Not far from home was the residence of the White Fathers, all bearded and dressed like Arabs in flowing white garments because they tried to convert North Africans. The most celebrated missionary at the time was the same Father Damiaan who had died caring for lepers on the island of Molokai in the Pacific Ocean and the return of whose remains I witnessed in 1936.

More information about missions stemmed from elsewhere. First some shops sported little angelic ceramic figures in white clothes with black faces on top of a piggy bank. The figures represented African children who had just been converted, and when you put a cent in the box the thankful convert nid-nodded in reply. Then there were calendars to support the missions. Every year a new calendar came to hang near our kitchen door, and on the reverse side of the page for every day there was a little story. One of these puzzled me so much that I still remember it. It was all about old men in Congo who carried off young girls as wives for some unmentioned reason that I guessed was not good.

Horizons beyond School and Home

At about the age when I started to attend St. Lievens school I also began to discover the "real world" beyond the confines of home and school. Little by little I gathered experiences along other streets similar to those that led from home or school, for example along the itinerary from school to the shop at the Melkmarkt in the very shadow of the great cathedral tower in the city center. Some favorite sights made such an impression that they still stand out in the welter of memories about them even today. One of the most impressive were the windows of the offices of the Belgian maritime agency, where one could admire large-scale models of different types of freighters, including the prestigious mixed freighters known as Congo-boats. Usually one could also admire huge posters for the colonial lottery on the corner of that building, although they nearly always showed the same picture of an elegantly coiffed Mangbetu lady.

Visiting the main department stores, especially the foremost of them, the Grand Bazaar (*grand bazar/grote bazar*) not far from the shop in the Melkmarkt, was like roaming the streets—only more intensive. The Bazaar was the most relevant landmark of popular culture in the city. Nearly everyone went to that vast emporium for almost everything imaginable. It was a genuine bazaar where every child's horizons expanded endlessly as he or she discovered an almost infinite variety of products that people might ever want for their homes, schools, offices, hobbies, leisure activities, vacations, and I believe even last resting place, for I am certain there was a discreet section for grave furnishings as well. Wise parents avoided bringing their children to the well-known rooms on the second floor where the lure of an irresistible cornucopia of toys inevitably led them either to buy some toy or engage in the exercise of a heart-rending deprivation.

The customers of the Bazaar were perhaps even more interesting than the goods on offer, for a motley multitude always thronged the place. Housewives in flowered frocks, gesticulating emotionally as they gossiped in the rich local dialect, formed perhaps a majority. They were the pulse of public opinion in town about the Bazaar, and they, more than any advertisement, determined the success of its sales. Yet one saw almost as many respectable prim bourgeois ladies carefully inspecting merchandise for flaws, or cagey farmwomen in town for a market or just on a shopping foray. One also encountered a great variety of men such as office workers, blue-collar laborers, students, longshoremen, sea-going sailors and their officers, but very few bargemen or fishermen, who had their own shops along some of the older quays. And there were nearly always lost children, blaring loudspeakers inquiring about their where-abouts, and frantic mothers looking for them. Indeed it seemed that over time an observer might encounter almost every conceivable kind of person there. Black people, clergymen, monks, or nuns were not exceed-ingly rare, but truly tall Mongol-looking men, turbaned Indians, or Arabs in flowing robes were—and we never saw a gypsy in the Bazaar. Most black people were transient sailors, for there may not have been more than a hundred Africans resident in Antwerp at the time, among whom there were probably more West Africans than Congolese (most of the latter, one suspects, were people who had jumped ship). It is hard to evaluate what exactly we children learned in that Bazaar, but the goods and the crowds certainly widened our horizons beyond anything we were taught in school or saw in the streets.

Father's shop in the Melkmarkt taught us very different things about the world, especially about atelier work and about religion. When we were brought there we often were rapidly pushed across the shop itself to reach the atelier beyond. So we only had a hasty glance at the store's discreet display of a few liturgical vestments, missals or psalters, and the like, and sacred vessels bearing a card saying "It is consecrated" (*Het is gewijd*), which in commercial terms meant ready for immediate use. Once there was even a complete foldable and portable altar "for your beloved missionary." The atelier beyond was even more interesting. A dozen young women sat there embroidering patterns of figures on flags with a great variety of various colored bobbins of threads nearby. We learned to distinguish between wool, cotton, and the more expensive silk thread from Lyon that sometimes came in tiny wooden boxes. The most expensive of these was gold or silver thread, which was kept in separate boxes apart from all the rest. This was actually a silk thread around which minuscule springs of gold or silver had been wound. Even more interesting was the working collection of saints. The shop had a basic template for a saint, to which one added the appropriate emblems to distinguish the particular saints. There were emblems for classes of saints such as martyrs, confessors-bishops, virgins, and so on, and symbols for individual saints, such as the particular instruments of torture used in the case of martyrs, a book or a miniature church for bishops, and so on. I realized there that the images and plaster statues of saints I knew were not as "real" as photographs but were produced completely according to convention. In the back of the shop lay a small courtyard with a loggia on one side facing a miniature Renaissance Italian style portico that housed the shop's office. Father's studio was also somewhere in the building, and on a few occasions I was allowed to watch him drawing or painting. Thus I one day saw taking shape a nearly life-sized greenish Salome, gazing at St. John the Baptist's head against a swirling background of black and blue clouds—too somber by half for me.

Visiting the zoo was the most exotic of all our outings, and we had a family season ticket to it. This was one of the foremost zoos in the world, set in one of the most beautiful and artfully landscaped flower gardens in the country. But it was relatively far from home so that we never visited it as frequently as I wished. The gallery of the most vivid mental pictures I retained from it includes the intelligent trunks of the elephants, the haughty look of the giraffes, monkey families, the catacomb-like snake house with its boas and always lazy African crocodiles, a walk inside the skeleton of a blue whale, a rocky hill inhabited by mountain goats, and especially the high bridge that led to it spanning a "Central Asian" gully, bare of grass, where stately Bactrian camels ambled and dromedaries posed. Then there was the celebrated okapi, a sort of neckless giraffe from the deep Congolese jungle that was then a recent scientific discovery. This animal had been brought back from the Congo in 1933 by our very own king when he was still a prince.

The dinner of the trained chimpanzees was intended to be a lesson in table manners, as our adult escorts never tired of pointing out. Anyway it was certainly the most memorable attraction of the zoo for my sisters. First one chimp invited the others to be seated at the table. Then they all wound their napkins around their neck and waited politely with their hands next to their plates until they were served. When the dishes were served, they helped each other courteously without overloading their plates and proceeded to eat neatly with knife and fork. The only item missing was saying grace! The whole performance would be inconceivable today, and it reveals how unsophisticated the ethics of animal science still were at the time.

Antwerp is a gift of the Scheldt's estuary, and its maritime character has made a strong impression on most of its inhabitants. Without doubt the most preferred and the most instructive outing in town for children and for adults alike was to the two wide terraced promenades built on top of warehouses facing the main wharves along the river Scheldt. Every other trip paled by comparison, even the zoo. These terraces were separated by a floating pontoon where small ferries landed and a wider stretch of quay where the tourist boats of the Flandria company were moored. The promenades themselves overlooked the wharves where oceangoing ships often moored. There the river was about 550 yards wide, and looking between the balusters of the balustrade when still a tot, I could barely discern the far bank. The spectacle on the promenades was always worth watching. The large vessels with gaping cavernous holds were loading and stowing all manner of goods with the help of cranes on rails from a train of railroad cars or unloading into the cars parked on the railway running along the quay. From time to time several cranes had to pull together to shift spectacular and huge machines, such as a whole locomotive, for instance. We learned to recognize the vessels' national flags and many of their company flags, we checked on their Plimsoll readings, we estimated their tonnage, and we recognized the state of the tides as the ships rose or fell on the river. We delighted in finding them throbbing under steam ready to set sail as the anchors rattled, cables were thrown, and a waltz of tugs began to ease them into the river, or the reverse as they berthed. Most of these vessels were freighters or mixed freighters like the well-known Congo boats, but a few were genuine liners. The Red Star line was the most famous of these. They specialized in third-class passage for emigrants from Eastern Europe, Poland especially, to Montreal, New York, or Philadelphia. But we rarely saw such ships set sail simply because such a throng crowded the promenades when they did that we small children could not see a thing. So we avoided such departures. And of course from time to time foreign warships, or just as rarely tall-masted schoolships on official visits, anchored there for a few days so that we could admire them close up.

All the while, as the freighters along the wharves loaded and un-loaded, canal boats from impressive *Rijnkassen*, or "Rhine vessels," to small barges were plying the river up and down according to the tides, riding light and high or heavy and low so that their gunwales barely cleared the water by an inch or so. Many came from or went to surpris-ingly distant destinations in neighboring countries or even as far as Switzerland. As they passed by, the barge women were often seen working in the gutters alongside the coamings of their decks to attend to various domestic chores, such as hanging wash or pulling water for cleaning the decks from special buckets that they dropped in the river. Besides these barges, there were dredgers, ferries, lighters, fishing vessels, ocean going tugs, tankers, yachts of various sizes, and even just small sailing boats. Many city children were keen to spot and identify every known sort and variety of vessel and floating device, just as others might be birdwatchers or car-spotters. No wonder that in such an environment I dreamed of becoming a ship's captain and could hardly wait to enroll in the official school of navigation not far downstream of the north promenade. Who knows? Without a war, I might well have ended in the merchant marine.

Toward War

In hindsight it is crystal clear that during the 1930s Europe was inexorably moving toward a world war. The impact of the Great Depression led to unrest everywhere, inflamed existing political grievances, and seemed to call for fast, all-encompassing, and decisive solutions that justified the rise of fascism. In Belgium specifically the main issues in politics during the early 1930s were the management of the Depression and the Flemish Question, followed not only by a general trend toward fascism in all parties but by the rise of explicitly fascist parties after 1935.

The initial fall of the stock market in New York that heralded the Great Depression occurred on the very day I was born, and the market collapsed only forty days later. Endowed with an economy that relied heavily on exports, Belgium had been most affected by the general rise in customs tariffs, the loss of the gold standard accompanied by the devaluation of the British pound (then the international reserve currency), and the frequent bankruptcies or insolvencies that wiped out savings and assets. The rise of unemployment that followed was so dramatic that the existing rudimentary social institutions were unable to cope with it. Then the usual prescriptions of severe budget and wage cuts failed, so that already in 1931 the socialists were clamoring for state planning as practiced in the USSR since 1928, and the Catholics, following the Vatican's lead, were pleading for a mixed economy based on the decisions of councils uniting employers and labor. Meanwhile fascists vaunted the decisive leadership of dictators.

By the time I was old enough to observe what was happening around me, the Depression had been going on for six or seven years, and its most dramatic scenes of distress had disappeared. By then a modest, albeit timid recovery, led by the diamond sector, was underway in Antwerp, and hence, although I had lived through the whole of the Depression, I simply was never aware of it until the worst of it was already over. But I did experience the political tensions that arose out of the Depression. At the time dissatisfaction with the whole process of decision making was widespread. Criticism centered especially on the Belgian parliament, many of whose members were suspected of habitual corruption. Hitler's meteoric rise in 1933 and his economic successes in the following years seemed to many to prove the case for decisive personal leadership backed by corporative organizations, as opposed to the endless dilatory compromises generated by Belgium's parliamentary democracy. By 1935 such sentiments led to the creation of the fascist party Rex in francophone Belgium and the transformation of the older Flemish Nationalist League (VNV), quickly imitated by its two splinter parties, which likewise turned into fascist parties of their own. For the general public this meant mass rallies for adults accompanied by spectacular theatrical shows of militias resplendent in uniforms carrying martial drums, flags, and, for Rex, even brooms to sweep democratic corruption aside. In the 1936 elections Rex achieved a stunning victory, especially among the economically independent lower middle classes who suffered the most from the Depression. However, disillusion already set in by the following year, and the elections of 1939 reduced Rex almost to a shadow of its former self as it turned into a party of fanatics, wholly committed to the cause. VNV and its splinters for their part did not make comparable spectacular gains in 1936 but continued to make a modest advance in 1939.

Despite the comprehensive character of the language laws, linguistic tensions did not abate after 1933, because the local administrators in many towns where influential francophile bourgeoisie lived simply refused to apply the laws requiring the sole use of Dutch and continued to issue only bilingual or even monolingual French documents. One result of this attitude was the secession of the Flemish members from the unitary Catholic party in 1936 and the formation of their own wing of the party. Another was continuing agitation among militants across the whole spectrum of the various Flemish political parties, from moderate cultural autonomists to the most virulent nationalists.

In contrast to the economic trends, these political developments had repercussions that even small children such as we witnessed. I was too young still in 1936 to be aware of the elections, but the agitation in the streets that began a year later certainly caught my attention, particularly the reports about the nightly antics of Florimond ("Flor") Grammens and his merry band in 1937 and 1938. Grammens was outraged by the impunity with which local authorities flouted the language laws. The bilingual street names were one manifestation of this breach, so night after night he started to whitewash French names on such signs in different townships. He always seemed to sidestep the local police, and every day gleeful newspapers had pictures and accounts of his latest caper. Eventually he was caught but soon was freed, because defacing street signs was not the kind of crime that could keep him off the streets for long. It also generated much support and continued to draw attention to the illegal activities of these authorities. Eventually the case was won, and by the onset of the war bilingualism had died out for the most part, and street signs in Flanders were becoming unilingual.

Schools were not immune from the reigning climate of confrontation. Every Flemish national day (July 11) fights erupted on the playground at the school of the Ladies between the Frenchies (*franskiljon*) and the Flemish-speakers (*flamingants*). One year many of the latter, including my older sisters, wore big broaches with the slogan "Speak polished Dutch." When a fight broke out and my sisters were overwhelmed by the other side, they began to stick their opponents with the sturdy pins of these broaches. Naturally, the parents of the victims complained, and the Ladies simply canceled all classes on that day. Meanwhile, at St. Lievens, the same day was more or less celebrated as a holiday with militant songs and Flemish flags.

As a result of the Grammens agitation, school-age children became more politicized. They began to wear broaches with the slogan *In Vlaanderen Vlaams* (Flemish in Flanders). By 1938 or 1939 groups of older students began to roam the streets after class chanting that phrase and blocking entry into shops that still had signboards in French only. My parents were adamantly opposed to such intimidating fascist-like behavior. They forbade us to have anything whatsoever to do with it, and moreover they appreciated quite a few French-speaking inhabitants of the city. But Father encouraged Flemish patriotism. When I was seven or eight I had already acquired a few martial Flemish nationalist songs, probably in the "song" classes at St. Lievens. Among them my favorite was a vaguely maritime one that dated to the pre-1914 era of militant students in the Flemish movement. It sounded ominously:

"Now [hear] the song of Flanders' sons . . . with its savage northern sounds . . . when the bird *blauwvoet* flies, [there is a] storm at sea"—and I would belt it out over and over again whenever I had a chance.

The last, highly visible presence of the political parties were their youth organizations, in shorts and shirts of various colors. The more militia-like among them liked to show off by flourishing Flemish flags (*vendelzwaaien*) to the sound of martial drumming. The most discrete of all the youth organizations were the boy scouts, who did not overtly flaunt any political ideology. Yet they belonged more or less to the official establishment whose values they adopted, and they recruited among the better-off middle class. But even among the scouts there were different associations. Our link was unsurprisingly with the one called VVKS, Flemish Association of Catholic Scouts. Two of my older sisters were girl guides, my older brother a scout, and I had just been enrolled among the cubs when we left Antwerp.

Street unrest was not limited to the Flemish movement but extended also to agitation against Jews. Some time after the mid-1930s, my sister Veva tells me, a broach appeared on the streets with the slogan "I boycott Jewish shops," no doubt an initiative sponsored by competitors of their shops. When she asked why some people disliked Jews so much, Mother told her that such people believed that Jews were cheating them in business, but that such beliefs were completely unfounded. One evening at dusk Father, who had been growing a beard recently, was walking along the street when he was suddenly accosted by a man who stopped right in front of him and spat before his feet shouting "Dirty Jew." In line with their overall policy of shielding the children from any grown-up unpleasantness, our parents never told us anything about this or similar incidents. All we knew about Jews beyond information in religion instruction was that there were many Jews in Antwerp, and that their religion was different from ours even though Jesus and the apostles had all been Jews.

I became first aware of international politics in 1936 through the photographs in the weekly magazine *Ons volk ontwaakt* (Our people wakes up) of the German military occupation of the Rhine showing ranks upon ranks of German soldiers as they advanced on March 7 through city streets, presumably of Cologne, and thereby initiated Hitler's first military action. Later that year I also saw a picture in a paper at a newspaper stand illustrating the "relief of the Alcazar" at Toledo by Francisco Franco's Army of Africa on September 27, 1936. From that time onward I remember pictures of the main events punctuating the continuing expansion of Germany, such as the Anschluß— the absorption of Austria—on March 12, 1938; and Neville Chamberlain's return home from Munich on September 30, 1938, to declare, as he stood by his airplane with folded umbrella in hand, that there would be "peace in our time." To us the most interesting part of this latter occasion, actually, was that here was a head of state who for the first time had traveled by plane to another country and back. Local omens also announced the approach of war, such as a small earthquake and not long thereafter a very rare appearance of an aurora borealis. More genuine than those omens was the sight of a little band of forlorn-looking men on the stern deck of a Japanese freighter waiting to sail to Yokohama, recalled home to their own wars.

Indeed, war was near for us as well, and with it came our departure from Antwerp for other environments. In 1939 I was a conventional metropolitan, bourgeois, easy-going, Flemish nationalist child, equipped with standard Catholic beliefs and ethics. With the exception of the beliefs and ethics, every part of this profile was soon to come under attack by the new situations in which I found myself. Inevitably such a rapid change was bound to leave a strong imprint on me. Hence it is suitable to provide here a quick sketch of the kind of child I was before we moved. Compared to other boys I was smaller, more agile, and endowed with a nervous, very active temperament. So my reactions were faster than usual, but that very quickness led me often to be too hasty, impulsive, impatient, incautious, and sloppy about outside appearances. I was also rather clumsy with manual tasks, even something as simple as drawing, and I was only adequate at arithmetic. However, I liked to read and was equipped with an excellent memory as well as a luxuriant imagination, traits that largely account for my scholastic results, especially in the more literary subjects. Yet I was quite obedient because I tended to accept at face value whatever interpretation of any concrete situation an adult in the family or at school presented to me, rather than questioning either their observations or their interpretation. Overall, then, I was a contented boy, safe and self-assured in a close-knit family and a school I liked, a boy for whom the appropriate intertwined virtues of honesty, trust, and loyalty were paramount, and a boy whose own personality was only beginning to emerge. This was beginning to be acknowledged by my siblings and parents, but beyond that in society at large, this emerging personality was still attributed by most outsiders to all the Vansinas, the family, rather than to Jan the person.

Right: Our front door, Antwerp. (family photo)

Below: Antwerp, ca. 1932. (anonymous photographer)

The family at home in Antwerp, 1932. In the back row from left to right are Father, Mother with Nico, Mietje, Annie, and Veva; seated in front of them are Bea and Chris; on the floor from left to right are Guido, Jan, and Rina. (family photo)

The family in Gooreind, 1932. From left to right are Bea, Veva, Rina, Guido, Mietje, Mother holding Nico and Jan, Annie, and Chris. (family photo)

Dirk Vansina in uniform, 1918. (family photo)

Self-portrait by Dirk Vansina, oil painting, 1920s. (family photo)

Façade of our parish church, St. Carolus Borromeus. (Fotografie Lukasweb, *Wegwijs in Sint-Carolus Borromeuskerk te Antwerpen*)

Salome by Dirk Vansina, oil painting, ca. 1938. (family photo)

First communion, Mother and Jan, August 22, 1935. (family photo)

The festive white suit.
(family photo)

Meezennestje cottage, Gooreind, 1930s. (photo Hoelen, Cappellen)

Wiezelo house in Bauhaus style, Gooreind, June 1939. (family photo)

Rural old lady in traditional dress, Gooreind, drawing by Suzanne Verellen. (family photo)

Canal and belfry, Bruges. (family photo)

Left: Villa Manon, 1940. (family photo)

Below: *Apocalypse* by Dirk Vansina, oil painting, 1940. (family photo)

Concert in the garden, Bruges, ca. 1940/1941. From left to right are Suze, Jan, Chris, Guido, and Nico. (family photo)

3

War Erupts

July 1939 to June 1940

A t Easter 1939 we moved as usual to Gooreind—this time not to the familiar Meezennestje, but to Wiezelo, a new house well outside the village proper. We stayed there during the whole spring trimester and commuted every school day to attend St. Lievens in Antwerp, approximately thirteen miles away. The household only returned to the Markgravestraat a few days before World War II broke out on September 3. At the time that move looked like a small variation on the usual state of affairs, but it was not. In retrospect, this was the first step in a transformation of our family from a typical, conventional bourgeois household into something strikingly different. Of course, our parents were both artists and as such already to some extent lived beyond the routines and mindsets of other bourgeois. But the summer at Wiezelo, and the further move to Bruges that followed at the end of that year, were to take us quite palpably outside our customary social circles. Cut off from our earlier network of family and acquaintances for the next three years, we were thrown back on our own resources. As wartime conditions, especially the procurement of food, forced major changes in long-standing respectable routines, we children were pushed to new levels of independence. Moreover, the effects of our social isolation were intensified because our group of siblings was large enough to prevent any outside group of teachers or classmates from having any significant influence on us. We became our own peer-reference culture, and as the war went on our existence could no longer be recognized as a typical bourgeois lifestyle anymore. I begin to detail the why and the how of this metamorphosis in the following pages.

Gooreind

The process really began that spring with the move to Wiezelo. Compared to Meezennestje, this large new summer home, nestled on an estate of perhaps seventy acres, was quite removed from the outside world — even from the tiny village of Gooreind. The village of Gooreind was and remains officially part of the municipality of Wuustwezel, whose town hall lies a little over three miles north of Gooreind along the Bredabaan, the main road from Antwerp to Breda in the Netherlands. Yet Gooreind was a distinct village on its own, and sociologically its population was also different from that of Wuustwezel.

About thirteen miles north of Antwerp, the west side of the Bredabaan became a built-up area, part of a small grid, and a little further on the east side of the road one arrived at the stately entrance to castle Posterijhof, the residence of my maternal grandparents, where they lived from 1905. The gate faced Gooreind's main street, which ran straight west from there to a circular square in front of its small church. The Meezennestje, where we had spent our previous summers, lay along this street not far from that square. South of the church and the surrounding grid lay a wooded estate of over two hundred acres, owned by Koch, an English banker who used it as a hunting lodge and a summer residence. All year around his estate provided work for a handful of foresters as well as for a large domestic staff and a throng of game beaters when he was in residence. The country north and northwest of the church was an open landscape of farms scattered on their croplands and meadows. Known as Boerengooreind (Farmers' Gooreind), this was the oldest part of the village, where people had settled at least eight hundred years ago. A few farms there were quite prosperous, but most made only a modest living. That part of the village was still not yet modernized and quite conservative. In the later 1930s a rural electricity network had only just reached all the farms, and drinking water there was still pumped manually from wells. Some of its older women still went to church on Sundays dressed in black with lace caps adorned with long, wide ribbons in the back, colored according to the liturgical color of the season.

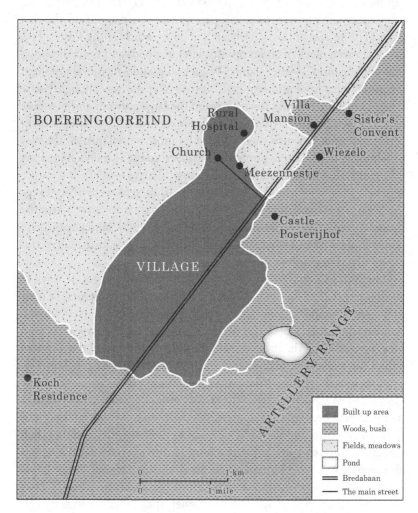

Gooreind, 1939 to 1944

Map labels:

BOERENGOOREIND

Rural Hospital

Villa Mansion

Sister's Convent

Church

Wiezelo

Meezennestje

Castle Posterijhof

VILLAGE

ARTILLERY RANGE

Koch Residence

Legend:

■	Built up area
▨	Woods, bush
⋮	Fields, meadows
◻	Pond
═	Bredabaan
—	The main street

Scale:
0 — 1 km
0 — 1 mile

Opposite the built-up village on the east side of the Bredabaan lay the Posterijhof, surrounded by more than fifty acres of parkland woods but nevertheless almost cheek to jowl with the cigarette factory along the Bredabaan whose profits had paid for its construction in the first place. To the east of the Bredabaan and going north of the Posterijhof, one first met a block of about seventy acres of woods and some meadows that became our residence named Wiezelo, a pseudo-medieval toponym meaning "meadows and woods." Next to Wiezelo was an eighty-acre estate of of similar land on which stood the large convent and novitiate of the Franciscan sisters of Mary, a missionary order. Continuing northward, that estate in turn was followed by more woodlands all the way to Wuustwezel. All these properties bordered to the east on a huge tract of uncultivated land of about three thousand acres—in effect a nature reserve—that constituted a military domain used as an artillery range for both short- and long-range ordnance. Hence in these parts the Bredabaan was the border between two very different landscapes: open spaces to its west and what amounted then to a large nature reserve area of woodland or brush to its east.

Gooreind's population was unlike that of most villages. It was not all that unusual to find two different categories of inhabitants, farmers in Boerengooreind and factory workers in the more densely settled area. Some of the latter, women as well as men, worked in the cigar factory; others cycled along the Bredabaan to the military barracks at the southern end of the military domain, while still others went to work in Antwerp, often as longshoremen. What was unusual were the activities of some rather lawless elements within the factory group of people. They made a living as poachers or as smugglers, for the Dutch border ran only five miles or so north and west of Gooreind as the crow flies. Among their smuggled imports cattle were preeminent, but everyone in the village also seemed to obtain butter and cheese from there as well. A few hardy souls among them also made a living as "foragers for metal." They poached the proving grounds for shrapnel, spent shells, and their cartridges so as to resell their metals, especially the valuable brass and copper. The prize was to find unexploded ammunition, especially of a heavier caliber. They defused the shell and then carefully retrieved and sold nearly all its parts. But accidents happened, and as a result Gooreind counted an unusually large number of maimed young people.

Public authority in the village was exercised by its fearless pastor, the Reverend de Wit, who ruled from the pulpit and also announced communal or governmental official communications from there. In addition the settlement boasted a single rural constable and a post office staffed by a mailman who spent much of the day doing his rounds on bicycle. Unlike most of the larger villages, Gooreind had no other elite persons such as a local aristocrat or a powerful lawyer-notary. No one here was really rich, no one had a car, and there was only one light truck. The biggest machine was still a windmill. I remember visiting it on a cart and watching from inside as its anchored sails were released and unfurled. Then a low, slow creaking made the huge millstone turn and shed a rain of flour into bags readied to receive it.

Wiezelo 1939

One summer day in 1938 I accompanied Father to a large patch of heather where Wiezelo was to rise. We met a fussy contractor and saw a few shallow trenches sketching an outline of a house. Less than a year later, here was a large, almost rectangular house, built according to severe Bauhaus principles, two floors high with a flat roof. It had several unusual features. Its outside walls had been built with the strongest brick known—a feature valued by my father, who had once run a brickworks himself. Its inner walls on the second floor were made out of a cardboard (certified to be nonflammable), which made it possible to alter the floor plan as needed. The house included a huge open main hall that covered well over half of the downstairs surface and boasted one of the widest picture windows ever made. At its shorter inner side rose a hearth in refractory brick, large and deep enough to hold an entire log at least five feet long. It was provided with two brick corner seats inside its mantel and a space for several chairs in front of it. Its chimney was so wide that when it rained outside, the drops also spattered into its bed of ashes.

I was too young to know what prompted the decision in July 1939 to move permanently from the Markgravestraat to Wiezelo, but I later realized that it did not primarily result from the threat of an imminent war. My parents had lived in Gooreind before. Mother had grown up in the Posterijhof, and Father especially preferred a rural life to an urban one. There may also have been financial considerations. The Depression had not been kind to investors, and by July 1939 the growing likelihood of war was apparently triggering the total loss of some sovereign obligations. Whether such considerations played any role in reaching their decision, the move was accompanied by a drastic reduction in domestic staff. With the exception of Miss Eva, none of the former servants wanted to move to the countryside. Instead two new Polish maids, Maria and Basha, accompanied us to Wiezelo. Soon their garlands of drying mushrooms from meadow or wood adorned the kitchen, and the smell of borscht permeated the house.

Life certainly acquired some spartan features. There was electricity, but its supply was unreliable, perhaps because of the long line through the woods that connected the house to the rural electric network. As elsewhere our water was drawn from a well by an electric pump intended to provide running water for the upstairs rooms, which were all equipped with splendid wash basins. But the system never worked, and we all learned in a trice how to prime the hand pump in the kitchen sink and get our water from there. The hearth heated part of the main hall, and its chimney warmed some of the upstairs rooms. Otherwise there was only a single small stove (coal or wood) in the kitchen and an even smaller one in Mother's office. Wood came from the estate, and we fetched it as needed from a barrow of faggots next to a stack of cloven wood and logs that lay at the far end of the spacious yard surrounding the house.

Under these conditions and in such an environment the children thrived. Apart from the smallest, there was no way we could be closely supervised. As long as we wore "play clothes," we were mostly left to our own devices. We had never known such freedom, but we also had to cooperate with each other as never before. Bomama's gift, the Arabian donkey and its trap, were the biggest attraction. Suske had his own little stable hidden under the trees near the house, and my older siblings knew how to harness him for rides and how to groom him. Then there were our bicycles, there was the waterhole, there were "Last of the Mohican" sorts of walks in the woods and more. I still remember my poor cousin Pierre reluctantly playing his role as victim of the "redskins" with a few high-spirited Vansina children, our skin dyed red with blackberry juice, dancing around the stake at the edge of the yard until some indignant adults came to the rescue. In creating this scene were we perhaps inspired by those huge South American murals at the school of the Ladies of Christian Education?

It was at Wiezelo also that I came to know my parents better, especially Father. In Antwerp he had been invisible for the most part. Here we all ate lunch and dinner together at a long table in the great hall, and Father presided. While still in awe of this imposing, tall, baldish man with the severe glasses and the ever-serious mien, I learned to recognize his moods and his predilections in classical music, where he rated Wagner the best. He would stay awake deep into the night to listen to the concerts from Berlin that were broadcast toward Latin America and that for some mysterious reason reached Gooreind with nearly perfect reception. Hence, little by little, he became less of a public personality to turn into a more paternal figure. From time to time some of his friends visited, and on one occasion we listened completely spellbound to the writer and master storyteller Ernest Van der Hallen when he recounted his adventures on a recent trip to Libya. Its most impressive portion was the description of the banquet deep in the Sahara given by a powerful sheikh for a few Italian officers and himself. Seated in a circle on poufs, the company conversed as dish after dish of exotic fare succeeded each other, culminating in the crowning delicacy: lamb's eye. Little did I realize then what Libya's colonial condition really entailed, nor did I then know anything about the long-fought conquest that preceded such "banquets" in the desert.

Our new home was located at one corner of the estate and a little over a hundred wooded yards away from the Bredabaan, from which it was screened by a stand of firs. Nature, not nurture, started at its door. For unlike the Posterijhof and to a certain extent even the sisters' convent, our house did not sit in a more or less landscaped park with stately lanes, giant rhododendrons, trees, grassy retreats, and the like. This estate instead looked like some sort of arboretum. Yes, there were a few avenues with beeches and poplars, but most of the terrain was occupied by woods of fir, locust, birch, and spruce, separated from each other by patches of heather and bush in which one espied an isolated native oak or a solitary bird cherry. Interspersed with the woods lay a few irregularly shaped meadows, only one of which was sizeable, and at the time it was rented out for raising sheep. Finally, at the diagonally opposite end of the estate from the house on the border road with the Posterijhof estate lay a small modern farm with a one-horse barn run by Frans Van Loon and his wife Net (Antoinette).

Not only was the estate not a manicured park, but it was completely left to run wild, despite efforts by Frans to keep at least the main alleys open. To us this was paradise on earth. While no one talked to us about nature, the environment, organic practices, and the like, we experienced them directly. On our own we soon recognized the different personalities of trees as diverse as stately beeches, poplars reaching for the skies, gracious silver birches, a melancholy elder here and there, a few leafy chestnut trees, some gnarled native oaks, and huddled fir. The notion of ecotone was foreign to us, but we "knew" where there would be forest undergrowth and where not, where to expect spontaneous clumps of rhododendron rather than huge patches of blackberry thorns. We observed the comings and goings of small animals such as ants, moles, voles, rabbits, the occasional red squirrel or toad, and even a rare hedgehog. We recognized the common early morning calls of the songbirds in the spring, naturally the cuckoo first of all, and who can forget the thrill of listening to the liquid trills of the nightingale on moonlit nights? During summer, hidden in the reeds at the edge of the water hole, we watched the dancing dragonflies, the occasional jumps and plops of diving frogs, and once or twice even the landing of a great blue heron in search of dinner. All in all by summer's end we were no longer just city children anymore.

Beyond the estate lay a sandy lane marking the edge of the forbidden military domain. From there onward one entered into a true nature reserve. It was a land of abraded ancient dunes of white sands covered in low bush, a fen or two nestling in their folds. Not far from its edge stood an ugly observation tower, topped with a cabin and a movable wooden arm. When it was raised above the cabin it meant that artillery exercises were underway and that someone with binoculars was watching where the shells hit. But when the arm was lowered, no observer had any reason to be there, and we could safely sneak onto the range. Anyway, we soon learned to distinguish between the claps of bursting shells and the fainter plop that signaled their firing. We learned, too, to tell the difference between the heavy guns from the fortresses north of Antwerp, well over ten miles away, and the field artillery only a mile or so from us. From time to time, the gunners made mistakes, usually when a fresh crew started its practice, and shells fell on the estates outside the range, a few times even rather close to our own home. Then Father phoned directly to a special number at headquarters to report the error, and usually the fire soon ceased. On one occasion that summer one of those misguided barrages set the locust wood alight, generating a forest fire that threatened the whole estate. Alerted by the smoke, men from Gooreind just as suddenly appeared as if out of the void and joined every one of us armed with branches and buckets of sand to halt the fire. Even I, branch in hand, gleefully beat down the flames until my arms ached.

Surrounded by nature, Wiezelo was an isolated place, and we learned that isolation has its own features. Reckoned in yards, our nearest neighbor was a villa Mansion across the Bredabaan and somewhat further up north. Our parents had once lived there, and a number of my sisters had been born there in the 1920s. In 1939, however, the villa was un-inhabited. On "our" side of the road the closest establishment was the sisters' convent. It was only a short ten-minute walk away by a path across the woods. Every weekday morning we followed it to attend mass behind a railing at the back of the convent's large church, and we were soon familiar with the peculiarities of the occupants' white and grey habits. We found out, without being much interested in it, that these sisters ran missions in India and in some parts of Africa. But we also discovered that they sheltered an unusually discreet lodger who looked like a bishop because he was wearing a ring and a large pectoral cross. Actually he was a Basque nationalist bishop whose identity was the reason that he needed to be in hiding. My siblings told me that he had found refuge in this isolated spot during the civil war when his side, the anticlerical but Republican government, was overwhelmed by General Franco's fascist armies. How they found out I cannot imagine, but I knew it was a secret, and no one was to know.

Yes, we were isolated, and the occasional shots of poachers at night or the traps they left in the woods for us to dismantle reminded us of it. Hence it was not wholly surprising to wake up in the dead of night to the melancholy sound of lowing and to behold a mass of reeking cattle milling around the house by moonlight. They had obviously just crossed over from Holland and escaped their drovers. Yet when the sun rose, not the slightest trace of their passage could be seen. I had watched this and yet it was evanescent like a dream. For, like the bishop, this was the sort of secret no one was supposed to know and certainly not officially. In this way, then, and well before the outbreak of war, isolation already taught us the virtues of discretion.

War Postponed

One day in August my older brother Chris and a sister or two decided to hold a speed trial on bicycles between the house and the closed entrance gate on the Bredabaan. On your marks, set, go!—and we took off at speed. Chris was ahead, our sisters dropped out halfway to the finish line, and I was catching up with him. Almost in front of the gate he swerved to the side, but I went on and . . . ran smack into it. I had won, but the bicycle was in a sorry state, and so was one of my shins. Once home the adults tut-tutted and got me somehow to the rural hospital next to the parish church where Wuustwezel's physician removed a piece of wire, stitched the wound, and dressed it with sulfa drugs, the newest class of medication at the time, for there were no antibiotics yet. Nevertheless the result: bed rest for umpteen days; no more play; a single puzzle; an aunt's gift of an "unbreakable" armored watch where numbers appeared in little windows to keep track of the hours, minutes, and seconds it took to heal; and a lot of boredom. One afternoon through the open window I heard a farmer outside talking to Father. He was asking whether war was about to break out or not. The answer was not clear to me but sounded more ominous than reassuring. It was my first intimation that war might strike us. Certainly we all knew the hectoring sounds of Hitler's voice over the radio that made those adults who could understand him quite distraught, but hitherto I had not internalized either the seriousness or the imminence of the danger that loomed. Now I did.

In expectation of a war there had been more preparations at Wiezelo during the summer. First Father, with all his experience from the trenches in the First World War, directed the digging of a large bomb shelter near the house. Its walls were entirely shored up with fir logs and its roof was also made with logs covered with several layers of grass sods, which also camouflaged the whole. Inside, a long zigzag trench gave access to several side rooms. One day also canisters of gasmasks in several sizes appeared, and we were each given one. Then each mask was carefully adjusted, and we were drilled in their use until we could don them quickly and correctly. Downstairs there also appeared sets of wooden shutters to slide before the windows at dusk so that not even a ray of light might filter out at night to betray the presence of a house. With these methods we were ready to cope with the last war.

During the third trimester, between Easter and July, we all commuted every day to our schools in Antwerp. This was a heroic undertaking. It was still quite dark when the first of us arrived on the Bredabaan to catch the regional bus in the early morning. As we waited the little lights of cyclists were already streaming by us on their way to work. Later the big headlights of the bus followed, and as the first child climbed aboard his or her task was to incite the driver to wait for the lagger or laggers. Meanwhile chaos reigned in the kitchen as one or more of us were still hunting for a shoe, a satchel, or a coat. The driver was wont to count on his fingers: 1, 2, 3, 4, 5 Vansinas . . . and, oh yes, there comes number six running, so off we go. Apparently, this scene recurred every single school day. Once on the bus I usually went to sleep for most of the one-hour trip until we were decanted at Antwerp's famous Central railway station. While the girls went their own way, Guido and I walked to our school half an hour away along wide boulevards roaring with traffic with me, just ten years old, in charge. True, the first week Victor had shown us the way, and sometimes Chris accompanied us, but after that Guido and I were on our own under my responsibility. Naturally along the way to school there were many distractions, starting with the railway station itself and the Rex cinema nearby. One of the most attractive scenes was the stand of exotic fruit at a weekly market on a square alongside one of those boulevards. That explains why the names of such faraway places as Santos, Brazil, or Jaffa, Palestine, soon became quite familiar. Still I was careful not to linger much at such spots.

Most of the time everything went smoothly, but not always. One day after school Guido blithely told me that he had spent the money for his bus fare on a delicious licorice known as a shoelace in the candy shop opposite the school. And I had just enough for my own fare. Not knowing what to do, we returned to the bus stop. At the time Guido was an angelic little boy with a head of golden curls, and he knew it. So as we approached the railway station he decided that he was going to beg just like some other little children he had once seen there. He darted in front of me asking ladies right and left and suddenly dived in an open door into a corridor that ended in a room with several ladies. As I arrived he was already pouring out his tale of woe, and I was about to stop him when, lo and behold, one of the ladies just pulled the coins needed from her purse and pressed it into his hand. Crisis resolved. Sometimes the girls would be late, yet the bus would not leave without them. Its driver merely continued to wait until they arrived, scolded them as they boarded, and only then did he drive away.

The trimester wore on, and signs of impending war became more and more frequent. The most obvious one was the disruption caused by the general mobilization. The full strength of the army on war footing comprised six hundred thousand men out of eight million people, and the absence of so many men from the labor force caused monumental headaches everywhere. Yet week after week nothing happened, and there was mounting pressure to grant the reservists leave to return to their farms or to other "essential" jobs on temporary passes. After a while there were only older workmen on the bus for the early morning journey to the city, but on the return trip in the late afternoon there were more and more soldiers on leave or absent without leave. They had the sympathies of the general public on the bus, as became manifest when it was searched by military police or even gendarmes. While the bus conductor loudly announced that the police were about to board, a few passengers could be seen suddenly sliding from their seats onto the floor to be immediately covered with whatever camouflage their neighbors had at hand from coats to suitcases or even baskets (remember, this was a rural bus). For these people all knew stories of hardship on the farms in the absence of their men. The bus met another obvious sign of increasing danger in a spot more than halfway from Antwerp when it had to negotiate gingerly what had started as a ditch across the road. Over time the ditch became deeper, its steep banks bristling with barbed wire and huge metal teeth, only to grow later still into a canal crossable by pontoon. It was then named the anti-tank canal.

When war was declared on Tuesday, September 3, the news was expected. For me that event drew less attention, though, than our return to the Markgravestraat a day or two earlier had. Although Belgium was not yet at war, by then the impending conflict had already triggered considerable changes in the country. Belgium had returned from an alliance with France and Britain to strict neutrality on August 1, 1936. That implied self-defense against all comers. So already on May 26, 1939, the king had decreed a general mobilization for the second time in two years. A first mobilization had been prompted by the threatening situation in the spring of 1938 but had been discontinued after Chamberlain's visit to Munich. This time even Father, then forty-five years old, volunteered or was called to Wuustwezel—I do not know which version is correct—but in view of his age and the number of his dependents he was rejected.

After our return to the Markgravestraat in September, radio and the newsreels at the Rex cinema near the railway station constantly reminded us of impending doom with images such as cavalry charging armor in Poland and, later in December, valiant Finnish soldiers on skis. The newsreels alternated with documentaries about the impregnable Maginot line in France or British warships patrolling the sea lanes. Yet actually there was nothing more than light skirmishing in the West, a situation known as the phony war—so perhaps there would be no "real" war?

These were the obvious signs of ominous danger. Other signs of approaching war were more subtle, and we children did not understand them. Thus on a weekend at the end of the summer I once saw a gypsy caravan, drawn by a horse, pass by at a good clip toward Holland, and I only thought how enticing it looked with its gaudy oval-shaped body with a little balcony at the rear and a smoking chimney pipe. Little did I realize that the sight was out of season, that the caravan was unusual because it came from central Europe, and that this anomaly more than likely had something to do with the impending war. Even as early as the spring of 1939 we also noticed that people on the bus traveled with more and more luggage as the weeks went by, but we did not fully realize that more and more people were beginning to hoard all sorts of commodities. Once war was declared the flow of imports, most of which reached the country by sea through Antwerp, began to slowly dry up. People soon sensed this. First speculators, then more and more ordinary housewives, began to hoard supplies of things they might need in the future. They were all betting that a genuine war would soon succeed the phony one.

Bruges

For the first time we did not celebrate Christmas in Antwerp that year but returned to Wiezelo. There one evening a few days after the holiday Father casually announced from the inglenook of the hearth that we were about to leave Gooreind as well as Antwerp, lock, stock, and barrel. He reminded us that Wiezelo lay in the field of fire from the fortifications of Antwerp and well beyond its anti-tank defenses, which we all knew. It had become too dangerous to stay here because the harbor of Antwerp was likely to become a major stake in the fighting as soon as hostilities broke out, and that might happen any day. By that time it would be too late to leave. The time was now, and all of us were to move to beautiful Bruges, the capital of West Flanders that advertised itself as the Venice of the North. That city had no particular military value and would be as safe a haven as could be found anywhere.

The impact of this news on our lives did not really sink in as I thought of it as something similar to the earlier move from Antwerp to Wiezelo. In any case I had only once been in a city outside Antwerp, and that had been a pleasant and exciting outing. Just the previous spring I had accompanied Mother to visit my sister Bea, who then attended a boarding school at Liège, a city on the Meuse River and the pearl of Wallony. For me it had been a series of firsts: traveling by electric train and by a huge steam train as well, looking up at "mountains" from the deep valley of the Meuse, being in a place where no one spoke Dutch, and watching the high swaying plumes of powerful fountains playfully rising from the river. Perhaps Bruges would be something like that? It was not.

Bruges came as a wholly unexpected shock. I seem to recall traveling in the back of a small truck for so long that I fell asleep. When I woke up in a strange room to the sound of a shrill steam whistle I realized that we had arrived, and I eagerly sped to look through the as yet uncurtained window at this Bruges. I appeared to be on a second floor, and below me lay a fairly wide street. On its opposite side an arched gateway bore the inscription La Brugeoise. That gave access to a bridge over a narrow canal that ran parallel with the street, and then a railway parallel to and beyond the canal. A long factory shed interrupted the railway behind, and the strident whistle emanated from a pipe that stuck out from its roof like a chimney. Beyond all of that lay featureless meadowland with scarcely a tree in sight. Was that industrial landscape beautiful Bruges? Yes, but not precisely so. Bruges itself was a small round and compact city with many medieval houses and monuments and crisscrossed by canals. It had a glorious past, first as an early capital of Flanders, and somewhat later as the main port and perhaps the richest commercial place in the Low Countries. But in the later 1400s its access to the sea silted up, and it declined precipitously in favor of Antwerp. In 1940 the city housed roughly a little less than a fifth of Antwerp's population, and its main revenue stemmed from tourism.

Our new home was villa Manon, no doubt a confectioner's delight in stone: rectangular, exuberant with excrescences, and topped by a wispy Turkish kiosk above the villa's equivalent of a central keep surmounted by the beginning of a steeple. This concoction, surrounded by a large walled garden and orchard, ornamented a suburb of Bruges, not far from the city moat and the drawbridge that gives access to the Katelijnestraat and from there leads to the celebrated city center. Inside the house on the ground floor, all was white marble, crystal mirrors, and lots of gilded scrolling, especially inside the large drawing rooms filled with the swathed furniture of the villa's owners. Those rooms were out of bounds to us as renters. Hence while we all slept on the first floor above, we spent the day in the basement floor below. The household was also reduced. Basha and Maria did not accompany us, and during the summer in 1940 even Eva left us, to the great regret of my sisters. They were replaced by a local cook, Zoe, and an "upstairs" maid, who turned out to be a thief. She was rapidly dismissed for stealing clothes, shoes, and small trinkets. But her successor stole even more and found herself even faster out the door. After that there were no more maids besides Zoe and a daily cleaning lady.

However, there was more to the situation than disappointed expectations or thievish maids. While we did not realize what was happening, any anthropologist could have told us that we suffered from culture shock. The first element of it was linguistic. West Flemish was a different language from ours. For instance, when the cleaning lady complained, *T'is gin avans da minder kuschen* (What is the use of cleaning?), we expected something like *Wat baat schoonmaken?* in standard southern Dutch (ABN). It took time for us to learn to understand the Bruges dialect clearly, and until then we often felt insecure. Then there were some local customs. In contrast to Antwerp, in Bruges no one ever seemed to be in any hurry, not even to catch a bus at the last minute. Except for a street or two in the shopping district near the great market, most others were almost completely deserted during working hours, and in 1940 there were no tourists to enliven the center of town. The Vansina boys were faced with yet another sign of cultural difference on the very first day of school. Clad as usual in short-sleeved shirts and shorts as we were in Antwerp, we were halted at the entrance of the establishment amid indignant accusations of immorality and told to return only attired in long-sleeved shirts with either regular trousers or at least shorts that came below the knee. Back home Mother was furious. She swaddled our arms in bandages and then accompanied us to school where she negotiated a compromise with the authorities. It was not an auspicious beginning.

We had barely arrived at villa Manon when the school year began again. The girls were all sent to the equivalent of the Ladies in Antwerp, an establishment called Hemelsdaele (Heavenly Vale), to which they did not easily adapt, in part for cultural reasons. My sister Rina points out that the nuns in Bruges were far more narrow-minded and inclined toward excessive piety than their counterparts in Antwerp. They pressured their pupils to join the "children of Mary," drafted them to march in processions, and encouraged them to offer votive candles. Their devoutness went so far that laughter was actually outlawed at school. For their part the boys were enrolled at the grade school of St. Lodewijks, a diocesan college like St. Lievens, but with quite a different ideology. Instead of the motto "All for Flanders, Flanders for Christ," this school was decidedly Belgicist. Mysteriously, its slogan *Ora et Labora* (Pray and Work) was borrowed from the Benedictine order, yet there was nothing Benedictine at all about it.

In principle the schools in Bruges followed the same curriculum as in Antwerp, yet with one significant difference: whereas grade school in Antwerp included six grades, here there were seven grades, and therefore my class in the fifth grade here went over much ground that had already been covered in Antwerp. But St. Lodewijks taught French, and St. Lievens did not. My class here counted some fifty pupils rather than the twenty in my former school, and the teacher was much less respected than had been the case there. Our teacher, a lay person, also acted as sexton at the cathedral of St. Salvator nearby, and when there was an important funeral service he was absent from school. Here as in Antwerp, classes were adapted to local culture. For example, a set mathematical problem could only be solved if one knew the height of Bruges' belfry, the proudest symbol of the city, and when I asked how high it was, a shocked silence at such ignorance was my only response.

My classmates and those of my brothers at this new school did not receive us well because we came from Antwerp, the successful rival. So we did not adapt well either. Our first reaction was passive resistance. As a consequence all four of us—Chris, Jan, Guido, and Nico—found ourselves frequently expelled from class for one reason or another and banished to the playground. It did not take us long to figure out how to achieve this end on purpose so that we could while away the time by playing there until classes were dismissed. Somewhat later the school figured out what was happening, and instead of exile we were now given extra homework in the form of writing sentences like "I will not disrupt class" a hundred times or more.

As we became more and more familiar with the customs of the people of Bruges, our opposition became less overt, and we apparently began to learn something, even though our discontent did not vanish altogether. Still, there remains a pleasant memory from that period: the visit of our class to Guido Gezelle's native home and museum. Guido Gezelle (1830–1899), a priest, was the foremost poet of nineteenth-century Flanders whose idyllic and nostalgic poems about nature and the waning ways of former rural customs remained unequalled. They were written in a limpid West Flemish tongue of unadorned simplicity yet were replete with musical harmony. His modest house was small and so quiet that you could almost hear a bird or two whistle outside. What I found most impressive, however, were the many drafts of his writing. I was of a boisterous nature, and it was a revelation to learn how much effort had been necessary for Gezelle to achieve the unpretentious simplicity of his poems. Endless peacefulness seemed to engulf that house, but meanwhile the war continued.

When the trimester finally ended and the Easter vacation began, my results, while not disastrous, were not nearly as good as they had been at St. Lievens. Somehow all the rebelliousness had been sublimated in the notation "application: less good," but then "politeness: very good" made up for it. Still, on the whole the detailed results were mediocre and included unadorned failures in such diverse topics as calligraphy, song, drawing, and even Dutch grammar. Seemingly no one paid any attention to them at home. However, a week or so later, Mother did something exceptional: she called me to her boudoir and told me first that St. Lodewijks did not suit me because the courses there were not challenging enough. So she had withdrawn me from that school and had managed to enroll me instead on short notice into the boarding school of the Abbey of St. Andrew Zevenkerken, near the village of Loppem and some six miles away from home. I was to attend the seventh and last grade of grade school there two years ahead of my class at St. Lodewijks, and she counted on me to succeed there "without any further nonsense."

This abbey school was very well known in West Flanders, and it was not remarkable that she had found this institution, but it was surprising that it accepted me because our family did not at all fit the usual family profile of their pupils. Why was I accepted, then? Was it because the monks there knew of Father as a member of the former Pelgrim movement and an artist striving to renovate religious art? Or did they know of him in some way through the business of the Melkmarkt? It was, after all, this abbey that published *L'artisan liturgique* (The liturgical artisan), the leading religious publication in this field. Or had my parents found a mutual acquaintance to vouch for them to the school? Or had it something to do with the impending war? For the war was nearing closer and closer. Had I not just read in the paper of April 10, on display at a stand next to the drawbridge at the city gate, that Germany had invaded Denmark and Norway the day before? Be all that as it may, I only knew that I had to get to the abbey as soon as possible.

So, all of ten years old, I was given a bicycle, loaded my gear in a suitcase on the carrier, and rode off to school the very next weekday morning. It was the first time that I was thrown to my own resources, and I was not very self-assured yet. Soon I arrived at a narrow late medieval city gate that I had to cross in busy traffic, and sure enough the heavy bike slid on the rough cobblestones, and I fell off just in front of a little van that managed to avoid me with squealing brakes. That snarled up the whole traffic. Bloodied but unbowed, I ignominiously fled the chaotic scene to a rich accompaniment of curses and after miles and miles finally reached the turnoff from the main road without further incident. Then, after I had pedaled a while along a quiet lane through a copse, suddenly an extensive complex of red brick buildings hove into view, clustered around and dominated by the grand abbatial church. This was St. Andries Zevenkerken (St. Andrew with the seven churches), one of the foremost Benedictine abbeys in Belgium at the time. As to the school itself, its entrance was discreetly tucked away at a right angle to the grand façade of the abbey, while the school buildings extended from those of the abbey but were otherwise entirely separate.

Moving to a boarding school was not a big issue for me because I had already slept elsewhere once. During the preceding summer in Gooreind my aunt Maria Brusseleers, who kept a well-appointed summer cottage on the main street in Gooreind, had invited me once to sleep over. I was allowed to go, clad in dignified clothes, after a refresher catechism on good table manners and fortified with recommendations not to let "the family down." From that occasion I only remembered the strain of a sandwich supper served by a maid, of waking up in an unfamiliar guest bedroom, and of the choice of jams and toast at the breakfast table. My expected performance seems to have absorbed all my attention because I do not even remember playing with my cousins.

On arrival at St. Andrews I found out that I needed all my wits about me just to keep myself afloat in these unfamiliar surroundings. I landed as a fly in the ointment toward the end of the school year when the last trimester had already begun, and I had to learn its customs and the habits of my cohort of fellow pupils in a hurry. They were quite different from what I had been used to hitherto. To begin with, the common language outside of class was French, even though all the subjects were taught in Dutch, barring only French and religion. Indeed, all the pupils and most of the monks were francophone and upper class. Secondly, and even less usual, nearly all the pupils who attended the school and all of my classmates without exception were of noble birth, and I had never even met a single nobleman before. So I had to become fluent in conversational and colloquial French in a hurry. It soon became apparent that I was the only commoner in my class, if not in the whole school, and henceforth I was scornfully teased as an "uncouth commoner." Moreover, nearly all my classmates recognized in me the sworn enemy of their class: a *flamingant*, or "convinced Fleming." Whereas our teacher merely called me Jean-Marie instead of Jan, the bullies taunted me as a "Flemish primitive" and other such witticisms. However, I was not easily intimidated. Impetuous by nature, and strong for my age, I did not take all this nonsense lying down but held my own in the occasional scuffles that broke out, and I boasted on occasion about my imaginary superiorities. And yet, in spite of all the antagonism and despite appearances, we slowly began to get used to each other.

I found the school itself quite attractive and very different from the earlier institutions I had attended. The windows of all the classes overlooked the extensive playgrounds and a grass field beyond, where we played field hockey. Ours was a class of fewer than twenty, and we had a devoted teacher who encouraged all his pupils and followed our progress quite closely. Many of the topics taught were quite interesting, and our teacher knew how to manage us, my then-turbulent self included. Also, I enjoyed the extracurricular activities. For instance, once the class attended a concert in Bruges. I had never been to such a thing, and the performance of Bach's Brandenburg Concerto #3 absolutely bewitched me. Another time we went to a swimming pool, where, of course, I had to "dare" and dive off the high board. I executed the dive so badly that I ripped the front of my swimming suit.

At the time I was besotted by geography and loved our textbook for this subject. Two of its pictures were really fascinating: one showing the Nile flooding Egypt, and one of an ivory statuette of Kwan Yin described as the Chinese Goddess of Mercy. The legend of the first one made it crystal clear why Egyptians had to be good at math: every year they had to recalculate the boundaries and the surface area of their fields. As for this Kwan Yin, I thought that she likely was their Virgin Mary over at the antipodes. So I started to wonder why God was made man on our side of the world and not on theirs. And when people died over there did they really go to our heaven and hell? That thought triggered a set of reflections that would culminate a few years later when I dreamed I had died. I woke up standing before a masked judge in a Tibetan temple with blue devils dancing all around us when the awful truth dawned on me. Not our creed, but popular Tibetan Buddhism on the other side of the world really was the true religion.

Then there was the time the teacher berated me with a rhetorical question during a geography lesson about Africa or Congo because I was not paying attention, and I retorted that my (mythical) "photographic memory" was so good that I did not need to be attentive all the time. So there and then he proposed a wager: I would memorize the map of the Belgian Congo and be ready to reel off all the major effluents of the river Congo at the next lesson. If not, there was a penalty. I set to memorizing with a vengeance, and my exposition of Congo's waterways got off to a great start. But alas, when it came to some smaller tributaries in the northeast here came a mistake! So I lost the bet, but it had been a decent run, and meanwhile I learned a lot.

As all of this was going on, the war was never far from our attention. A large bulletin board in the main hall of the school displayed comparative tables of the armed forces of the main combatants: troop strength, numbers and firing power of different classes of warships, types of aircraft, and varieties of tanks. Gains or losses could be registered but affected only warships during that period. In the evenings we adored playing a board game between rival fleets for hours. There were destroyers and battleships in miniature with gun batteries that could be taken off when they were "hit." And I did write an essay at the time of which I was very proud. It was all about the king of the rats and the war against the mice, and it essentially consisted of successive victory bulletins proudly giving tallies of the slain, the wounded, and the prisoners of war interspersed with comments such as, "Oh, how much misery that caused." There was no war yet, but already my sensibilities were hardening.

War Erupts

May 10, 5:35 a.m.: Germany invaded Belgium, and its planes destroyed nearly the whole Belgian air force conveniently assembled at the military airfield of Melsbroek near Brussels. Not much later I awoke in my cubicle of the dormitory as a monk was frantically shaking me and shouting, "Wake up . . . wake up. It is war!" or some such cry. Whatever it was, he was in a hurry. I was still so sleepy that I could not even manage to slide a leg into my trousers, and the more I fumbled the more hurried he became. Finally his maneuver succeeded, and I was now awake enough to look around me and outside. There I saw in all the windows of an aisle parallel to ours helmeted soldiers anxiously peering at the sky. But there was no time to ask questions, for by now I was running helter-skelter down the stairs to catch up with the other boys, who were hurrying to the refectory. There I learned that the soldiers were scouring the skies to detect German planes and especially paratroopers. The war was barely a few hours old, and yet apparently a great rumor about paratroopers had already engulfed the whole country to reach us here. Imaginary paratroopers were reported everywhere in the most varied disguises and preferably in nuns' habits. In fact, airborne troops had actually landed by glider on top of the key Belgian fort Eben Emael just west of the Meuse and north of Liège, and paratroopers were also dropped on a large scale in the Netherlands to secure the main bridges over the great rivers there.

Gradually the chaos at school subsided, and we were all shepherded outside in front of the great church entrance and the school's own entrance to the side to wait for parents to pick us up. The weather was superb. Unusual for Belgium, there was barely a cloud in the sky. Little by little, more and more cars of various makes kept turning into the roundabout there to pick up children and their luggage. There were so many that around noon there was almost a traffic jam. How I managed to get back home I do not recall, but when I arrived in the early afternoon, while a plane was slowly circling like a lazy hawk high in the sky, most of my siblings were milling around in the garden. The older ones were practicing how to dig foxholes in case of need, while little Suze was patrolling the gravel paths on her scooter.

In the days that followed, Father continued to paint an impressive picture he had started earlier. More than six by seven feet large, it showed the four riders of the apocalypse bringing famine, war, illness, and death. Some of us watched as he depicted the boots of Death on its white horse in the guise of Belgian army boots. What made it all the more fascinating was that he was putting a left boot on a right foot. Nobody dared utter any remark, and so the left boot is still on the right foot today. Meanwhile every day the frontline crept nearer and nearer.

Soon Mother, who had qualified as a nurse during World War I, had us help her in cutting up bedsheets and turning them into dressings before she left for a field hospital near the *béguinage* in Bruges. A week or two after the onset of the war, I accompanied her there once to carry more stuff, and we came across the following scene. Behind their common entrance gate the houses of the lay sisters called Beguines had been built in a large semicircle around a central green. That space, where they used to sit when the weather was good to fashion the most delicate lace, was now occupied by a jumble of grass-green tents, emblazoned with large Red Cross emblems, which made up the field hospital. Mother left me at the entrance to wait for her while she entered one of the tents. As I waited I saw all around me dazed and wounded soldiers, on crutches, on stretchers, or sitting by themselves with bloody bandages. Most of them were obviously in shock, smoking aimlessly, keening wordlessly, or just staring with vacant eyes. Almost no one was talking to anyone else. Every so often the scene was shaken up as one or several sturdy little field ambulances raced in as fast as they dared and suddenly parked higgedly-piggedly anywhere to release stretcher bearers and their loads to race to the triage tent. This is how I learned that the face of war was not the heroic one of Polish teenage aviators in a storybook I had read at the school library, but this melancholy mess of smashed-up men. A few days later, near an exit of the main market square, I witnessed a queue of pale-faced Tommies nearly scared out of their minds reluctantly boarding trucks to leave for the front line less than an hour away. Where, then, were the heroes in all of this?

At home we all now received the gas masks that had been kept for us by Mother and practiced taking them out of their canisters, donning them, and breathing through them properly in the shortest possible time, all with strict orders—nay, imprecations—not to start playing with them.

Before then, unbeknownst to us, the British destroyer *Brilliant* had entered the harbor in Antwerp on May 14 and had organized the evacuation of 26 allied merchantmen, 50 tugs, and 600 barges. Before leaving on May 17 the sailors also disabled storage bunkers for motor vessels that were holding 150,000 tons of oil. Meanwhile a general panic had gripped Belgium as almost every functioning car in the country, loaded with refugees and mattresses, was fleeing before the advancing German armies ever further southward, far into France. Indeed, during the very last days the government also joined these fugitives. Life was becoming more surrealist by the day. Was it then or later that young Nico came home one day with an exciting story about how a great shadow had dived above him over the street to spray a stream of firecrackers on its cobble, or did this account of a fighter plane machine-gunning some streets happen a few days after the Belgian surrender? No one in the family remembers when, and so it might have been either a German or an English plane.

Then, one morning official tricolor Belgian edict posters suddenly blossomed near the newspaper stands where grim people clustered to read the news. They apparently informed the public that the city was almost surrounded and requested the population to remain calm. It was a lovely sunny spring day, and while we played in the garden we again saw overhead one or two German planes leisurely circling high up, spinning whimsical vapor trails. At that point our parents announced that we were to leave the villa and move to the house of Samuel de Vriendt, an artist painter and an old friend of Father, far within the city proper on the opposite side. So, except for the two youngest, we all received tiny backpacks with bottled water and rations of military biscuits that we were not supposed to eat, as well as a strap with our now-familiar gas masks. We left on foot in a long single-file line, proceeding through the very heart of Bruges and its main square to a somber and unknown house facing the church square of St. James. A dark corridor brought us from the door straight to a large room at the back whose windows opened on the canal (*rei*) that flows behind the wall of the house.

There we bivouacked mostly on the floor, and I passed the time looking at a huge wall map in brilliant colors of a country I did not know: the long defunct Austro-Hungarian Empire. The map dominated the atmosphere of the whole room and its melancholy view on the canal as if it had just been hung there, and time had stood still in that room ever since. Could one imagine a safer refuge than this to wait for the resolution of the situation? Anyway, no one among us seemed upset, even when our provisions were checked, and it became apparent that some of the younger siblings had munched on them en route, and one or two had actually managed to eat the whole lot. Nevertheless, some supper was rustled up for us from somewhere. Then we went down to a cellar that had been propped with additional thick supports in wood, and there we all went to sleep.

The next morning we were told that the army had surrendered, and the enemy had entered Bruges. Then came a ring at the door. I was then in the front parlor and could look outside through a peephole. I saw a polite well-dressed man in *feldgrau* with a bar of insignia on his epaulettes and shiny black calf-length boots talking to someone on the threshold with an almost apologetic air for his intrusion. That was my first sight of a German soldier. Then some noise drew my attention toward the square in front of St. James and—surprise—the whole square was completely filled with empty buses, including the most luxurious tour buses I had ever seen. Had German soldiers really entered the city in the guise of military tourists? But no, the first ones apparently arrived on heavy motorbikes. Most likely the buses had been the conveyance of the impeccably turned-out squads that paraded later that morning, behind their bands, singing as they went from the market square to city hall on the Burg square. They stood out in sharp relief against the clusters of wholly exhausted and unkempt Belgian soldiers here and there who looked as if they had just emerged from their trenches.

Well before that parade, however, several of us managed to get out onto the street to see what else was noticeably new, and there was this huge, sturdy truck painted in a dressy grey pulling an almost identical long trailer. Until then I had never seen such a big truck nor even one with a trailer. So that was what they drove on the famous *Autobahn* pictured in magazines and occasionally featured on newsreels. Later that day, after the parade was over, I accompanied Father to the Burg square where our own dispirited troops were discarding their rifles on a big heap as they sullenly went on their way to captivity, except that from time to time one of them would just vanish in a flash among the multitude of silent sullen onlookers. They threw their weapons away, but there were no flags. Little did I know then that all the regimental standards had just been hidden in a now bricked-up cache in the abbot's apartments on the side of the choir of the abbey of St. Andrews, my new school.

The next day already the children returned again in single file to villa Manon and passed again along the newsstand near the Katelijne gate where German poster edicts, in black and white headed by an eagle with outstretched wings, had replaced the Belgian ones. They were issued by an office called *Kommandantur* and told the public what to expect and what was forbidden—*Verboten* was a word everyone learned very quickly. When we arrived, the entrance gate to the garden stood wide open, and Mother was distributing soup and biscuits to ragged slovenly soldiers. The street was pocked here and there with heaps of discarded rifles, bullets, and bayonets without anyone to guard them. The house itself was a disaster area. Fleeing civilians or soldiers had found refuge there, leaving a trail of considerable damage and mayhem behind them as they left. When we left the house two years later, this event triggered a major lawsuit for damages by the owner against us, the renters—a suit, I am happy to say, the owner lost. Later that day, as darkness fell, Chris went to the greenhouse to help Father dig up the sacks of coal that had been hidden there, to fuel the house's central heating system.

Nevertheless, a day or two later civilian life had apparently seeped back into its humdrum peacetime ruts, even though the battle over the evacuation of Dunkirk, only about forty miles away, was still raging and would not conclude until June 4. We heard about it, and we heard about the fury of Winston Churchill and the French authorities with the "villainous king" (*le roi félon*) who surrendered rather than fight to the complete destruction of his army and the civilians of the city. Yet to the people of Bruges and to us, Leopold III was the monarch who saved them and us from ruin, who had remained with his troops rather than run away like the politicians, and who was loved for it.

A week or so after our return to villa Manon, I went back to the abbey school, and classes resumed. For whatever else might happen, in the Belgian mind children should never lose a school year, and we had lost almost a trimester. When I returned to St. Andrews I found the situation strikingly different, and much more to my liking. There were now only a few pupils, perhaps because most of the others were still in France, where their families had fled the fighting. Some Benedictine teachers had also left because of the war and had been temporarily replaced by other monks from the abbey. As a result a good deal of improvisation reigned. Classes became informal, we sped through the curriculum, and discipline was quite lax. During recess we did very much what pleased us, whether it was playing croquet, watching older boys play tennis, timidly trying our own hand at that game, or simply reading in the sun. For some reason there was no access to the school library, and when I asked once for some reading material our novice supervisor found a little illustrated booklet that came, he said, from the mission. Thus I learned that the abbey had a mission field in the province of Katanga in Congo. The booklet was a first reader in "Congolese" for schools there, with many illustrations of enviable, jolly black children having a good time. It was, I recall, entitled *Bwana Yesu mupulushi* (Lord Jesus the savior), written in Sanga, a language spoken in rural parts of Upper Katanga. That was my first encounter with a Bantu language. I used it to try to learn some of those Congolese words by heart, no doubt to boast about it later. Thus a few hurried weeks concluded my grade school education. Final exams came and were successfully passed, and we were sent home. In the end Mother had succeeded in using the upheavals of that momentous year to make me skip a grade.

4

Hungry Years

July 1940 to Summer 1943

A tall fisherman, clad in oilskins, was heaving a fish even taller than he
was on his back: That was the label of the bottle of cod liver oil to which
I was addicted. It was early summer now, I was back from school, and
overall daily life was returning to its usual ways. The violent storm of
battle had passed by us, and even the occasional lone British fighter plane
diving over the city to machine-gun at something or other on a main
street was gone. Yet my novel hankering for cod liver oil signaled that
some things had changed. All manner of goods had first rarefied and then
disappeared altogether from the shelves of the shops, especially anything
edible. Imported foods like coffee, chocolate, cocoa, bananas, citrus
fruits, and most tobaccos had long since vanished, but it also became
quite difficult to find even milk suitable for babies and children, genuine
bread, any kind of meat, and many vegetables. Hunger was gripping the
land while food rationing was not quite in place yet, the black market was
just starting to take shape, and it was too early for any harvests.

As we sat in the spacious kitchen at meal times the lack of food
was evident. For lunch there were mostly soups made of greens, often
accompanied by one potato per person. At dinner we received a slice or
two each of something that was called bread but was mostly some sort
of chaff on which we could smear a syrup of supposed apples or pears
that tasted like soap or sweetened dandelion flowers, and as a special
treat we were each given one big tablespoon of cod liver oil. One's
stomach kept quiet for an hour or so after each meal, but then hunger
began to gnaw again. It gnawed and gnawed, quite unlike the occasional
empty stomach one had known hitherto when skipping a meal. Now
one felt hungry nearly all the time, day and night. At times it felt like

cramps, and at other times it became merely a familiar dull ache accompanied by listlessness and lack of appetite. Or does one call *appetite* that occasional yearning for food with tears in the eyes? We children were still fairly easily distracted from our hunger, but even so we were always on the lookout for something to eat. This was the kind of hunger that can turn into a famine over time.

Luckily for us, the period of extreme deprivation lasted only a month or two at most, though at the time it seemed like an eternity. From then onward the situation improved somewhat: rationing kicked in, a black market of sorts began to function, and some vegetables, fruits (cherries first), and later grains were harvested, although that fall the crucial potato harvest failed. Nevertheless, despite a steady increase in its national production, Belgium continued to depend on imports for absolutely essential foods such as cereals during the whole war, and all those imports were under German control. Hence the situation improved only a little, and the pursuit of food remained the most constant feature of the war. In a test of words by association, the cue *war* is still bound to evoke *hunger*.

The Abbey School

By September, however, I was back at the Abbey of St. Andrews school to embark on my secondary education. What had been a hasty decision in May "to find a school for Janneke" had now become a long-term commitment that would deeply influence me. The modern abbey of St. Andrews was founded in 1899–1900 by a group of Benedictine monks from Maredsous, a monastery in Wallony, south of Namur. It replaced an earlier one that flourished on the same spot between 1100 and the French Revolution. In 1910 the abbey opened its school, and by 1940 both abbey and school were prosperous communities of about 120 monks and 120 students. Its large complex of brick buildings, huddled around an imposing church and cloister in a neo-Italo-Byzantine style, vaguely recalled the ancient abbey of Monte Cassino, revered by all Benedictines. At that time Dom Théodore Neve de Mévergnies, scion of a noble family from Liège at the other end of the country, was its abbot, and most monks, like those at Maredsous itself, still came from Belgium's French-speaking rural nobility and especially from landed gentry in Flanders.

The community closely followed the spirit and usually also the letter of its ancient rule. For example, it stressed the Benedictine vow of poverty and plain living, although this policy had led to the acquisition of an especially expensive—but properly rustic-looking—set of eating bowls for the refectory. The understanding of "labor" was no longer limited to work on the farm, as in ancient times, but the balance between work and prayer as prescribed by rule was carefully followed, and this accounts for the contemplative aura that surrounded the whole institution and for its letterhead motto *Pax* (peace). Yet despite this meditative bent, the abbey was not wholly unworldly. Its hiding of the standards of the Belgian army is but the most extreme example of worldly intrusions in the minds as well as in the buildings of the congregation. The special mission of this abbey was the careful preservation of the Roman Catholic liturgy in all its facets, including that of liturgical art, and most of the abbey's income appropriately stemmed from the sales of its Roman missal. Not surprisingly, the celebration of the liturgies was especially impressive, as was the appropriate Gregorian chant. The long Holy Saturday morning services, which I watched from a side balcony over-looking the choir, remain unforgettable to me, and particularly the invocation *Fiat Lux* (May there be light) at the foot of the choir, followed by the striking of pure new fire from a silex stone well before dawn at the very onset of the sacred drama. This spectacle made one feel the direct continuity of the faith over nearly two millennia and justified all the arguments about the relevance and central role of the liturgy.

Apart from its main activity, the abbey also directed missions in Katanga and maintained the boarding school I attended. That school was unlike any other on in the country, barring Maredsous, because it recruited its pupils primarily among nobility, especially the landed gentry of ample means in Flanders, a milieu that considered itself to be part of the cream of the country. Given this situation, it is not surprising that to a certain extent the school's model was the British public school in general and Eton in particular, albeit with less stress on the importance of sports, with less use of the "word of honor" system, and without the British reliance on student "prefects." In my time a monk named Dom Feuillen was "prefect" of the whole school, and he was responsible for its practical management. Also, unlike most British public schools, this one did not favor a Spartan regime, and it completely eschewed corporal punishment. On the other hand, the school's special sport was field hockey, not plebeian soccer, and its dress code echoed Britishness in that its formal suit included knickerbockers with knee socks, and its uniforms were all tailored by a single clothier, the Union des drapiers. In addition, there were standard sports outfits, tennis "whites," and even an official swimming suit emblazoned with the abbatial crest.

Nevertheless, despite its British resonances, the abbey school belonged first and foremost to a proper Benedictine tradition. It stressed learning above sports, and its definition of learning referred to classical humaniora, a curriculum that had evolved from the standard medieval one. Ordained monks, teachers or not, were addressed as "Father" but were always referred to as "Dom" for *dominus* (lord) as they had been in the Middle Ages, to set them apart from brothers, and they wore the distinctive habit at all times. In its understated way the institution also viewed itself as preparing a crop of boys destined to be leaders in the next generation. Hence it carefully instilled a sense of refined knowledge, manners, taste, and deportment that was and often still is referred to as "culture," and it used various ancillary programs as well as judiciously chosen excursions to achieve this goal. However, even more care was given to the religious formation of its pupils.

When I returned in the fall of 1940 it was wartime, and many traditional features of the school had to be abandoned. It was now impossible to insist on the proper uniform; a suit with short trousers sufficed, at least in the lower grades. The school had ceased to offer such amenities as individual piano or violin lessons, and there were no more educational excursions, albeit with one exception—a visit to a vitamin factory in Bruges, where we were led up and down steel ladders along snaking pipes and trembling vats. Whatever the cutbacks, however, the school retained its core ethos of training elites for leadership roles, an ethos to which I was somehow completely tone-deaf. Today I realize that my situation resembled that of the only native child in a school for colonials. Still, I was at the abbey school, and I had to conform to its conventions, whatever sense of rebellion they might generate. Nevertheless, the recurring refrain in my school reports for those years—"Jan must learn to control himself"—indicates that my efforts to conform did not always succeed.

In addition to the subject of religion, the school taught Graeco-Latin humaniora, one of several officially approved curricula for secondary education. At the time the parents of children who completed grade school had a choice between different "streams" of secondary education leading to different career opportunities, according to the ability of their children as measured by their academic success in grade school. In this particular stream, teaching was focused first on Latin (five hours a week) and Greek (four hours a week from fifth grade onward), and then on Dutch and French language and literature. After them came the lesser branches in order of importance: mathematics, including geometry and algebra; history; geography; sciences (a grab bag in the lower grades); and the so-called third modern language, the fourth one being optional. In our case the language, not surprisingly, was German rather than English; indeed, during the war English was not taught at the abbey school. Each class had fewer than twenty students, and most of the major branches in a grade were taught by the same main teacher, who was therefore able to closely follow the progress of each student he oversaw. In the sixth grade our main teacher was a creative monk, who loved the theater and was always organizing a play or a sketch, while in the following grade it was a visiting lay teacher who replaced a monk who was still in a prisoner of war camp.

Judging by the plethora of memories they left me with after all these years, their teaching was certainly impressive. Here I am reciting the first Latin declension *amo, amas, amat*. Barely a year later—a bigger boy now—I am repeating to myself the Greek declension *pipto, pesoumai, epeson, peptoka*. I see myself desperately struggling with Euclid's proof of the square of the hypotenuse, but also lovingly detailing the peninsulas of the coast of Honshu. Two reminiscences in this medley stand out. In the first, our teacher is using a set of bones in a magisterial demonstration showing that the fins of a whale are actually arms. "How could this be?" I wonder. In the second, I am gazing in wonder at the fine carving detail of finger-long figurines dating to prehistoric times (15,000–7,000 BCE) in the abbey's own collection of Magdalenian art. I could not even come close to this quality of work even with modern iron tools, let alone with the sharp edge of a stone. And those people were "primitive"? Or, were they perhaps primitive elites?

Life in our boarding school followed daily routines that for the most part did not strike me as very unusual. Still, there were some special features. Daily mass was not memorable, but the practice of singing hymns was, especially those set to music by Bach for Lutheran services, including some written by Luther himself. Lunch was the main meal, and we ate it in silence as someone standing at a lectern read to us from a book chosen for this purpose, exactly as if we were in the refectory of the monks. Sometimes the book was the biography of a saint or another remarkable person, sometimes it was some edifying or instructive story, but from time to time it was light reading such as Jerome K. Jerome's *Three Men in a Boat*, the only one of all the readings I recall.

Physical activity was also unusually important at that school. For a short period twice a day we practiced field hockey, and afternoons on half-days off were usually devoted to matches between competing school teams. These matches were the most exciting events of most weeks, and their highlights were endlessly rehashed afterward. I was quite proud to be a goalie—that impressive figure, clad in leg and abdomen guards, who must be ready at any moment to charge out of his niche to block a bullet-like puck in the middle of a stampede . . . or miss it. Then there was physical education in a specially equipped hall whose tiled roof was held up by a framework of large rafters. I knew from long ago that I was good at climbing ropes, but I learned now, from exercising on the high beam, that I kept my balance easily and had almost no fear of heights. Walking rope, I discovered, was no problem. So I acquired the strange habit of going to the gymnasium when discouraged or when I had enough of the world, climbing along a wall to the rafters, and walking along on one of the main beams as far as the middle of the room, to be by myself and out of reach. It worked. Once a teacher arrived in the hall to see a boy high up there. Not daring to call out to me, he went away, no doubt for reinforcements—time enough for me to make a quick getaway. I never heard a word about it, so I continued with the practice, and the rafters remained my safe haven.

As there were no more excursions apart from the one to the vitamin factory, the only remaining extracurricular activities were the school plays that we produced for our comrades and for some outside visitors on a real stage built at one end of the gymnasium; there were even entrance tickets. The first play in the fall was about how Saint Nicholas saved three little children from being slaughtered and pickled like piglets by sheltering them under his cloak. I was one of the three children, and in this era of food shortages it was not difficult to imagine the story. On Mardi Gras 1941 we produced Hans Christian Andersen's story about the little girl selling matches and a play about the Trojan horse in which I played a "Russian rabbit" as I announced very proudly in a letter home. A year later I played a local youngster blowing in a conch in what was a major production about a story of conversion at a mission station in the Pacific—not in Africa. Apart from plays our sixth grade also performed as a choir. Most memorable about that was that before every appearance our teacher tickled our throats with a chicken feather dipped in wine. This is where I learned my first Congolese song, *Uele, O makasi o malibe*, a paddler's song about the Uele River. No one there seemed to know then that it simply meant "Uele, tough river" in a Europeanized pidgin.

The first year culminated in my confirmation in the faith on June 20, 1941, along with nine classmates. We had been prepared for this all year long, first by a thorough exposition about the nature of sacraments and why they were central to Catholic doctrine. Then followed an analysis of the sacred drama of the mass, after which I was allowed to serve mass in those seven chapels of the abbatial church for any monks who required a servant. All that led to a further exposition about the holy ointment or chrism. The ritual itself was impressive. The choir held two thrones for two prelates in full pontificals, and at the appropriate moment we knelt on the steps there for the renewal of our baptismal vows in the hands of "our" abbot, followed by the administration of the chrism by Mgr. Lamiroy, "our" bishop of Bruges. In passing we also learned something about ecclesiastical politics: the episcopal throne was by tradition one step lower than the abbatial throne. Because of the war any celebration after the confirmation ceremony was perforce subdued, but Mother was there and took me for a tour through the countryside in an open carriage. Indeed, the war was not over: two days later Germany attacked the Soviet Union.

Anyway, there was no way to forget the war; every day the greater or lesser shortage of food reminded us of it. Although fortunately the abbey ran its own farm, food was still scarce, especially during the shortage of potatoes in the fall of 1940. We received very little—just one potato a day per boy—and one day two older boys simply stole mine from my plate. Soon I began to try out anything that looked edible, including berries that were supposed to be poisonous. They did not send me writhing, but neither did they provide much sustenance. It was then that I became addicted to toothpaste, blotting paper, and the erasers at the end of pencils, so much so that I remained hooked to these delicacies even after the situation had eased somewhat. Still, as late as the following spring I had to get rid of a very long hookworm that had incubated in me from a bad piece of meat. That had been a terrible experience. I felt unwell, and as I hoped to relieve myself, I felt a piece of string in my bowel that I grasped and began to pull out. I pulled and I pulled until I was wholly free of it, and then I discovered that it was not a string but a horrible sort of endless centipede. At the time I had never heard of hookworms or the like, and I could not imagine where this nightmare worm came from, except that it certainly had something to do with something devilish in myself—it had to be "my fault," and it was my shame. This left me absolutely terrified and devastated for a few moments. Then I picked myself up and behaved as if nothing out of the ordinary had happened. But still I did not dare to mention the incident to anyone at all, let alone call for medical attention.

The net effects of the food shortages during that first year at boarding school are clear, thanks to a series of measurements. Between early September 1940 and April 8, 1941, at age eleven, my weight remained completely unchanged at 35 kg (77 pounds), even though I had grown 13 cm (5.2 inches). Compared to the weight loss suffered by most adults in the year after May 1940, this was actually not bad. In contrast, however, during a period two years later, between January 27 and April 20, 1943, when the situation had somewhat improved, I gained 2.6 kg (almost 5 pounds) but grew by a mere 1.3 cm (0.52 inch). Probably the food shortages between 1940 and 1945 stunted my growth a little and kept me relatively thin.

As the war wore on, shortages of other items also became more and more pronounced. By early 1942 the only good cloth that Mother could find for a school jacket was of a vivid grass-green color, so that I and Guido, who had joined me that fall, set off to school fully expecting to be treated as "frogs." At that prospect Guido simply "lost" his coat somewhere, while I kept mine and merely shrugged off the teasers. By then also most of the heels and soles of my socks were gone, but my shod feet still looked presentable. Not much later, though, I went through the soles of my shoes and hence started walking around in hockey boots, only to lose their soles as well. This I managed to hide from all prying eyes until a fatal walk with the class on a Sunday afternoon. It had rained, and suddenly the pupil behind me noticed naked footprints in the mud and began to wonder loudly what sort of mysterious savage might have trod there before us. The upshot was that Mother had to find a spare pair of suitable shoes somewhere in a hurry. She did procure a pair, probably from one of my older siblings.

Another indirect effect of the war, especially in 1942, was the sudden unexplained appearance of sundry people among the school staff. Thus for a few weeks a new foreign scholar taught us Greek. His name was Obolensky, and it was whispered that he was an émigré Russian prince, somehow on the run from somewhere. In our first-year German class the teacher was a monk we had never seen before, evidently more fluent in German than in French. He had been the abbot of a monastery in Czechoslovakia, and he regaled us from time to time with a story about the sinful wealth of these institutions there and how their wealth had led to their downfall. But we never learned whether he himself was Czech or German. I knew perhaps the most intriguing of all the monks because I was his regular servant at mass. He was Dom Lou Pierre-Célestin Tseng-Tsiang (Lu Zheng Xiang), and in this case his presence at the abbey was not caused by the war. He had joined the monastery many years earlier. Dom Lou had been China's first prime minister after the fall of the Empire and the proclamation of the Republic. Not long after we first met in 1942, he published his reminiscences *Souvenirs et pensées*, or in translation *Ways of Confucius and of Christ*, and he gave me copy of the book signed in Chinese and in French. In 1942 he used to talk to me about all sorts of topics after mass: how to add or subtract various layers of silk clothes according to temperature and season, how to use certain objects, how characters represent ideas and words, but he sometimes also spoke about ceremonies and judgments at the last imperial court, how he once was prime minister and minister of foreign affairs of China, and how he refused to sign the Treaty of Versailles in 1919. At the time I conceived of the world as a sphere-shaped medal and considered China to be the reverse image of our own world, or perhaps it was the obverse, and we were the reverse. This made the country particularly intriguing to begin with, and ever since those days China and things Chinese have held me spellbound. I might well have ended up as a sinologist, but at the time I did not even know that such a specialty existed, and the exigencies of wartime did nothing to encourage this embryonic interest.

Indeed, the war was always with us, in more direct ways as well. On our Sunday afternoon school walks we sometimes crossed platoons of German soldiers marching to their sergeants' shouts of *Eins, zwei, drei, vier*, a cry that we soon mimicked to perfection. Then they burst into song. Their repertoire, however, was rather limited, so that we soon recognized the most familiar tunes, including the nostalgic "Lili Marlene," which became so famous that Allied troops adopted it as well. But my own favorite was "Erica" ("On the heather blossoms a little flower, Erica"), because it reminded me of Gooreind.

Moreover, there was always news about the war, often dramatic news. At first, and especially during the Battle of Britain, Dom Feuillen, the school prefect, appeared every evening in the study hall with news from the BBC, but later such bulletins grew scarcer and scarcer. Later still our sixth-grade teacher could not hide his admiration for the capture of Crete by German paratroopers. But then he was an unusual person. For example, he had studied Arabic and one day wistfully proposed to teach the language to those of us who were interested, though nothing came of it. Then two days after confirmation and barely three weeks or so before the end of the year came the invasion of the Soviet Union, signaling a major change in the course of the war. Over the summer the newspapers were full of it, and when fall came and we were back at school, we began to follow the German advance daily on a map in the dormitory by listening to both the official radio and the clandestine BBC. By mid-December a huge itinerary from Smolensk to Moscow appeared one day on a tall wall in the fashionable Noordzandstraat at Bruges in which Moscow was indicated by a huge Christmas star, and every day the little light of the battlefront advanced toward it. But then the light got stuck as the German army did not make it, and the whole display vanished before Christmas, thus proving to everyone that German might was no longer inevitable destiny: it had actually been checked.

During the same fall it gradually also became obvious from the fragmentary remarks of our teachers that this new conflict was causing a split in Catholic milieus, between those who clung to the old belief that communism was the greatest threat to the world and those who viewed Nazism in that role. That debate acquired substance on a day in late February or early March 1942, when an alumnus from the school appeared unannounced for lunch at the high table in the refectory, in the guise of a veteran of the eastern front clad in full SS uniform, boots included. The effect was at once boorish and malignant. In one instant this apparition by itself succeeded in uniting practically the whole school against him without any need to utter a single word.

Out of Place

The first impact at home of the occupation occurred, according to Veva, not long after I left for St. Andrews to return to villa Manon. It began with an inspection of the whole house by a sergeant accompanied by a small escort to assess its capacity for quartering soldiers. On leaving, he wrote "7 Men" in chalk in large letters next to the front door. They arrived a little later and were met in the entrance hall by our Mother at her most supercilious, who ordered them in her own brand of German to leave their boots downstairs, to climb the stairs to their quarters two floors higher in their socks, and to do so quietly, so as no to disturb the children sleeping on the floor under them, and they obeyed her. When he heard what was happening, Father, pallid with apprehension, was off to the *Kommandantur*: "I have eight daughters at home and hence it would be highly irresponsible to lodge seven young men so near to them." The result was the disappearance of the seven men in exchange for Hans, a twenty-five-year-old officer, and his batman, Willy, and for the occupation of the rear half of the garden, most of which was an orchard, by a military field kitchen and its attendant horses. They had their own gate at the back of the garden and in this way had access to an alley behind its wall so that their coming and going did not bother us.

Father soon found out that Hans was a teacher by profession, and they both rapidly discovered that they shared similar views on many issues, to the extent that no sooner would Hans arrive home every day than he went to discuss one or another of these with Father. Pretty soon Father was passing outlawed anti-Nazi literature to him such as the Catholic prewar magazine *Kirche und Volk* (Church and People) or banned novels or philosophical texts. Not only was Hans a Catholic himself, but he had also been a member of the Guardian Angel movement before the war, a movement that actively tried to wean rabid Nazis from their ideology. His batman, Willy, was a Bavarian barber around forty years old with six children. That explains why his room was always redolent with the refined fragrance of all sorts of lotions and the walls covered by drawings made by his children. One day he broke down at the sight of our Marleen—two years old at the time, the very age of his youngest daughter, whom he had not seen for more that a year. There he sat weeping on the bottom step of the stairs, while Veva could not believe what she saw: a soldier in tears.

Many months passed, until one day in late May 1941 Hans was caught in possession of forbidden books. That led to a search of the house by "three men in black," according to the badly frightened maids, who had sought refuge in the kitchen and were still sniffling when the children returned home from school. The men must have terrorized our parents with dire threats because they never mentioned anything at all about this visit to any of us, and no more outlawed books or magazines seem to have remained in Father's library. Indeed, the atmosphere in those days was such that even when I came home from school in July none of my siblings told me anything, either. Hans and Willy moved out one afternoon a few days after the incident. As he was going Hans told Veva that he was being sent to Russia and that he did not think he would survive the then impending war there.

Meanwhile the season of great hunger broke out. At the villa Manon the first help with that shortage of food came from an unexpected quarter . . . the field kitchen in the backyard, as the cooks there fell into the habit of bringing us the remainder of their dinner, usually a very thick broth full of meat. Once, when the cherries were ripe, the cooks arrived as usual with their heavy soup kettle, followed by two very young conscripts, carefully carrying their helmets filled to the brim with cherries for us. No doubt the whole episode was inspired at least in part by the general policy at the time to win over the civilian population. The kitchen remained in the yard until late summer, and it was only then that hunger really began to bite. All that was only a Band-Aid, perhaps, but it came at the right time.

Nevertheless, the most urgent day-to-day concern of my parents remained the provision of food. This was true even after the introduction of rationing in August by means of food coupons or tickets, because the rations were insufficient, especially for children. Each month each family was allocated a number of coupons or ration tickets according to the number of persons in the family, so that outright starvation was avoided.

There were coupons of several kinds: for bread, for potatoes, for vegetable fats (rarely butter, and later usually canola, a.k.a. rapeseed), for sugar, for meat (20 percent of it in bones), for milk, for coffee (actually its substitute, chicory), and soon afterward also for textiles and coal. The quantities of each item varied and tended to decrease as the war wore on except for the absolute essentials, cereals and potatoes, where they increased. Perhaps the most crucial item was unadulterated milk for babies and infants, and that was almost impossible to find except on the black market. Vegetables and fruit were not rationed. People began to grow those where they could and hoarded sugar for making preserves. Tobacco imports from the Americas or Southeast Asia also vanished, so that cigarettes or pipe tobacco now contained a mixture of some locally grown tobacco with a good deal of finely chopped-up grasses. As to tropical products, I would only discover or rediscover them after the war.

It was customary in Belgium, even in these circumstances, to hold women primarily responsible for feeding their families, and so they were the first to cope with the whole issue of food sufficiency. Mother did what she could. As it happened, villa Manon had been rented with a full-time gardener named Middernacht (Midnight) who tended its lawn, flowerbeds, and fruit trees. So like most housewives Mother turned the garden into vegetable patches. The lawn was the first part to go and became a plantation for carrots. Later a potato field took its place, but someone denounced us to the authorities, and we were fined for growing clandestine potatoes. We also kept a pig, called Wannes. Wannes was our pet and hero. He knew his name, and when he heard the call he always managed to break out of his sty and come barreling along as fast as he could, ears flapping in the wind. Most of us loved to see him coming, but he scared Bea to the point that when she saw him coming she clambered up a tree as fast as she could. He was also greedy beyond belief and had even figured out a way to get at the apples off our fruit tree by charging as hard as he could against its trunk, which then provoked a shower of still green apples, which he devoured in no time at all. We loved the spectacle. Of course, all that interaction was no good: it prevented the pig from fattening as it should, and it threatened to make his slaughter truly traumatic. Wannes was slaughtered while I was at school and caused quite a drama indeed. After the first recriminations and lamentations were over, the children were still so shocked that they refused to eat any part of Wannes for a long time before they relented, and one of them, Veerle, never did.

But even all of that was not enough; one also needed access to the black market. Our main problem in Bruges remained that, despite appearances, we were essentially displaced persons, without access to our network of family, old friends, and neighbors, and therefore we were bereft of information and mutual help. We could not return to Wiezelo because the German army had requisitioned the house as lodgings, and despite Father's repeated efforts it had so far proved impossible to dislodge them. Meanwhile, as aliens in the region of Bruges, we had at first no way of procuring food from the countryside on the black market.

So, starting already in the summer of 1940 and continuing for two years afterward, Mother often rode off on her bicycle, equipped with a sturdy luggage rack and two big canvas bags in search of food, ready to buy whatever she could find. She would be on the go all day, mostly along rural country lanes. It was, of course, illegal to buy rationed food on the side, and there was always a regiment of controllers on the lookout for suspicious characters traipsing along the roads. Hence the need for all those quiet rural lanes. This was also why Mother always carried her official marriage book with her, a document that enumerated all her twelve children. Should she be caught with her supplies on her way back, those papers were produced in an attempt to convince the controller to let her pass. Most of the time what she found were innocuous vegetables such as carrots, leeks, cauliflower, or beans, though sometimes she also had a cereal: buckwheat. Once in a while, however, her foraging resulted in some anxious moments, such as the day when she was caught with several badly hidden hams. On that occasion her marriage book did not help, but by bluffing about her connections to various local potentates, some of whom she barely knew—and, I suspect, by abandoning part of her catch to the controller—in the end she still managed to escape with most of the meat.

By 1941 a team of my siblings consisting of Bea and usually Chris (and more rarely Veva, who was less efficient) joined the search. Every Wednesday afternoon during their weekly half-day off from school, they made the rounds on their bicycles, stopping at the well-known larger farms in the vicinity of Bruges and beyond, sometimes as far as twenty miles away. Nearly always they returned with large quantities of vegetables, but on occasion they had nothing more than perhaps a few pounds of fruit to show for their efforts. All in all, though, the family managed to scrape together sufficient amounts of food, even though it came at a price far higher than was sound for the family's budget. The resulting menus depended on the kind of vegetable brought back by these expeditions. Rina recalls the uses to which a haul of leeks was put: breakfasts of dry war-bread with stewed leek, leek soup and stewed leek for lunch, fruit from the trees in the garden as a snack, and in the evening bread with leek pie. Others recall similar waves of menus fashioned from carrots, lettuce, beans, and cauliflower as well. At least there was never any need to admonish, "Children, eat your vegetables."

There were very few breaks for anyone during those years. The most memorable one is known in Belgium as the miraculous herring catch. In 1942 the fishing season unexpectedly turned out to be more bountiful than anyone had ever seen hitherto. The boats ran into shoal after shoal of herring in such quantities that this fish fed the whole country for quite a while as the new Belgian beefsteak. So exceptional was the event that even cardinal Van Roey wrote a special pastoral letter of thanks to be read on Sundays from all the pulpits in Belgium. Another kind of major break for us came from the shop at the Melkmarkt, which stocked various sorts of textiles for flags or church vestments. By the second year of the war, first aunt Maria de Moor raided it for her daughters, and then my sisters followed. Silk for artistic flags was well adapted to turn into ladies' clothes, although the colors were usually sharp and bold. Vestments were often adorned with discreet devout motifs. And what of it, if one of my sisters wore a loud silk dress, or one sprinkled with a discreet pattern of small invocations? After all, this was the time when worn-out clothes were refashioned inside out, and when stockings became unavailable, women were reduced to paint them on their legs in appropriate colors, right down to the darker shades signifying the seams. Leather for some reason had soon become extremely rare, so that wartime shoes were mostly made out of canvas cloth and cardboard, but they were not at all waterproof, and their soles wore out very quickly and required constant patching.

While at St. Andrews I first and Guido later were fed by the abbey school and its farm, in return for our rationing coupons. That was not the case for the other children. They had to bring their lunch from home and did not receive any food at all at school, which caused a great deal of resentment. While some lucky pupils were in the position of eating white bread, others had to settle for a sort of brown magma. One day our Nico, who had only the substitute imitation bread, gently whispered in his neighbor's ear just as the latter bit into his succulent sandwich: "My father is a controller," with the result that the poor child stopped eating right away and hid his lunch. Then in January 1942 Winterhulp appeared. This was an official organization funded by charity and organized by the former colonial lottery. One of its goals was to provide all school children with soup, milk, biscuits, and vitamins. But the authorities in Nico's school wanted the children to also bring bones for the soup. Nico knew there was nothing like that at home, but as luck would have it he happened to notice some bones on his daily route to school, and he would routinely dip into this stockpile to secure the required quota. Eventually someone realized that these were human bones. The enquiry revealed that Nico passed every day next to a small ancient cemetery adjacent to the cathedral of Bruges where they were digging air-raid shelters and carelessly throwing the excavated soil and the human remains it contained near the street, where Nico found them. Such was the situation that the school did not even make a drama about it but simply released him from the obligation.

Understandably, then, the mood at home whenever I returned from St. Andrews was often subdued, all the more so because none of my other siblings, except for my oldest sister, adapted well to their schools. Frictions were frequent, and even clashes were not rare, especially involving St. Lodewijks and Nico. One incident is enough to illustrate the atmosphere. Nico's master had placed a plaster piggybank with a nid-nodding black child in his classroom to raise funds for the missions and insisted regularly and forcefully from that day onward that his pupils should bring coins to fill it. So, on leaving the classroom at playtime one day, Nico took the whole abhorrent object and carried it to the playground. There he proceeded to smash it, shouting: "Come on, you guys, and get all your money back!"—whereupon a great scramble for coins ensued. Following a series of such episodes, my parents decided to withdraw all my brothers from St. Lodewijks and place them at other schools, and that is how Guido joined me at St. Andrews in September 1941.

We spent all our holidays, including the long summer vacations, at villa Manon. There, apart from a very few excursions to Bruges, we spent our time "doing nothing," that is, only playing in the garden, because the situation made anything else out of the question. I vaguely recall a few outings rowing on the canals of Bruges and a few visits to museums or churches. However, there was not much to be admired there because most important portable works of art had been removed to safety for fear of bombardments, except for massive sculptures such as Michelangelo's *Madonna*, which duly impressed me, even more every time I saw it. Another exception to this dearth of artwork was the reliquary shrine of St. Ursula inside the medieval dormitory of St. Johns hospital, where the Ursulines (the nuns of the order of St. Ursula) had been nursing the sick ever since medieval times; since it was still used as a hospital, the building was considered safe from attack. In a rather genteel way, the last panels of this masterwork of the fifteenth-century painter Hans Memling depicted two scenes of violence that reminded one of comparable wartime outrages: the impending martyrdom of Ursula at Cologne by decapitation and of the eleven thousand virgins with her at the hands of archers.

But the outing that left the strongest imprint on my imagination was of a quite different order: a visit to an exhibition at the Masonic lodge of Bruges. In Belgium the Freemasons were a secret society that constituted the backbone of anticlerical forces in the country. The society, it was rumored, recruited its members among the political, economic, and intellectual elites and derived its strength from the mutual assistance that members secretly gave each other to advance in their careers and to thwart those of their opponents. They were quite influential and feared precisely because their membership was undisclosed, and popular legends about them abounded. The Freemasons were sworn enemies of the Nazi regime, and hence when their lodge was found, the German occupiers organized an exhibition about them there, essentially to reveal that hitherto secret membership and to ridicule their activities. The exhibition was a sensation, and all Bruges flocked to it. I was impressed when I saw it, and not just because it exposed the rituals of a secret society, however attractive that in itself would be to any young boy. What struck me most was the dark cubicle-like room where aspirants to membership passed a fearful night before they were questioned (I imagined a sort of catechism) and inducted. The paraphernalia of their lodge merely seemed quaint, but the legend of Solomon's temple, its architect, and its masons struck me as an alluring poetic dream, while the cabbalistic signs held all the attraction of mysterious words in an unknown language.

Besides the above, my mental album of reminiscences from those years consists almost entirely of domestic scenes, such as playing mass in children-size vestments using slices of carrots as hosts and Guido as mass servant, furiously stomping on a shoebox with fake knobs rigged by Chris to resemble a radio, or playing a role in "The Rich Uncle from America," a play we children had invented and performed for our parents. The most significant image in that album undoubtedly was our huddling altogether in the severe winter of 1941 on December 7 next to the real radio to hear the announcement from Cardinal Van Roey that he had joined our king Leopold in morganatic marriage with Miss Lilian Baels. Only later did we learn about the attack on Pearl Harbor and the entry of the United States into the European war. At the moment itself we children were wholly absorbed by trying to grasp what "morganatic" might mean, and we had no inkling at all about the political significance of the event for the future of the country. Yet two aspects of this marriage upset the Belgian public: that the king had married a commoner was the least of them; the more shocking one was that he, the commander of our army, would be insensitive enough to marry at a time when most of his troops were languishing in prisoner-of-war camps.

Nearly every day during the vacation Mother took us to attend mass at the church of the small Benedictine abbey of St. Peter in Steenbrugge, not very far away. Actually, this was not an institution hitherto unknown to her, for Father had been an old companion of its abbot, Dom Modestus Van Assche. They had both been active in the Flemish anti-war movement centered on the annual pilgrimage to a commemorative tower on the Yser River, next to the trenches of the First World War. So it came about that the four Vansina boys were invited a few times to the abbey during the summers of 1941 and 1942 to weed the orchard and incidentally pick up the fallen fruit and eat some of it, as well as to lunch with the monks in their refectory.

Here, then, I found a small Benedictine abbey with a very different outlook on the world than that of the large abbey of St. Andrews, and yet their spirituality was practically the same: they shared the same interest in liturgy, the same mixture of work and learning, the same general emphasis on peace. Yet the differences were considerable. First, this abbey was not rich, and its monks ate not from artfully made rustic ware but from unadorned cheap plates. These monks had been recruited from less prominent families, and they all were Dutch speaking. In 1941 their abbot traveled to Germany as soon as he heard about a railway accident that had befallen Flemish prisoners of war returning home— an initiative I could not imagine Dom Neve at St. Andrews would ever take. Steenbrugge definitely felt more rural, but not less learned for all that. Its specialty was Syriac patristics, that is, the study of the Syrian fathers of the church and the publication of their texts in the original, something definitely more esoteric and otherworldly than St. Andrews concerns. I drew the comparison between the two but did not come to any conclusion, apart from learning to distinguish a religious spirituality from a secular ideology.

Turning Points

In August 1942 Father once again had biked the seventy miles to Wiezelo and was told this time that the house would be vacated immediately, but the family had only three days until the end of the month to occupy it. If not, the military would return. As I was just then leaving home for school, my account here has to rely on the reminiscences of some my sisters. According to Veva, on arriving in Gooreind he discovered that the inmates had found a Flemish flag and were using it as a curtain, whereupon he set off for the *Kommandantur* in Antwerp full of rightful indignation. As we already saw with the story of the Belgian flags hidden at the abbey, in those days flags as symbols had unsurpassed value. When father told the officers there about it, they relented and decided to let the house go. So he returned posthaste the seventy-plus miles to Bruges, and within three days, by the first of September, the whole household was moving clothes, utensils, furniture, and all to

Wiezelo. All sorts of supposed neighbors in the Baron Ruzettelaan, people whom we had never seen before, suddenly turned up in numbers to help us move, but in the chaos of this hasty evacuation they actually filched whatever they could, including a few pieces of furniture, as well as Veva's own winter coat and her raincoat.

Rina remembers helping Mother carefully pack dinner sets and trunks to be sent on and then the exodus itself. Led by Mother, they traveled by train, every child wearing a gasmask around the neck and a backpack containing some underwear and dry food. The elder children each held a younger sibling by one hand and carried a pot or pan or something else in the other. Once in Antwerp they went two by two behind Mother to the square where they were to catch the tram to Gooreind. They must have made a newsworthy sight, because everyone on the sidewalks without exception halted in their tracks to gape at the procession. Meanwhile Father had already raced back on bicycle to Gooreind with Bea. There they found the kitchen to be unusable for lack of a stove. Bea began therefore hesitantly to prepare their meal on an open fire, when salvation in the shape of Net from the farm appeared and helped them out. Then, after the family and the luggage had safely arrived, Father returned with Veva to Bruges to start cleaning villa Manon, a job that took them more than two weeks. On that occasion he discovered an antique piece of chocolate turned white with age, which he gave Veva as a surprise to celebrate her eighteenth birthday.

By the spring of 1942 the whole character of the war was changing. The Soviets had not been crushed, and the Reich now began to require a new level of war efforts from the populations it had subjected, including us. On March 6 it was decreed that Belgians could be forced to work in the country itself, but many people became only gradually aware of this as it affected their families—in our case it was late fall before two of my sisters were called up for this compulsory service. In July the flood tide of German expansion reached its highest points at Stalingrad in the USSR and at al-Alamein in Egypt, and everyone, including me, was well aware of it. Meanwhile in Belgium the first roundup of Jews took place in Antwerp and in Brussels, but neither the students at the abbey nor the children of the family in Bruges heard anything about it, despite the fact that nearly everybody in Antwerp or Brussels itself must have been well aware of this. Next on October 6 the mobilization of Belgian men to work as forced labor in Germany via the paramilitary Organization Todt was decreed, and in the following months most adults and all young men became acutely aware of this, and so in later months did children like me. By November the tide turned, and German power began to ebb, never to recover. What we did not know was that serious armed resistance to the occupation had first been organized by communists after the invasion of the USSR; nor did we know that the bulk of the recruits for this resistance was provided only later by the growing numbers of men who were called up as forced labor in Germany but refused to go and hid as best they could.

Even though I and others were only vaguely aware of these turning points at the time, they certainly affected me. In March 1942 the winds of change broke up the school, and by the first of September they allowed our displaced family to return to its "natural" milieu.

The visit of the SS alumnus to our refectory turned out to be an omen, because soon afterward on March 25 disaster struck. Abbot Dom Neve was ordered by the Germans to vacate all the premises of the abbey and the school within a week except for the church itself and the farm. The abbey was to become a headquarters for the Organization Todt, which was then building fortifications all along the coast. And so, at one stroke, the orderly routine of this great abbey and its school came to a sudden end.

Perhaps that day was a disaster, but not for everyone. To me it proved to be a blessing in disguise. With the passage of time I found the strict supervised routines and constant ideological elitist indoctrination harder and harder to bear, despite the school's and the abbey's other attractions. Our teachers may not have been aware of it, but a few of my older schoolmates were just as antagonistic to me as they had been before the war—only more careful. They still saw me as a sworn enemy of their French-speaking noble estate. They were the ones who had occasionally stolen my food, and a year later they were still out to harm me. Then several of them suddenly seemed to warm to me and taught me an Italian song beginning with the words *Bandiera rossa trionfera*. I did not understand the words, but my schoolmates claimed it was a martial Italian song. In fact, it was the Communist International song, and its opening words meant "The Red Banner will overcome." If I had ever sung this in public I might easily have been denounced to the occupiers. Somehow I found out what the words meant and kept quiet.

At the time my school reports reflected nothing wrong, but I felt more and more that I could not withstand such a toxic atmosphere any longer. The following detail well illustrates the source of my feelings. Before he left his abbey, Abbot Dom Neve de Mévergnies gave a touching thank-you speech in French to the local population. One of his monks then translated this in Dutch for the benefit of those who were being thanked. By 1942 this sort of situation had not occurred anywhere else in Flanders since the end of the First World War, and it was precisely this kind of feudal or pseudo-colonialist atmosphere that I found so intolerable at that time. Ironically enough, had the speech been in Latin that would have been quite acceptable!

After the buildings of the school were occupied, the institution was saved by a number of its noble and well-off alumni. As its directors almost instantly laid out a practical course of action, several barons in the region among its alumni were contacted and within a few short days agreed to place their castles at the disposal of the school. The available space was then assessed, and it was decided to break up the school in two blocks. The three grades oldest in age (grades 1 through 3) would move to the castle of Bellem in East Flanders, while the younger grades (grades 7 through 4) would move into castle Het Blauwhuis at Izegem way south of Bruges near Courtrai in West Flanders. The move itself was helped considerably by the offer of transport vehicles and fuel by a few alumni business managers in Bruges or its vicinity. In the immediate future the three youngest grades, including Guido's and mine, were sent home, while the four older ones were to help with the moving. Since there were only ten days left before the Easter vacation, most of us simply viewed this as a vacation bonus. Nevertheless I remember the solemn procession of convent and school all around the premises, including the farm, chanting the litany of our Lady. As we sang *Sancte X, te rogamus audi nos* (Saint X, we beseech you listen to us), the feeling overwhelmed me that through this chant we were actually talking to one saint after another, and it struck me how living that supposedly dead language, Latin, really was.

A Wandering School

As a result of these changes Guido and I turned up at the end of the Easter holidays in April at Het Blauwhuis in the small city of Izegem in the south of West Flanders. The castle turned out to be a very large building in a severe late-eighteenth-century classical style, set in a small park with a number of dependencies on the side that even included a so-called orangery, albeit one without orange trees. I was delighted by it all because it completely lacked the atmosphere of an ordinary school. First, there were only seventy-three students in all, the tables of our refectory were laid out along the grandiose corridor at the foot of the grand staircase, the students were lodged in groups of three or four on the top floor in what had been about twenty servant rooms with dormer windows, and the four classrooms were set up in the drawing rooms. All the floors downstairs were parquet, and hence we could not wear shoes but walked around in a sort of over-sock. At the rear of the house lay a wide lawn around a pond stocked with carp, and behind that a tiny wooded hill covered a cavern or icebox where we were told blocks of ice had been stored during the summer. To make it even better, that spring was unusually sunny. But there was a shadow side: German soldiers were still quartered in the dependencies on one side of the castle behind an old stone trough and its water pump. We never went along that side, but one day as our class was going out for a walk we saw a bare-breasted soldier washing his torso there and flanked by two others, arms at the ready. What could that be? That, we were told, was a deserter who had been caught and was to be shot later in the day. True or not, I believed the story then.

Apart from our ordinary classes we also learned different unconventional things. That spring, for instance, we each were given a small plot next to the pond to grow carrots, radishes, and lettuce from seed, and we learned to plant, weed, and water these plots as needed. The project became a great success. On another occasion our class repaired to the attic for a lesson about nobility. There we looked at a document showing the genealogy of the noble owners of the castle, illustrated with their coat of arms and mottoes. We were given some explanations about rules of descent and the changing composition of the coat of arms from generation to generation. When we returned in the fall some sheds in the park had been furnished with workbenches and closets, and one of these became our lair. Our class of eighteen was divided into three teams, and each team was provided with its own Latin motto and coat of arms. That was the occasion to teach us the rudiments of heraldry and its specialized vocabulary. Then the teams were supposed to compete with each other in producing linotype art. We began, of course, by designing our own coat of arms, according to a written description of it, cutting it into linoleum and printing it. Even though I was still not a good draughtsman I took to linoleum like a duck to water and was soon carving houses and landscapes more or less after drawings provided by other team members. Needless to say, only an aristocratic school like ours could have deeply interested its pupils in such a subject!

I was delighted with the move to Izegem because of its novelty, because it resulted in a more relaxed disciplinary atmosphere than had been the case at St. Andrews, and because the breakup of the school had removed all those older pupils who had so pestered me there. Our class walks and excursions around Izegem in a hitherto unknown country-side, often along country roads meandering between farms, were part of that novelty. This was flax country, where much of the land was given over to the cultivation of that grass, whose fiber is obtained by retting the plant after harvest. Retting is the maceration of flax plants in stagnant water until they rot enough to easily separate their fibers. After retting, the fibers are dried and ready for weaving into linen cloth. As we soon discovered, however, the major drawback of that operation is the heavy country air it produces. A tenacious stench envelops the whole country-side at harvest time and hangs on seemingly forever afterward. During that period tatters of rotting flax could be found anywhere, even high up between the wires on the telephone poles along the roads, where it became stuck when wagons passed underneath that were stacked with flax as high as on any hay wain.

From time to time our walks led to a surprise at the rural seat of one or another alumnus of the school. I will never forget the day we arrived at a farm to be given each a huge sandwich of genuine white bread, something I had not seen in over two years. Another time we were al-lowed to loot an old apple tree in an orchard where we were also shown how to pluck apples for marketing from carefully bred trees by capturing each hanging apple in a sort of sock so as not to bruise it. Once we arrived near a village where the monk who chaperoned us gave a graphic account of the last battle that was fought there in 1940 and in which he had taken part. One trip on bicycles remains especially unforgettable. It brought us to the city of Ypres ("Wypers" to British soldiers), ruined during the First World War, and the trenches at nearby Passendale (Passchendaele) where so many British soldiers had died. It was a sunny early spring day, and the long, seemingly endless lists of the names of the fallen glistened on the commemorative marble wall—but what for, I asked myself? Not even a further afternoon of fun on one of Flanders' largest lakes nearby managed to dispel that thought.

Besides the novelty, the relaxed discipline, and the disappearance of older bullies, another advantage of Izegem was the small size of the student population there. That and our division into heraldic teams probably explain why I finally made two friends that year. The ebullient one was André de Maere d'Aertrycke, with whom I went exploring and daydreaming all around the estate. We climbed the icebox hill and imagined it to be a crag in the Alps. André planned to follow in the footsteps of one of his forebears and become a "pioneer conqueror in Congo," and I felt an equal vocation as pioneer adventurer but not as a warrior. The only available remaining slot was that of missionary, and so that is what I would be. In due time André really did become a colonial administrator in Congo, and I became an anthropologist-historian there. In contrast to André, my friend Jacques Willemot was the quiet one. As a newcomer to the school and the only other commoner in our class besides me, he felt lonely, and so we used to abscond to quiet corners together to study and talk.

And then it happened again. On March 15, 1943, ten days before Easter, we were expelled again, this time from Het Blauwhuis. So we pupils helped the staff move the school's belongings elsewhere as needed and then left on Easter vacation before the onset of the last trimester. On our return we found that we had a common dormitory on the top floor of a factory, our refectory was housed in a local convent called Ave Maria, the soccer field of the city became our playground, and our class met on the ground floor of a shoe-making factory where a corner of the floor had been partitioned off . . . and there we were, snug as a bug in a shoe. Apart from the endless noise made by the machinery, it was an intimate room, quite effective for teaching. In fact, I seem to recall more from what I learned in that room during that single trimester than from the two other trimesters at Izegem combined, especially about religion— a subject on which Dom Xavier, our teacher, expounded in depth, well beyond the usual considerations. It was probably there that I first was told that when it came to ethics and sin, one's well-informed individual conscience was crucial. If one went against one's conscience one sinned; if one followed it, even though others equally well informed did not, there was no sin. He did not mean this to apply to matters of faith, where the authority or magistery of the Catholic church was absolute. Later in life, however, I gradually realized that it is impossible to separate ethics and faith completely and that one must always be true to one's informed convictions.

Dom Xavier became more of a parent than a distant authority figure to me and others. He closely followed my teenage readings from the tales of the Comtesse de Segur and used her masterwork *Les malheurs de Sophie* (Sophie's misfortune) frequently as a parable to demonstrate the folly of my pranks and what would happen to me if I continued to act on enthusiastic impulse rather than after mature consideration. There was no study hall, so we learned our lessons where we wanted, as long as Dom Xavier knew where we were. For me and Jacques Willemot that was often in the warm folds on the roof of the factory out of the wind, or next to a concrete wall. A few times the whole class settled in the trees of an old orchard while Dom Xavier walked in the grass below us. And so life went by until the end of the school year in July 1943.

By then traveling to and from school was much more difficult than it had been in September 1942, because the family had moved from Bruges back to Wiezelo. The trip from there to Izegem entailed the following: first a steam tramway for a few miles, then an electric tramway to Antwerp for about one hour, then ten minutes or so on foot from the square where the tram arrived to the railway station, then a little over half an hour by electric train to the station of Brussels North, then half an hour more on an always crowded tramway across the city to the station at Brussels South, then more than an hour by train from Brussels to Courtrai, and lastly in one way or another about fifteen miles to Izegem. Counting the time waiting between conveyances, the whole trip took around six hours. I was then thirteen and responsible for Guido as well as for myself. Usually all went relatively well, but one trip, the one back to school after Easter vacation 1943, did not. We left Wiezelo as planned, arrived at the railway station, and bought tickets as usual. We found a long train standing at the platform. The first wagons were empty but they all had notices saying *Nur für Wehrmacht* (Only for the army) stuck on their windows, so we traipsed alongside with our luggage, including the violin, until we found coaches we could board, and away we went. In Brussels, too, all went well until we arrived at the platform where people were waiting for the train to Courtrai. Knots of people were strewn all over the platform, each one around a hill of all imaginable sorts of luggage. As the train steamed into the station the expected surge into the wagons began but froze almost instantly. Suddenly nobody moved as a motorcycle with a sidecar manned by *Feldgendarmerie* roared on the platform, passed by us, and disappeared toward the head of the convoy. We waited and waited until a conductor's whistle blast signaled that we could board. A huge stampede followed during which somehow Guido and I were propelled on the train but only as far as the articulated bellows between wagons, where we became completely stuck between bodies and luggage.

The train shuddered and began to move, but still we remained stuck. And so we traveled for about half an hour until all at once the convoy braked hard and came to a dead halt. So sudden was the action that the sliding door to the carriage where we were stuck flew shut on Guido's left hand and may have broken some little bone there. But there was no time to check. We were in the middle of nowhere. The outer doors opened, and everyone poured out as fast as they could move to dive helter-skelter into the nearest ditch. We were being strafed by an Allied plane, and while neither Guido nor I even saw it, the rat-tat-tat of its machine guns was unmistakable. A little later all became quiet again, people cautiously emerged apparently from the earth as if this was the day of the Last Judgment, and everyone rushed back to their compartments and their luggage. This time I made it into a carriage, but Guido was delayed just enough to be stuck outside in the bellows again.

Apparently nothing vital had been hit, and the train moved off again. On the seats in the compartment sat two girls surrounded by a sea of mostly young men both seated and standing. Presently some of them began to tease the girls, whereupon one of the two started to giggle, flirt, and preen. In turn that provoked some of her neighbors to start pawing her and the other girl as well. At this point an older man next to me muttered something about how a kid should not be there, and lifted me off my feet and passed me on, violin case and all, like a parcel, to his neighbors who shoved me out of the wagon altogether into the articulated bellows next to Guido and then managed to close the door. I was too young to realize what was going on except that the commotion continued for quite a while. Meanwhile the train sped on relentlessly to its destination. That trip was my first intimation that the fury of war was returning to the country.

5

Ominous Horizons

July 1943 to September 1944

As the tide of the war first wavered and then turned decisively against Germany, every ripple of its fortunes seemed to impact almost instantly on the hitherto usual practices of the occupation, and every change in those practices pulled Belgian civilians deeper and deeper into the vortex of war—forcing them into positions where they either had to collaborate with their occupiers or else throw in their lot with the Resistance. From late 1942 onward, every passing month slowly but inexorably dragged everybody, civilian or military, further and further toward a final resolution. Try as one might, no one escaped this undertow of history, not even in our family.

July 1943 arrived and with it the summer holidays in Gooreind. Although in my eyes life in Izegem was rather enjoyable, it seemed to me that Wiezelo was bound to be better because it was home, and one could never be as much at ease elsewhere as one was at home. In retrospect it strikes me now that after the last harrowing trip by train I should have been quite apprehensive about the return journey, but I was not. I knew that the air war was intensifying and the frequency, if not the scale, of bombing in Belgium was steadily escalating. Yet somehow I did not connect that fact with the potential danger to travelers. The same impulsivity and lack of foresight my teachers rightly kept deploring apparently also had some advantages. In the midst of all this turmoil Gooreind seemed to be an insignificant and hence a safe place, and the prospect of spending an eternity playing and roaming through wood and bush with my siblings, almost wholly unsupervised by adults, overwhelmed everything else—including the fact that this "eternity" was to last only six weeks or so.

A Safe Haven?

The Gooreind of 1943 still looked like the place we had left three years earlier, though here too the war had left its mark. To begin with, there was a brand new and larger church in a style described as "local rural barn," a form well adapted, it seemed, to the farming portion of the population. The parish was still in the hands of Pastor De Wit, but this man's influence had grown considerably because he was now in charge of the local food stamp program. Now he was counted on to turn a blind eye and ask no indiscreet questions as he distributed rations to all the young men who had gone underground rather than be drafted for forced labor in Germany. Occasionally he might also provide for one or two mysterious newcomers. On Sundays his church was full, and his sermons were as fiery and ad hominem as ever, but most of the men stood at the very back and escaped to a nearby pub as soon as he began to preach, to return to the church only when the sermon was over—a habit they got away with for a time, until Pastor De Wit managed to have the sexton close the doors behind them, thus locking in his reluctant flock for the duration of the service. But even Pastor De Wit had been powerless to prevent the confiscation of his main church bell for the war effort, so that now only a small tinny-sounding bell remained to announce baptisms, burials, and disasters, or to call the faithful to mass. As always there was a yearly procession in which the holy sacrament made its way under a swaying canopy through the fields while onlookers prayed for rain and a bountiful crop. To watch this bucolic scene, one might imagine that the war was passing over Gooreind, yet the almost canary yellow canola crop (rapeseed) in some of those fields told another story. Canola was a new crop, grown for the oil used in the ubiquitous margarine that had now replaced butter. According to the injunctions of the clandestine BBC to patriots of the Resistance, however, it was a devil's weed to be destroyed on sight. These injunctions stemmed from the Belgian government in London, which mistakenly believed that canola was exported to Germany for its war effort. But in Gooreind no one heeded that command. Hence for those who could see, all was not as peaceful nor timeless as it seemed. But I saw nothing at first. To me Wiezelo was still a safe haven out of the current of history, and I enjoyed a sense of security as illusory as any such feeling is in wartime.

Frans and Net's farm on the Wiezelo estate did not look very different either from what it had been earlier. Indeed, the technology of farming could be described as of hoary antiquity. The cereal fields were first plowed by a single coulter plow, pulled by the same single horse that later also pulled the rectangular harrow with the driver on top of it, and the manure cart after that. The farmers sowed by hand, and scythe-swaying men reaped the harvest with their women at their heels to tie the barley or rye in orderly sheaves for conveyance to the barn, still by the same faithful horse. The men threshed the harvest by hand with wooden flails on the barn floor, raising an unholy cloud of choking dust as they did so. After that the grain was stored in bags, and the men pitched the stalks for straw into the barn loft using a three-tined pitchfork. Yet this seemingly stubborn adherence to hallowed tradition was but an effect of the war, a war that left most farmers without affordable chemical fertilizers, fuel, or even enough electricity. For the same reason, sheep no longer grazed on Wiezelo's great meadow with its picturesque sheepfold—Frans and Net had been forced to sell or slaughter all of them one by one well before our return in late 1942. Suske den ezel, the donkey, was also gone. Now he pulled the vegetable cart of the market gardener across the Bredabaan. Here as elsewhere the shadows of war were visible for those able to see, but I was not among them.

Access to Gooreind from the outside world by public transport had also regressed as the prewar bus service had been discontinued, no doubt due to the lack of gasoline and tires. From Antwerp a regional electric tram line ran to a terminus a few miles south of Gooreind. From there onward an antediluvian steam tram had been pressed into service again. A small, almost square locomotive, usually fueled by coal and made in Liverpool around 1870 as attested by a shiny brass plaque on the engine, bravely pulled two or three miniature railway carriages with open rear platforms and swaying hurricane lamps inside them. In the dead of winter one ordinary little stove heated each carriage. Passengers had to beware of fiery or sooty cinders. Indeed, when the weather had been very dry and hot for a while those cinders could and actually did ignite a forest fire along the train's route at least once a year. The engine was not very strong, and during rush hour it often happened that it did not make it to the top of the single almost imperceptible incline on its route.

Then all the passengers got out, the menfolk helped push the contraption uphill, and once over the top of the hump everyone embarked again. But this was certainly preferable to days when the steam tram did not run at all, and there was no alternative left except walking.

When Guido and I returned in July three of our sisters were no longer there. The oldest, Annie, was now a registered nurse and had found a job at a sanitarium called De Mick in Brasschaat, the main town between Gooreind and Antwerp. Mietje and Veva, the two others who were over eighteen, had been drafted for the *arbeidsdienst* (forced labor service), and I knew neither where they were nor what they were doing. There were no more maids at all in the household. Every morning Net came over from the farm, mainly to cook lunch. The children were now responsible for all the other chores. For the boys, myself included, these usually included peeling potatoes, cleaning vegetables, pumping water, carrying bundles of washing once or twice a week by bicycle to the laundry in Wuustwezel, doing errands in the village as needed, and carrying logs and faggots from the woodpile to the hearth as required.

In addition Chris and I were given occasional tasks from time to time on the farm. I especially recall the potato harvest. We uprooted the plants, picked the potatoes, and gathered the foliage in heaps to be burned later, after it had dried somewhat. At first it seemed like fun, but by the end of the first afternoon I was frazzled and had acquired a healthy respect for farm work in general. We returned dirty beyond description but filled with pride, and with a slice of genuine farmer's bread in hand. Later we also helped somewhat with the grain harvest by gathering the cut stalks in bundles behind the scythe swayers for the women to build up sheaves behind us.

Back from school I imagined myself to have returned to surroundings familiar from 1939, though some of them were clearly not. Certainly the care and concern for food were new. Now there was a pig in a sty out of sight but quite near to the house, and its slaughter in the backyard became a major event for us that we were forbidden to watch. But there was the anguished scream as the butcher cut its throat. Then Mother, Net, and the older girls all began to rush around with pots, jars, pitchers, large basins, and any container at hand, to the yard and back to the kitchen, to save every possible part of the animal. We younger children were definitely not wanted there, and it all reminded me, paradoxically, of the hustle and bustle that had surrounded births in the Markgrave-straat. Soon Net was making black blood sausage followed by white sausage, while in the cellar hams were being hung up and cuts of meat pickled with salt in three-foot-high stoneware crocks. That was to be our meat supply until the late fall, when the next pig should be ready for slaughter. However, when fall came our pig was stolen on the night before it was due to be slaughtered, and at the time in Gooreind that was that. Another pig was then raised, only to be stolen again, but the next one eluded the thieves and provided us with meat in the spring of 1944.

One or the other of those pigs also caused a fire. Mother was smoking some neatly wrapped-up hams in the hearth one day, and their fat was dripping along the great chimney's walls when the soot that was coating the chimney all at once caught fire, sending spectacular flames skyward. Upstairs the little metal hatch that gave access to the chimney in one of the rooms soon began to glow red-hot, threatening to set fire to the supposedly flame-resistant cardboard walls there. Thereupon Chris and I began racing up and down the stairs with pails of water to throw against the hatch while others filled buckets at the pump and passed them along at the foot of the stairs. Despite ominous hissing and a cloud of steam whenever a pailful of water hit the hatch, the tactic slowly succeeded, and the conflagration remained limited to the chimney. But the hams were reduced to cinders.

The scarcity of meat was responsible not only for this spate of pig stealing, but also for a sharp increase in the number of poachers now encroaching on the estate in quest of small game. As it happened, Chris made friends with one seasoned poacher — reasoning that since he could not beat them he might as well join them. So he learned the trade from his new friend, who demonstrated how to recognize the paths followed by rabbits and hares, to set snares at the right height, and to lure pheasants with aniseed — useful lessons all purchased at the reasonable cost of assisting his instructor in defending his turf from competing poachers. And so from time to time Chris returned with a much-appreciated hare, rabbit, or pheasant for the family pot.

Other major mobilizations, especially of the womenfolk, also occurred when beans were harvested and when the berries were ripe.

The boys peeled Himalayas of beans and peas while the women stored them again between layers of salt in those huge brown crocks of the cellar. In season the children collected various berries everywhere in huge quantities for making jam. They all disappeared in our largest stew pans to be cooked for hours. When ready, the froth was skimmed off for use as spread on our bread, and after cooling the jam was poured into jars and more jars until these filled a good part of the available shelf space along the cellar walls, where they joined jars already filled with strawberries earlier in the year. Those were smuggled in from a Dutch village just north of the border, renowned before the war as "the world capital of strawberries" but now bereft of its usual outlets. All that jam provided the spread for our slices of bread in the winter. So all in all, I found the food situation better than in Bruges, but I was still hungry enough to consume blotting paper, toothpaste, or erasers whenever I had the chance.

Clearly our nutrition was still deficient, especially in proteins. That is probably why we were all frequently plagued with toothache and perhaps why our dentist in Antwerp claimed that the Vansinas were his best customers and their teeth the worst in town. Gooreind also provided some relief from other shortages. We all wore wooden clogs as a matter of course and ran around in rags, justified as clothes for playing, all summer long to save on decent footwear and quality clothes that could no longer be found at any price.

The four boys and the three so-called small girls spent most of their time that summer playing together, but it was to be the last one for that. As ordinary toys, like everything else, were long gone by now, they made their own. The girls had found a way to fashion little people out of acorns and twigs, and the three older boys played with men made from sections of thin logs that sixteen-year-old Chris sawed in secret using a stationary electric circular saw no child was supposed to even approach. Provided with limbs and faces, they made up the population of three countries adjacent to each other, next to a shallow but large sandpit that belonged to the girls and Nico. No country was named, and the loggers were not really soldiers, yet war sometimes did erupt among them. The game consisted in a competition to develop one's territory as best one could with whatever useful trash could be found. There were several rich sources of rubbish in the area, the greatest trove being an old barn with discarded boxes, spools of ribbon, and metal molds for cigars dating from the time the nearby factory manufactured cigars rather than cigarettes. Those molds seemed predestined to make bunkers and bridges, the metal cigarillo boxes fitted out with wooden wheels made vehicles, while the wooden cigar boxes were great for paneling the inside of the log houses, and the industrial ribbon enabled the construction of a funicular railway. The great junk pile of the Franciscan sisters yielded much less, but some of the finds there were treasures, like the old stove that became a splendid underground house. Chris made his country the most modern by far. It had smooth highways used by all manner of vehicles (wheels were fashioned by the same electric saw), and it sported the railway. Guido's country displayed the grandest palace, with paneling from cigar box planking. Mine, the furthest away, boasted of its un-spoiled nature (I did not work much at it!) and its sturdy population living in miniature log shelters.

Once again we failed to notice how much our play had to do with the real war and with the propaganda surrounding us, even though we freely insulted each other as "capitalist" or "communist." In a further echo of reality, Guido's country was one of elegant, decadent, wealthy, urban living, whereas the territory of Chris was all corporate and milita-rized efficiency, and my own faraway realm of rough men relied mainly on the advantages of its vast remove for purposes of self-defense. As for Nico, he protected the sandpit of the smaller children with a secret weapon. That consisted in a genuine mortar shell he had found on the artillery range. Someone had kindly removed its detonator, and now Nico provided it with coat-hanger wings to turn it into a guided missile. Little did he know that he was prefiguring German V-1 flying bombs by a year. Today it strikes me how much each of these different "countries" reflected the personality of its creator.

But we did not always play near the house. We roamed about the whole estate and sometimes well beyond so that they had to call us for lunch using the powerful call of a real cow horn. We went swimming in a rectangular pool near the big meadow, or far beyond the estate in Keiven, a fairly large fen that lay half in the military domain and half in an adjacent property. We went hunting for berries or wildflowers, and we fashioned hidden retreats in the woods, usually under huge and thorny wild blackberry bushes where we kept treasures.

When it rained we read. Most of us devoured the tales of Karl May about noble Indians and cowboys in North America, and we read or reread Hendrik Conscience's *Lion of Flanders* and some of his other novels. I loved the old comic strips of the Breton servant Bécassine in Paris—we had no access yet to the most famous of the Franco-Belgian comics, Tintin—and at someone's urging I read Hector Malot's two-volume *Sans famille* (Paris, 1878), translated as *Nobody's Boy*. This is the most melancholy and strangest child novel ever written in French. Malot intended it not for children but for adults, to provide a moralistic socialist-realist perspective on the France of his day. But clearly the combination of a heroic performing poodle with the adventures of a young foundling turned it into a children's classic. That book made the most profound impression of everything I read that summer. It tells the adventure of a foundling reared by a woman who sells him at age ten to the director of a circus of performing animals, where he befriends a poodle and a monkey. They move all around France with more downs than ups. By the end of volume one the poodle, the foundling's only genuine companion, dies, and the boy's master is jailed. In volume two things perk up somewhat when his master is released, although he dies soon thereafter, and the hero is then forced into an apprenticeship to a brutal gardener. But the man is jailed for debts, and the foundling hits the road again, this time with a young Italian violin player. Eventually he finds his real family and all ends well for everybody.

However far from the mainstream we might have been, the world beyond still reached us occasionally. From time to time family visits or trips to Antwerp—if only to see that dentist—interrupted this almost idyllic life. We liked some visits more than others. I was delighted when cousin Jacqui, a tomboy if there ever was one, came to play, and all of us got along famously with all the children of Uncle Joe, Mother's youngest brother, who lived in Brasschaat, the main town on the road to Antwerp. A go-getter, as a young man he had traveled extensively in the Caribbean and Mexico in connection with his father's business. Now, during the war, he had founded a brand-new business producing cigarillos and cigars in his own factory south of Antwerp, and he even owned a small if old car in which he once brought Chris back from Turnhout to Gooreind after emergency surgery for appendicitis. I vividly recall the occasion when he invited a few of us to stay over for a weekend. We learned the game of Monopoly, became acquainted with figs and more, but most memorably we watched a clandestine film. It documented the German bombardment of Rotterdam during the 1940 campaign, and I would never forget its stark images of buildings turning into flaming waffle irons before they collapsed. That event had been the first bombardment of any city during the war and a precedent later invoked by all belligerents to justify all the subsequent attacks, including those that were then occurring in our country as well.

War Renewed:
What I Knew

Before I started to write this book, I had no idea of the full impact of the war on my family during these years, as so much of it was kept from us in the name of what can be called a culture of silence. It was not only unnecessary to share information with anyone who did not need to know, but when it came to sensitive matters in the context of the war it could be dangerous. That was especially true with regard to young children, who might not really grasp what it was all about, might misunderstand what they were told, and would be too garrulous to keep information confidential. This culture of silence ran deep, not only in our family but generally in Belgian society as well. However, it follows from this that I must now sharply distinguish between what I saw myself or knew at the time and what I did not. The air war and the destruction it caused were highly visible, but other effects of the struggle were not. These included clandestine operations to evacuate downed airmen to safety; the forcible drafting of labor to work for the war effort in Germany, a situation that drove many of these draftees underground and into the arms of various Resistance groups; increased pressure on civilians to collaborate with various authorities; and the deportation of Belgium's Jewish population. I discuss first the war I saw and later the happenings of which I was unaware.

The earliest bombardment of an urban target in Belgium occurred at Mortsel, a suburb of Antwerp, on April 5, 1943. In eight minutes' time 936 people were killed, of which 209 were under fifteen, and about 1,600 people were wounded, 600 seriously. The news shook the whole country and made people realize that a shooting war had resumed in

Belgium. Mortsel was also the deadliest of all bombardments in Belgium, so severe that from then on everyone began taking bomb shelters and warning sirens seriously—and there were many more small attacks to watch out for. Shortly after Guido and I had left Izegem at the end of the school year, the railway station at Courtrai was the target of one such operation, and as the months wore on other incidents followed.

Several times in Gooreind that summer we witnessed a fleet of bombers in almost cloudless skies, usually on their way back from Germany, while those on their way to Germany passed us as darkness fell in the early evening. Because sound travels much faster than planes, the noise of the engines always announced the imminent arrival of these fleets. First we would hear a seemingly endless swelling wave of rhythmic vibrations emanating from several thousand engines, droning in unison far above us. In daytime the bombers then came into sight, like tiny toys flying in V-shaped formations with lead and wing planes around the main body and perhaps a few stragglers apparently trying to catch up. They passed through a sky punctuated by little evanescent, harmless-looking cloudbursts from flak shells bursting among them as the guns on the artillery range went into action. In any case, harmless or not, we never saw any hit, but we were well aware of shrapnel rustling all around us. One formation followed another, all heading west toward safety over the Scheldt estuary. At the very end of the parade, as the wave of vibrations began to recede, a few damaged planes appeared, sometimes trailing a plume of smoke behind them. At night we only heard the noise made by engines and flak, while all one saw were searchlights crisscrossing the sky. From time to time, one of these caught a plane in its beam, like a little silver fish, and tried to hold it steady for the artillery. After the passage of such a fleet we would wake up in the morning to find thin long strips of reflective silver paper everywhere. We realized that they came from the Allied planes, but we did not understand then that they were thrown out to disturb radio communication on the ground.

One day as I was crossing a street in Antwerp an extraordinary sight halted me: everyone in the street had stopped walking and was looking up into the sky without uttering a word. Looking up, I saw two fighter planes dueling each other high above Antwerp's harbor, ducking and weaving or climbing and diving around each other, until suddenly one of them went into a tailspin and began to fall. At that point, or a moment later, everyone along the still speechless street began to clap as a white blob, obviously a parachute, began drifting downward. At that distance no one could really distinguish one type of plane from another. Were people applauding the victor in the belief that a German fighter had been shot down, as I assumed at the time? Or were some of the bystanders perhaps applauding the pilot's survival? I will never know, and neither will any of the other spectators in the ad hoc audience that formed on the street that day, for soon everyone began to walk again, still without any comment. After all, in those days who could trust whom in a city rife with both collaborators and resisters?

The war further intruded regularly into my field of consciousness through news bulletins on the official radio. All summer long there were frequent program interruptions to announce success in the battle of the Atlantic with the sinking of so many gross register tons of shipping by packs of submarines. That summer also I once encountered a parade of sailors on the Meir in Antwerp, perhaps on their way to a submarine, lustily singing as they marched: "And we sail, we sail against England," to which the boys on the street mockingly added, "on the other side"; in Dutch this reply, *aan den overkant*, rhymes with German *gegen England*. Certainly the submariners were not aware that they were referred to in Antwerp as "fish fodder." Most of the daily news, however, was a steady diet of German retreats, camouflaged by propaganda and punctuated from time to time by a resounding defeat in the Ukraine, a defeat that was always explained away by much talk of tactical hedgehog positions. Only here we were familiar with genuine hedgehogs, and we knew all about the usually hopeless character of their defensive positions. The only German victory on land at that time was the liberation of Mussolini, then held on the Gran Sasso, the highest peak of the Apennines in central Italy. In a daring raid he was rescued by air on September 12, 1943, and then created his own Italian Republic in northern Italy, piling up ever more misery there. But to claim this rescue as a victory merely underlined how deep the Reich's fortunes had already fallen. So, gradually over that summer the conviction grew in the family that Germany was about to lose the war. The question now was merely who would arrive first, the Allies or the Soviets, although it was just possible that those vaunted secret new German weapons, mysteriously labeled V-1,

V-2, and V-3, with the *V* for *Vergeltung* (retaliation), would arrive first and reverse the fortunes of war.

We children also could read the news in the daily newspaper, but I did not pay much attention to it at all, because it was either the most predictable propaganda or very local news that had nothing to do with us. The first year we were back in Wiezelo Father decided that we should honor the Flemish national holiday on July 11 by raising the flag from a pole near the house. No speeches, no songs, just the flag, and I recall that I found this a natural thing to do. Were we not Flemings, while Belgium was merely the state in which we fitted, part of a practical arrangement in the world at large? As some villagers in Gooreind expressed it, we were now "under the Belgians" just as we had been "under the Dutch" before and "under the French" before that, and always "under somebody" before that as well.

War Renewed: Hidden Struggles

All during this period the older members of my family were undergoing struggles about which I remained wholly unaware. The situations of Veva and Father are particularly telling in this regard. After the move away from Bruges Veva enrolled at the Catholic University of Louvain in October 1942 to study Germanic philology. But around Christmas the students were told that they would not be allowed to take their examinations in July unless they had a certificate showing that they had done six months of *arbeidsdienst* (labor service). The university authorities had provided their enrollment files to the Germans for this purpose. Nothing further happened until the end of March. Then a peremptory notice arrived at Wiezelo calling up Veva to work at a munitions factory in Essen in the Ruhr area. Father simply forbade her to go. By chance the bombardment at Mortsel took place at that time, which saved her. My parents knew of an alternative organization called the VADV (Vrijwillige Arbeidsdienst Vlaanderen, or Volunteer Labor Service Flanders), whose founder and head was actually some sort of cousin of Mother's. He arranged for her to "volunteer" and fulfill her obligatory "labor service" in that fashion. Both Veva and Mietje "volunteered." They went immediately to an official medical examination by a German physician who provided them with a *Rassenschein* (racial certificate), labeled "Arian, Westfalian Type." Then they went to a castle in Mortsel where the VADV was camped. There they assumed brown uniforms with seven buttons on the jacket, which soon became a major headache. The uniforms had to be kept spotless at all times, or else, and the supervisors turned out to be much stricter than the SS inspectors who twice came to check on the operation. Their working clothes, however, were no-nonsense sack-like dresses in blue cotton well adapted to their jobs of clearing up debris from the bombardment and assisting the survivors. Four months later, on August 31, after severe rioting in the camp, they were dismissed on the condition that they would return after December 1944 for another six months of service.

Meanwhile, faced with the conscription of large numbers of students that spring, the university authorities decided that when released the draftees could start attending second-year lectures and take their examinations whenever possible. So in early fall Veva made her way to the university at Louvain for her oral exams. She had joined a girlfriend at Mechlin, and they were about to travel from there to Louvain in a truck running on gas produced by burning wood. They had just left the town when some fighter planes suddenly dived out of the clouds to strafe the streets around them as well as the nearby railway. Then suddenly bombs were dropped, and the next moment a cloud of choking dust arose and obscured everything behind them, while simultaneously they heard the shrieking of the numerous casualties that resulted. That shrieking was so piercing that it even surpassed the roar of the explosions and the shaking caused by houses crashing to the ground. The three young people in the truck were petrified for a moment and then fled at break-neck speed toward Louvain. Once there Veva went to take her first oral exam and realized only then that in the commotion she had completely forgotten everything she had studied. Demoralized, she abandoned any attempt to sit for any of her other exams and returned home. She told Father what happened, but he upbraided her, she claims, for her lack of courage in giving up. From then onward she unconsciously managed to completely avoid passing through the town of Mechlin for many decades until one of her friends made her realize that she was suffering shell shock, or posttraumatic stress syndrome, as we call it now, a condition still erroneously assumed to affect only combatants and not civilians. As to her further studies, she soon was forced to abandon them because of the worsening bombardments—especially on Louvain—and their attendant traffic stoppages.

As the war progressed, especially after the invasion of the USSR, efforts by both camps to recruit civilians to their cause also increased. From the start Father refused to be coopted by the occupier or the local fascists. Foreseeing an increased demand by fascist parties and their youth movements, he immediately put an end to the production of flags at the Melkmarkt, disbanded his atelier, and attempted to replace some of the lost revenue by selling devotional gifts such as rosaries, prayer books, and the like. In 1941 he still thought that his voice could make a difference, and he accepted an invitation to speak at the small Yser pilgrimage that year, where he delivered a poem about the Boerenkrijg of 1798, a short-lived guerilla war against the French revolutionary occupation by the farmers in the hinterland of Antwerp in defense of "altar and hearth." The symbolism was obvious, but his address made not a jot of difference and may simply not have been understood. Later on he was courted more and more by collaborating Flemish milieus but flatly turned down all their tempting offers. He refused to resume the direction of the literary journal *Volk* that he had founded and directed before the war, refused to assume the mayoralty of a coastal town in West Flanders, and later he refused to accept a professorship in art history at the University of Ghent. On the other hand, mindful of his obligations to his large family and well aware of his vulnerability ever since the incident with Hans and the banned books in 1941, he did not join any Resistance group. He was so careful that already in 1940 in Bruges he forbade Veva and Bea to continue the secret jargon they had invented based on the Polish that our governess Miss Eva had taught them. And yet . . .

In the late summer or early fall of 1943 a few mysterious incidents occurred at Wiezelo. One night I was woken up by the tramp of heavy boots and low voices out in the corridor. Curious to see what the commotion was all about, I opened my door and saw one and then another German officer with red lapels on their uniforms turn into the corridor from the staircase and disappear toward Father's studio around the corner. Someone, probably Mother or an older sister, shushed me back into the room. The next morning I was simply told that, no, I had not dreamed this, but I was not supposed to have seen anything and better forget all about it. Obviously there had been a meeting there, I realized, but what was it all about? At least once more I was awakened by similar noises but prudently stayed in bed. The morning after one such occasion I walked into the studio and found a large chart in German, apparently forgotten there. It showed production figures for tanks, artillery, and planes in the Soviet Union compared to the figures for Germany and proved that the USSR was now out-producing Germany and was projected to achieve massive military superiority in the near future. I did not understand this very clearly, but the drift was unmistakable, and obviously this too was something I should not have seen.

Chris later told me that one day he was roaming beyond the edge of the estate near the military camp when he became aware that soldiers stationed here and there, arms at the ready, had cordoned off the estate behind him. When he asked Father about it, he was told that probably an important general had passed through the area. What was that all about? Two decades after the war a reporter pressed Father for the details. "Someone told me," remarked the interviewer, "that many kinds of people used to visit here during the last year of the war." To this my father cryptically responded, "Germans of the German resistance met here. They were looking for points of contact. But such a range of differences in dissent left a weird impression on the ordinary spectator." In other words, Wiezelo seems to have served as a safe house for meetings of a German military resistance. Had these meetings anything to do with the failed putsch against Hitler on July 20, 1944, a plot that involved most of the high command of the *Wehrmacht* on the western front? My siblings and I will never know, nor will we know how Father came to be drawn into this or anything else, because long after his death Mother destroyed a whole trunkful of his papers. So we can only speculate fruitlessly about this issue.

Like many others in my situation, I have often been asked what my family knew about the persecution of the Jews during those fateful years of 1942 to 1944. The answer is "nothing." During those years the Nazi censorship, combined with the all-pervasive fear and with the culture of silence in the family, was such that nothing at all filtered through about the Jews' plight, even though in 1942 the deportation had taken on a highly visible character, at least in the four cities where they officially lived, of which Antwerp was one. On June 3 of that year any Jewish person over six was forbidden to appear in public without wearing a yellow star. On the same date the SS and their Flemish counterparts carried out the first raid on Jews in Antwerp, and on July 22 they conducted a similar raid in Brussels. A first convoy of prisoners was sent by train to Auschwitz on August 4, and from then onward the hunt for Jews continued until early 1944. In all, around ten thousand Jews from Antwerp were removed to concentration camps. Even in Antwerp itself, very few people realized the scale of the operation, and beyond the city most Belgians had no inkling of what was occurring. My parents must have known something but did not tell us anything. Even teenagers were so afraid that they kept what they heard or saw strictly to themselves. For instance, I learned only in 2012 that Veva had once seen a Jewish man wearing a yellow star at the railway station in Antwerp near a telephone booth. There was a long line and he seemed to ask for a volunteer, someone to place a phone call on his behalf, but no one in the line even dared take notice of his presence there. As was typical at the time, she did not tell anyone at all about this incident.

Still, I recall a single exception to this silence. Sometime at Wiezelo in 1943 I heard Mother answering one of my older siblings about Jews. In 1940 she was renting out a shop in the Carnotsstraat in Antwerp to a Jewish fur dealer, Mr. Rubinstein. She was saying that while Jews did not exactly share our culture, they were no less honest for all that. Indeed, they were more honest than many other folk, and she then cited Mr. Rubinstein as an example. He had always paid his rent on the dot until the outbreak of the war. He and his family had then hidden for some time in the shop but suddenly vanished in thin air one day. Yet even in this dire circumstance, he had left a fur as a gift of appreciation for Mother.

Nor did I hear or know anything at all at the time about Jews in hiding. Veva knew Katharina Korosmesei, a Jewish girl who had been a book illustrator by trade but was now hidden in an upstairs room of the Melkmarkt. But she too suddenly disappeared one day. Only after liberation did Net talk about a "Bulgar" hidden in the village. Chris, for his part, had apparently heard a rumor about a Jew hidden in Gooreind who came sometimes to swim in the same fen we did. Neither Veva nor Net nor Chris told anyone at the time anything about what they saw or heard, nor did my parents ever mention Miss Korosmesei. Due to this almost universal culture of silence, very few people knew much of anything about the deportation or its consequences, and no one had any idea of what was really going on in the Reich until the very last weeks of the war, when the horrors of the concentration camps were revealed one by one.

Interlude:
A Traveling Establishment

September came and with it time to return to school. This time I was to go to a brand-new location: the castle of Bellem, halfway between Bruges and Ghent. But the Germans suddenly requisitioned the castle, so that the formal beginning of the academic year was postponed for a week or two as the administrators sought new accommodations. So, as carefully instructed, I alighted from the train one afternoon at the designated station, crossed the track, and walked along a rural road further and further away from any built-up area until I finally reached my destination: a large cottage at the shore of a large pond. The school was housed there, or rather it was encamped there. Beds, running water, electricity, and heating were all conspicuous by their absence and replaced by straw mattresses on the floor, a water pump, a few carbide lamps, and cold. The pupils, however, were all there and in high spirits. Yes, this was a school, because there were classes, but otherwise it was a holiday camp of sorts. The lack of light did not allow for any study in the evening, so we frolicked around in the twilight near the water or on the pond. The great sport was to wait until it was really dark and then throw bits of carbide (at least I think it was carbide) on the water. That substance floats on water but starts burning, and it was great fun to watch these little flaming islands float away on the slightest current. Apart from that there were also memorable walks along the wooded alleys of the great park of Bellem castle nearby. It was a splendid park laid out in imitation of the renowned royal estates around Paris and just as pleasant to walk in.

That situation lasted only a few weeks. Then we were allowed into the castle on the other side of the railroad. That mansion was more grandiose than the one in Izegem. Access to it was preceded by what had been a great lawn before the war, flanked by two-story-high dependencies on the sides, one of which had been converted into classrooms. There were ample playgrounds, another large park behind the buildings, and a moat or ditch around the whole. As had been the case at Izegem, we were all lodged again in the servants' rooms under the roof in the main building. The moat was the center of attention for me and André de Maere. In our free time we managed to punt all around it, even though it was now covered with ice. So we played arctic explorers, breaking two poles and even one iron bar during our ice-breaking operations, but we crashed through every obstacle to free this circumpolar moat. We also fished a little, and each of us caught about sixty feet of electric wire, while André even managed to sell his "catch." No wonder that after some mixed academic news my letter of December 10, the last one before Christmas and our return home, concluded: "In general the situation here is excellent!"

To the school manager, though, food and food stamps remained the main concern, as shown by his October 21 letter to Mother: "Madam, I had barely received the envelope with the food stamps when I forwarded it to Loppem. However, in reading your letter attentively again, I became aware that you would eventually ask me to return the potato stamps. Please find them included herewith, with apologies for the delay in returning them: I had to fetch them myself from the abbey." Almost as an afterthought he added the following: "Jean is well and I am well pleased with him from every point of view."

Two days before Christmas we were home and expected to return by January 6. But once again the castle was commandeered unexpectedly by the German military, and this time the school decided to leave the vicinity altogether. It sought and found refuge in the quarters of the Jesuit novitiate for Belgium in a suburb of Ghent, Drongen (Tronchiennes), and that is where I alighted on January 6, 1944. We, the Benedictines, were housed in part of a wing four or five floors tall within a complex of similar buildings. However, it took some effort to adapt to a very different mentality. Strict punctuality, order, and silence prevailed, and we had to be as quiet as mice. The Jesuit spiritual approach was quite different from the Benedictine one. If the latter might be described as intimate, understated, and introspective, the Jesuit one was flamboyant, militant, and extraverted. Their chapel walls were painted all over with scenes of the exploits of their order in past centuries, to the point that once inside you could no longer find your way out, for the door itself was part of a painting and its knob was almost unnoticeable. This bold, triumphant stance visibly came as somewhat of a shock to our Benedictines, who kept repeating to us ad nauseam how grateful we all should be to our Jesuit hosts for allowing us into the novitiate, their most intimate establishment.

Although we mere pupils did not mingle with the novices, we were duly impressed with the aura of clockwork order and utterly Spartan atmosphere that seemed to surround the very buildings they occupied and it reminds me in retrospect of the atmosphere of a boot camp.

So we too tended to be more subdued than usual. Our classes were less animated, and somehow immersing oneself in the nuances of Latin grammar seemed an apt occupation for the setting. But this exterior angelic obedience was accompanied by an increase in interior tensions. I began to sleepwalk, and my roommates discovered that they could ask me questions that I would answer in my sleep and order me around. Once again our bedrooms were just under the roof, on the highest floor above the gutter line, and my classmates found out to their delight that they could make me go sleepwalking in the broad gutters—until I woke up one night and found myself in the gutter quite far from my room. During recess we often walked among the poplars along the banks of the nearby river Lys (Leie) toward a bridge. We were told that this was a spot to be avoided, as it could easily become a military target. Similar worries about safety also explain why, in sharp contrast to earlier practice, we were only rarely taken on longer walks. The only excursion I recall was a visit to the medieval castle of the counts of Flanders in the middle of the city of Ghent at the waterside, the stuff of every boy's dreams. There were forbidding medieval walls with pinnacles for archers, machicolations, a great hall, dungeons filled with an array of evil instruments of torture, and last of all the little palace added on top that was a residence of "our" Emperor, Charles V, although not his birthplace, for he was born in Prinsenhof, a nearby residence on the opposite riverbank.

This visit was our only major diversion during the whole spring trimester, although by chance I stumbled one day on a little newsworthy scene. A small car was stationed at the curb near our entrance, a very rare sight at the time. As I was watching it curiously, one of the monks arrived in the company of a middle-aged man and helped him into the car. Then he informed us that the man was Prince Charles of Saxe-Coburg, the younger brother of King Leopold. It was just a small bit of gossip at the time, but then none of us knew that barely four months later this man would replace the king, at that time held captive in Germany, and become the Regent of Belgium. But apart from this exception, day after day at the time looked equally grey and dull, and study became the center of our lives, all the more so because we had no access to any kind of newspaper or radio. I still wonder how we managed to hear eventually about the great scandal of that spring concerning Dr. Marcel Petiot, the serial killer of Paris. On March 11, 1944, the newspapers first announced his arrest in Paris by the Gestapo. He claimed to help Jews, members of the Resistance, and even criminals on the run to flee to South America, but actually he murdered them, stole their valuables, and burned their bodies in his furnace.

Dreary day continued to follow dreary day until April 10. That evening, after we had gone to bed, the sirens suddenly began blaring around us. That meant an air raid, and we all hurried down to the vaulted cellar. Soon the staccato barks of the flak were heard, and almost as soon they were muffled by the dull rumble of explosion after explosion, while our cellar shuddered in horror at each hit, and veils of dust drifted down from its ceiling. We were all huddled close together as it went on and on, and we were nearly in despair when the all-clear signal finally sounded. This had been a major bombardment of some of the railways around Ghent a few miles from us. We did not learn it at the time, but it inflicted over 1,000 casualties—428 dead and 724 wounded. For the school and for us this was but a preamble. More heavy bombardments came during the following weeks, culminating in the major attacks on Louvain on May 12–13. Those were so heavy that they triggered the country's administrative authorities as well as its bishops on May 14 to order the immediate closure of all schools. The next day the equally heavy attack on Courtrai underlined the wisdom of that order. All these bombardments were, we are now told, aimed at misleading the enemy to expect a landing on the Belgian coast. Hence civilian casualties by Allied fire were, so to speak, just unfortunate victims, the proverbial eggs that generals break to make their omelets.

When the news broke, we were first told that it was of paramount importance for us and for society in general that the school year should not be reduced, that our education should not be interrupted, that it was now our patriotic duty to continue our studies by ourselves. We were then told to return home as quickly as possible. There we would receive our lessons and assignments every week by mail, and we had to return our completed assignments in the same fashion. But this time I was not allowed to travel by myself. Father estimated that it was too risky for a child alone, and he came himself to fetch me. All went well until we reached the railway platform under the great glass barrel vault of the main train station of Ghent. In contrast to the situation just a few months ago when the platforms were overflowing with passengers, this time around very few people were waiting. After a while the public address system informed us that our train was coming in, and we could see it approach from a distance, until it suddenly halted just before entering the station. It was apparently being strafed. Father took me by the hand, ran to the safest place he could find to be out of the way of flying glass, and crouched with me at the very edge of the small wall and a huge metal buttress that supported the vault. It sounded like a sudden shower of hail passed several times over us, and some glass was flying around. Then a few moments later it was all over, and the locomotive slowly steamed into the station. It passed in front of us, and we could see quite a few bullet holes in it. Clearly the drivers had escaped injury, and so we went on our way and reached Wiezelo without further incident.

Countdown

At this point everyone expected an Allied landing soon somewhere. If successful—and success was far from guaranteed—the Allied armies would prevail more likely than not and would eventually reach and liberate us. Even children like me realized that we were now in a countdown toward decisive events. At the same time, though, Wiezelo was isolated enough to escape much of the restlessness felt elsewhere. Hence I settled down right away, studied my lessons, and did my homework undisturbed, for strangely enough, the mail continued to arrive and depart as imperturbably as if nothing out of the ordinary was happening.

This schooling by correspondence continued until halfway through July, when the examinations arrived. Our teacher trusted us to act honestly in answering these tests "on our word of honor," and I did.

Meanwhile war fever grew. I observed that when the fleets of bombers now came overhead they had protective fighter planes prancing all around them like sheep dogs around the flock and that they now flew toward Germany in broad daylight. Also, unusual events began to occur. One day in May or early June there appeared a couple of soldiers in the woods who began to measure the thickness of the trees and cut marks in most of them. That soon attracted Father, who was told that trees of suitable diameters were to be cut and the poles set up in all open fields so as to prevent paratroopers or gliders from landing. The only recourse he had was to argue over the diameter of each tree. So he began to measure them himself as well and found, of course, many more unsuitable trees than they did. Still, most of the trees were destined to be cut, especially in one wood. A private Belgian lumber company then appeared and began to carry out the job. But the work was halted before great damage had been done, because somehow we obtained a reprieve. Then the poles, nicknamed "Rommel stakes" after the famous field marshal then in charge, or "asparagus stalks" after their appearance, were planted in the fields and meadows, with barbed wire strung every which way between them. As this operation occurred during the growing season, it destroyed the crops standing in the fields and hence promised food shortages in the fall.

When the Allies landed in Normandy on June 6 the suspense reached a peak that lasted for a week or so, because another landing on or near the Belgian coast was expected soon. For a day or two public transport was seriously disrupted. Hearing of the landings, St. Victor in Turnhout released its boarders, Chris among them, and sent them home. Chris made it by tram as far as Antwerp. But then there was no more public transport, so he trudged nearly thirteen miles on foot, suitcase in hand, to rejoin us at Wiezelo. A few days later it became evident that landings on our coasts were not imminent, and the regional trams were back in business, although their schedules became more erratic by the day. Meanwhile, and unknown to all of us, King Leopold III was deported to Germany the very next day after the landings, no doubt for fear that he would soon go underground and escape.

Unusual events continued. On June 8 Marleen, our youngest sister, was to celebrate her first communion during the daily morning mass at the convent of the Franciscan sisters next to us. All decked out in white, with matching veil, shoes, and even gloves, she came in the early morning mist with Mother and us along the path to the church through the wood. Unexpectedly a soldier took shape in the mist and stopped us. A number of others appeared, rifles at the ready, and I saw two German tanks carefully hidden among the trees. I was astonished to notice how low-slung they were, but I did not look for long because another soldier came forward and told us to proceed between two rows of them. Innocent little Marleen in white came first and suddenly one of the soldiers, probably their sergeant, presented arms, and all the others followed suit as we continued on our way to church. We will never know why they would do something like this, but it probably was sheer nostalgia for homes with small children dressed up in white for their first communions.

By mid-July my examinations were over, and the Allies had finally broken out of the front in Normandy. The conspiracy to kill Hitler failed on July 20. As a consequence Alexander von Falkenhausen, the general in charge of Belgium since 1940, was arrested on July 29 as a party to that plot and replaced by two much more dangerous persons, a Gauleiter and an SS general. The combined effect of these events was to weaken the occupation forces significantly, to render them more insecure and hence more dangerous, to embolden Resistance fighters, and to enrage the armed militias of collaborators, all against the background of increasing bombardments, strafing, and further Allied advances. For us this meant that with every passing day life became more and more unpredictable and more menacing.

That summer, even after my examinations were over, I played far less outside near the house out in the open, primarily because it was just no longer safe there. Instead I spent much of the time in my room reading. My tastes had changed: children's books fell out of favor, as did most novels except for Jules Verne. Now I preferred tales of exploration, such as *About Wolves, Bears, and Bandits*, concerning Siberia, or accounts of Sven Hedin's travels in Central Asia. I was painstakingly going through the many volumes of the series *Panorama de la guerre* (Panorama of the War) that dealt with World War I. I had also discovered lyric writing and was most impressed by Rainer Maria Rilke's *Die Weise von Liebe und Tod des Cornets Christoph Rilke* (1906) in its Insel edition (Leipzig, 1930), a ballad in prose translated as "The Lay of the Love and Death of Cornet Christoph Rilke." The passage "Riding, riding, riding, through the day, through the night, through the day. Riding, riding, riding," about an eighteen-year-old bugler on horseback, seemed to me then romantically most appropriate to the times and perhaps my place in them.

Notwithstanding the changed circumstances, however, when the weather was warm and beautiful we were still outside, especially to trek in twos or threes all the way to go for a swim in the fen well beyond the castle's estate. One day Bea and I were all alone and happily swimming around when we suddenly heard the scream of a diving plane, and a neat straight row of little fountains popped up near us. We were being strafed! So we dived in the hope that the water would protect us from being hurt, and we went for the shore. By then the plane had gone around and was already coming in for a second attempt, but we reached cover in the bushes on the sand dunes just in time, and this time the bullets stitched a pattern a little further away from us. I was indignant because it was clear that we, two children, were the target of this attack since no one else was around. By then strafing was happening more and more frequently. I still recall four attacks in all in which I was involved during that summer, and nearly every one of my siblings had similar experiences. Most of these occurred along the roads, so we learned along which roads the deepest ditches ran, and hence where travel on foot or by bike was the safest. In spite of the danger, aunt Maria Brusseleers, who was spending the summer in her villa on the main street of Gooreind, often came to visit accompanied by her second daughter, Jacqui. Jacqui, a genuine firebrand of about my age, was always ready for all manner of wonderful stunts, with my admiring sister Rina in tow.

That summer a strong contingent of Russian soldiers from General Andrey Vlasov's army arrived in Gooreind and occupied the Koch castle mansion and estate south of the built-up area. These were Soviet forces who had been under Vlasov's command and went over to the German side with him in 1942. Distrusted by Hitler, Vlasov's first units were moved to the western front. Some of the ones in Gooreind had the names of their nationalities on shoulder patches. Given my interest in

Central Asia, I was thrilled to find a Kalmykh among them, the Kalmykhs being the only Mongols still living in Europe. These troops were much less disciplined than Germans, they drank a lot, and some rapidly found girlfriends in Gooreind. They also built a large and well-guarded weapons depot in the domain they occupied. But its sentries were no match for Gooreind's seasoned smugglers and poachers, who managed one night to steal a large amount of goods from it. When this was discovered their commander let it be known, naturally by way of Pastor De Wit, that if everything was not returned within twenty-four hours he would blow up the whole village the next morning, and his threatening soldiers patrolled the built-up area of the village for most of the day. By the next morning they found everything in place again at their depot, and the incident was forgotten.

It was now August, and the situation was becoming more and more volatile. In the province of Limburg, east of Antwerp, chaos was said to be growing. Even the newspapers reported that in some villages execution and counter-execution by members of the Resistance and collaborators had escalated nearly into civil war. They did not report that endangered people fled, but they did. One of Mother's cousins, the physician Jan Kerkhofs, nicknamed Nondepie (In the name of nonsense) after his favorite swearword, was among these from the Resistance side. He first found refuge with us for a little while and moved somewhat later to the villa of aunt Maria Brusseleers in Gooreind itself.

Time moved inexorably on. Paris was freed on August 25. A few days after that Father decided to go to Antwerp by bicycle for a day or two to settle some business before our supposedly imminent liberation. Hence he was not home the next day as I was in my room lustily hitting the keys of a noisy antique Underwood typewriter with its staccato noise. Suddenly the door opened, and in came a German soldier to check on me. A patrol had been passing next to the house when they heard what they thought was the rattle of a machine gun. They drew their weapons and went to investigate. Apparently somebody had seen them coming and got Mother double-quick. I do not recall whether it was the same patrol that assembled us all as they inspected the house. Somehow Mother managed to get them into her study, where a big bookcase against the wall was filled with bound editions of all of Goethe's works, plus other classical German writers. That convinced them somehow of our good faith, and they left.

The next day was September 3. The Allies reached Brussels and the outskirts of Antwerp while everyone deserted all the roads. The following day they took Antwerp and its harbor, where thanks to the Resistance, including cousins Piet and Jan de Moor, none of the crucial locks and other installations were destroyed by the retreating Germans. The next day BBC even announced that Allied tanks had reached Breda in the Netherlands. That was nonsense, and we knew it because we had been watching the highway like hawks all day long in expectation of their arrival and had seen nothing of the sort. In reality on September 4 the Allies were unexpectedly pinned down on the bank of a large canal on the northern edge of the city, as the Germans fought to deny the use of the port of Antwerp to the Allies.

As a result of this situation Father was prevented from returning home, and so was our aunt Maria Brusseleers, who was cut off in Gooreind from her family in Antwerp. Our village was now completely isolated from most of the country, and at Wiezelo we were also plunged in a total news blackout. No one knew how long this situation would last, certainly not that it would take more than six long weeks before it was resolved. But Mother understood right away that until that moment came she was very much on her own, although she and aunt Maria could advise each other. Still, there was a silver lining; namely, she had a stock of flour. She had long been planning to celebrate Father's forthcoming fiftieth birthday with white bread and cakes and had therefore been patiently hoarding flour for many months. That flour would now be a last resort in case of siege.

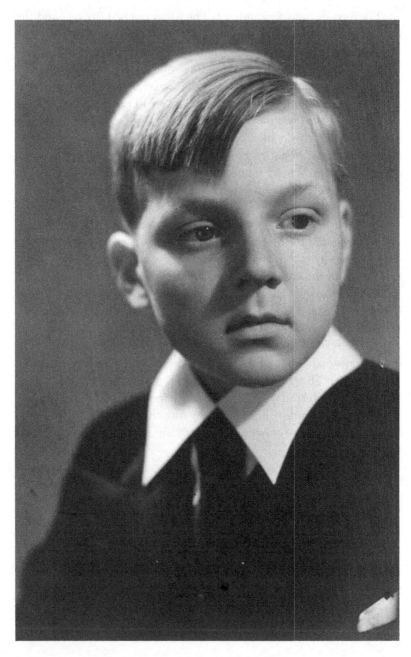

Jan's confirmation portrait, June 1941. (photo by P. Muylle)

Left: Dom Lou Pierre-Célestin Tseng-Tsiang (Lu Zheng Xiang), 1943. (from *Souvenirs et pensées*)

Below: St. Andrews abbey with school in right foreground, 1930s. (photo by Ernest Till, Abbey of St. Andrew Zevenkerken)

ABBAYE DE ST. ANDRÉ PAR LOPHEM LEZ-BRUGES.
(VUE PRISE EN AVION.)

S. A. B. E. P. A.

Classroom in a factory, Izegem, 1943. (from Dom Christian Papeians de Morchoven, *1942–1992: 50 ans*)

Three little girls astride the farm horse. From left to right are Frans, Marleen, Veerle, Suze. Note the lack of shoes and flimsy wartime dress. (family photo)

Jan returns home from Het Blauwhuis, late March 1943. (anonymous photo)

The hearth at Wiezelo, 1942. (family photo)

The main meadow and sheepfold at Wiezelo in winter. (family photo)

Annie as nurse at the sanitarium De Mick, 1943 or early 1944. (anonymous photo)

Castle Posterijhof before its destruction by cannon fire in 1944. (anonymous photo)

Canadians advancing during the Battle of the Scheldt, October 1944. (photo by Donald Grant, Department of National Defence, National Archives of Canada)

Cinema Rex obliterated by V-2 missile, December 16, 1944. (Stadsarchief Antwerpen)

Liberty ship unloading boxes of ammunition, Antwerp, winter 1944. (photo by U.S. Signal Corps, Stadsarchief Antwerpen)

Still fifteen, yet ready for university? (photo by Polyphoto, Antwerp)

Jan and Nico on jerricans rafting on the waterhole, summer 1945. (family photo)

Marleen and Jan sledding and skating, winter of 1946–1947. (family photo)

The family after the war, 1947. *Front row from left to right*: Chris, Annie, Suze, Mother, Marleen, Father, Veerle, and Mietje; *back row from left to right*: Guido, Rina, Bea, Nico, Veva, and Jan. (family photo)

The complete first-year history class of 1947 on an outing. Jan is the boy between the two monks. (anonymous photo)

"The historian's lair": the university library at Louvain. (Catholic University of Louvain)

Oral examination at Louvain. The examiner is Professor Jozef De Smet. (photo by Robert Martin, Catholic University of Louvain)

The first professional meeting: symposium of Dutch and Flemish historians at Muiden, Netherlands, 1949. Jan is first row left. (photo by Forebo Blaricum)

6

Unravelings and Outcomes

September 1944 to September 1945

The period that followed left a deep impression on me and all my siblings over ten years old, to judge by the number, variety, and overall intensity of our reminiscences. Each of us recalls incidents that others in the family remember differently, or not at all, and nearly all of these recollections retain a strong emotional flavor. Some can be shown to be false memories, either elaborated at a later date or originating in dreams or nightmares rather than in reality. Whatever their source, the abiding power of such memories indicates how strongly our experiences affected us at the time. Indeed, it is to this next year of my life—from September 1944 to September 1945—that I trace some of my most fundamental principles, including my attitudes toward intolerance, war and peace, adversarial politics and political leadership, and above all ideologies and nationalism. These times were momentous, however, not only for me and not only for my family. As historian Martin Conway has pointed out, the politics pursued by the Belgian government between fall 1944 and fall 1945 had long-lasting effects, and ultimately resulted in the breakup of the Belgian unitary state before the end of the century.

After the British-led forces were halted at Antwerp, it became evident that the Allies could not use the harbor without clearing the banks of the whole estuary of the river Scheldt from German hands. At first Field Marshal Bernard Montgomery tried to bypass this task by securing the bridges that gave direct access to Germany through the eastern Nether-lands and invading Germany itself. However, that operation (September 17–25) failed, and the clearance of the estuary became unavoidable. What is known as the Battle for the Scheldt began with attempts to cross the canal just north of the city. Only on October 3 did Canadian and Polish troops succeed in this effort. They then advanced toward the village of Woensdrecht in the Netherlands that commands access to the northern bank of the river between Antwerp and the North Sea. Over the next thirteen days a fierce battle followed involving armored vehicles and much artillery, with heavy Canadian losses before they finally took Woensdrecht on October 16. The town of Brasschaat, between Gooreind and Antwerp, and just beyond the eastern flank of the Canadian advance, was liberated between October 3 and 5 as far as the main barracks of the artillery domain, only two and a half miles south of Gooreind. Gooreind itself followed only on October 21 after the conclusion of a further three-day-long tank battle two miles or so northwest of its built-up village.

And so for six long weeks after the liberation of Antwerp, we remained just behind the front lines—neither occupied fish nor liberated fowl.

Six Weeks under the Guns

There were three of them crouching in a deep squarish pit, partially covered by fir boughs and weeds, in the middle of a patch of brush. That morning Mother had called me to accompany her and to carry a big basket containing some items folded in linen. Taking a path in the direction of the farm we proceeded until we glimpsed its roof in the near distance. Here my mother halted, put her finger to her mouth to stop me from chattering, and left the path with me behind her. Walking through the dense undergrowth she came to the pit. Its three occupants, hearing us coming, fearfully looked up at us but relaxed as they recognized Mother. They looked exotic to me—somewhat oriental but not Mongol or Chinese, more likely Turkish—and they had obviously escaped from captivity, as they wore some kind of ragged uniforms. One of them had a large dressing stained with blood around his left side; he had apparently sustained several broken ribs during their escape.

Mother unwrapped the basket, took dressings and remedies from it, and began to dress the wound, while I gave bread and apples to the two other soldiers. They said little in low voices—more whispering than speaking—and in a language neither Mother nor I had ever even heard, let alone understood. When they saw the apples they looked pleased, and one said "*alma ata*," pointing first to himself as *ata*, then saying *alma* as he pointed to the apple. Later I found out that Alma-Ata was the capital of Kazakhstan, and *alma* meant "apple" in Kazakh as it does in all other Turkish languages.

Afterward Mother called me from time to time for the same errand. Once, when she was dressing the wound, I crept on my belly twenty yards or so further from the pit to find myself staring at the yard between the barn and the house, where three German soldiers were busying themselves with a horse-drawn cannon. I prudently crept back.

Later I learned that these presumably Kazakh escapees had appeared soon after the liberation of Antwerp, and Mother, no doubt after consulting Net, had arranged for their shelter and concealment near the farm. Every day she went to feed and care for them, each time taking a different child with her, including even six-year-old Marleen. No doubt if she met a soldier on the path she would look like a wholly innocent woman on an errand.

The state of the wounded man worried her, and she wanted a doctor to see him. But whom could she trust? She turned to her cousin Kerkhofs, the member of the Resistance who was now hiding in the cottage of her sister Maria. At first he refused to treat them, just as he refused to treat anybody in the village, civilian or military, because he presumed the three men to be enemy deserters, presumably runaways from the Vlasov troops. But Mother kept insisting, and in the end he came once, examined the patient, and left her with instructions for his care.

We will never know who these men were nor where they came from, only that they were as afraid of the Soviets as they were of the Germans. After liberation our adopted fugitives left us, and we never heard of them again. Every child that had accompanied Mother on these furtive trips had been sworn to secrecy, and after years of seeing the posters warning that *Feind hört mit* (The enemy listens too)—signs prominently placed in post offices and railway stations, among other places—we were all so deeply indoctrinated in that idea that we never mentioned the runaways even to each other. Only in 2012, as I was writing this book, did several among us compare stories. Mine was contrary to that of several among my siblings who maintain that the soldiers were Azeri from Azerbaijan. Chris remembered that when he unpacked the apples one of the refugees exclaimed *yabloko*, the Russian word for "apple." That they spoke Russian was not surprising for men who had presumably served in the Soviet army. All in all the divergences between what each of us had figured out separately from the others are substantial. For me they were prisoners of war and had escaped from one of the infamous German railway gangs used to repair bombed tracks, while some others hold that they were Vlasov deserters. I am certain that the wounded man had crushed his chest in jumping from a moving train, but Chris is just as certain that the blood was from a bullet wound. Conclusion: we will never know.

As the frontline approached we were hit from time to time by some mortar shells, but nothing to compare to the situation of my eldest sister Annie. She was one of two nurses at the sanitarium De Mick outside of Brasschaat, in the middle of extensive woods, when the place was suddenly hit by a genuine barrage of Allied shells. The manageress of the institution fled to seek refuge in the woods, and Annie's fellow nurse sat petrified in a corner of the kitchen. In contrast, the physician in charge, Dr. Lardot, who lived nearby, came instantly running to the clinic, where he and Annie alone managed to evacuate over fifty-four patients to the safety of ditches in the surrounding woods. The buildings were completely destroyed. After the bombardment the doctor and Annie removed the patients one by one to the nearest hospital, some distance away. Later on the local Resistance decided to recognize this valorous act, as well as to stress its own importance, in a little ceremony at that hospital and gave Annie a medal.

In Gooreind we were still several weeks away from a similar outcome. At this stage the shooting was more desultory, at least at first, and followed a definite routine. Every morning it was quiet. Then, around lunchtime, some artillery fire was exchanged. Most of it was incoming, but from time to time we heard a few outgoing shots as well, not always from the same place. It seems as if that horse-drawn cannon I saw on our own land was being used to cover a wide area, firing a few rounds first in one place and then in another, to give the impression that there was more artillery around than there really was. By four or five o'clock there followed a tea-time lull, but as dusk fell incoming artillery fire resumed and continued long into the night. As the weeks went by, the shooting became more intense and lasted longer. We had to find shelter more often, yet even so, when there was a pause we all ran around to look for the largest, the warmest, or the shiniest piece of shrapnel to boast about.

Foreseeing the kind of witch hunt that would follow liberation, Mother decided that parts of Father's correspondence with various Flemish poets, artists, musicians, and writers could easily be misconstrued by overly eager members of the Resistance, thus jeopardizing his future. Still, these papers meant much to her husband, so she entrusted Veva with the task of hiding them. Veva took the canisters of our gasmasks, stuffed the papers inside, and buried them in various drainage ditches, where they could be retrieved later on. She obviously did not know that ditches were actually watercourses. When she tried to locate the canisters later, she found that they had drifted away. She recovered only one, which had landed in a thorny blackberry bush.

Day by day the shelling seemed to become worse and worse. If we were outside but near the house when a bombardment unexpectedly began, we tried to dodge the shells, running zigzag under cover of trees wherever possible to avoid the feared shrapnel, and then made a mad dash through the last open space before the house. One evening as just such a bombardment was ending, we all noticed a glare in the sky toward the village. We ran out to find out what it was and realized that the tobacco factory was burning. Mother had gone in the main meadow to have a better look and realized that the castle Posterijhof was going up in flames as well. There she stood in tears—the only time ever I remember her crying—as she watched the flames consume the home of her childhood, with all its emotional associations to her family, and saw it collapse completely in a dense shower of sparks. A few days later, as the shelling continued to intensify, I began to worry more and more about our situation. The steady routines were breaking down. Earlier, we could plan mealtimes to coincide with the interludes between firing. Now we had to take advantage of any random hiatus to cook. Net also visited us less often than before, though she appeared whenever she could. Moreover, throughout this period she somehow managed to milk the farm's cows in an open meadow, day after day, whether there was shelling or not, because (as she explained) "surely the children have to drink milk," and that included us as well as her own.

One afternoon when the gunfire was particularly relentless I convinced Mother to let us sleep in some safer place. Hence, that evening we all slept on the floor of the potato cellar lying on bags of potatoes, violet from the color of their sprouts. That was the first night of what became a very long wait for the end of the siege-like condition in which we were now living. The next morning we emerged from the cellar, and everyone went up to their rooms to check for damage. Imagine Marleen's surprise when she found an inch-long piece of shrapnel on her pillow, where it had landed after flying in through her open widow. That shocked all of us into accepting, once and for all, the necessity of sleeping in the cellar until it was all over.

By day, however, we could still move around somewhat. The younger children, including me, stayed close to the house whenever possible. But it was still essential to leave the relative safety of our home to fetch bread from the baker in the built-up part of the village. We boys seem to have taken turns at this task in three shifts (the two youngest, Guido and Nico, counting as one), and along the way all of us found the need sometimes to dive into the ditches to avoid strafing airplanes. Once I saw an open German staff car brake to a stop as its occupants flung all four doors open and plunged into a nearby ditch until the danger had passed. Chris and most of my older sisters met with similar experiences and took them in their stride. But Guido and Nico were once so frightened that they were released from the errand from that time forward.

Meanwhile in Gooreind the situation was rapidly changing as well, and rumor more than direct observation kept us informed. Net always had some news to impart, the older children still went to the village regularly, and Jacqui visited nearly every day. By this time the Vlasov troops had left, to be replaced by Germans, partly SS and partly army. They established their headquarters in our aunt Maria's villa, and for a short while a general referred to by a fancy pseudonym resided there. After the welcome departure of those commanders and their security guard, a huge reel of telephone wire, taller than me, appeared one day on the square in front of the church, where I saw it myself one Sunday. It was rumored to be "1.2 kilometer long." One night the whole bobbin disappeared, and the next morning the commanding officer, reportedly a circus director in civilian life, put out a placard claiming that he needed "650 meters of wire" by the next day and threatening to blow up the whole village if he failed to get it. And, just as in the case of the Vlasov soldiers, by dawn the stolen wire had been returned.

As the situation worsened, we stayed more and more in our cellar. The nightly artillery barrages, continuing now for most of the night, often prevented us from sleeping soundly. I listened to the succession of explosions sometimes louder, then again fainter, but never absent for long. All I wanted was tranquility and safety. I kept thinking that soon the front would move away. The Allies, whom I imagined in some sort of German uniform but in khaki, would be there. Everything would become quiet and safe, there would be good food and plenty of it, and a contented peace would envelop us all.

One night as we were sleeping restlessly in the cellar, Mother awoke from a doze and told us that she had just had a vivid dream. Two German soldiers carrying flashlights knocked on the front door and asked for shelter against the artillery barrage in our cellar. In her dream she refused them entry because we were occupying that space, but she told them that they could shelter under the heavy billiards table in a downstairs room. Barely a few hours after she had told her tale, there was a loud knocking on the door, there were two soldiers with flashlights seeking refuge, and everything happened just as she had foreseen, except that there was also a third soldier behind the first two. We had all heard the dream and were all dumbfounded. I still have no definitive rational explanation for what happened, although I can surmise several scenarios. The dream certainly dealt with a foreseeable kind of event; indeed, it was not the only one of its kind. On another evening two soldiers at the kitchen door, claiming to be Poles forcibly drafted into the Wehrmacht, asked to hide in the house until liberation. But that situation was far too risky to accept under the circumstances, so Mother turned them away, and they left without further ado.

We were then in the very last days of the occupation. In contrast to my older siblings, I do not remember much of this time, probably because I no longer left the immediate surroundings of the house, except to attend church. But Veva and Bea went regularly to the rural hospital near the village church to treat an open wound on Veva's leg. The clinic was run by a German army physician who treated civilians and military indiscriminately, attending to everyone in the order of their arrival, regardless of their status. Veva recalls once being cared for before a soldier wearing a dressing around his neck who had arrived after her. Chris, curious as can be, was often on the lookout near the burned-out factory just beyond the edge of our estate. Once he was chatting there with a bunch of young villagers when a large military truck passing on the Bredabaan suddenly burst a tire and lurched to a stop. Many young SS soldiers jumped out of the back, surrounded the onlookers, and began to search them for the weapon that they presumed had been used to shoot out their tire. Chris knew that one of the crowd was supposed to be a member of the Resistance and hoped that he did not carry any concealed weapon. He did not. A little later on the same day two men in civilian clothes suddenly appeared there out of nowhere and asked him in polished Dutch, not in dialect, for directions to reach the next village to the west of Gooreind's by using shortcuts. He thought they were spies or perhaps paratroopers, but they could have been just as well members of the Dutch Resistance.

And so came what turned out to be the last day of the occupation. That day Rina and Jacqui found villa Mansion abandoned with its front door wide open. They went to investigate, but while they were upstairs they heard voices downstairs. Luckily for them there was a tall and empty water cistern, and they helped each other hide in it. After the voices subsided, Jacqui managed to get out by standing on Rina's shoulders, but she had to call on someone with a ladder to free Rina. Later that day Bea arrived at the same villa on her way home when soldiers hidden in the trees, arms at the ready, shouted at her, "*Sperrgebiet*" (firing zone), but she shouted back in broken Dutch-German, "I do not understand," and crossed the road anyway. That afternoon, when the only older person at home was Chris, some soldiers arrived on a mission to requisition all the bicycles around. They took those they found on our property, gave him a proper receipt for them, and disappeared. That intrigued Chris. He followed them to the gate on the Bredabaan, where he witnessed a steady trickle of soldiers marching, riding, or cycling northwards toward the Netherlands. The same day soldiers commandeered the horse at the farm. Apparently they understood what a disaster it was to deprive a farm of its only horse, because they promised Frans that, once in the Netherlands, they would leave the animal in a field on the side of the road. They also gave him a receipt. As soon as feasible, either the next day or the day after, Frans followed in search of his horse. He found it in the Netherlands unharmed, peacefully munching in someone's meadow along the road.

Meanwhile, the rolling thunder of the artillery barrages was growing worse and worse each night, and on that last night the guns roared almost until dawn. But we were lucky, because it was all small-caliber field artillery now, and a fir wood just south of the house protected us from most of it. Most of the shells were either intercepted by the tree-tops, which they decimated, or they overshot the house to land in the alley of beech trees beyond or in the great ditch at the boundary of the Franciscan sisters' estate. Hence the house escaped unharmed apart from pockmarked brick walls.

Metamorphosis

Dawn came, and with it an eerie silence fell over the land. As I woke I heard nothing more outside our cellar. It was all over. Somewhat later, Mother hustled us in single file as usual on the path to hear mass at the sisters'. Veva, however, who was heading up the queue, suddenly came to a halt: a dead German soldier lay across the track. She called Mother, who curtly told her to step over the body and to continue on her way. When we followed, Mother placed herself in front of it and guided us around it. I did not even see what the obstacle was. After mass a few of us ran to the gate, curious to see if anything had changed. It certainly had: the Bredabaan was littered with boughs and branches, and the smell of bleeding tree sap was pervasive. In the far distance one could see whole large beech trees lying felled across the road, no doubt to slow any advance along it. Just across us in the alley next to villa Mansion, facing our entrance gate, stood the skeleton of a large burned-out military truck, already looted of its wheels and parts of the engine. True or not, we took this to be the work of the Resistance.

We then walked toward the village to see if there were any Allied soldiers. The first one I saw near the burned-out factory looked almost like a Martian to me. He wore a beret, not a helmet, a leather jerkin and battle dress, a kind of clothes I had never seen before. He reminded me of a mechanic in overalls, all the more so because he stood near an odd vehicle. That was just as weird. It looked more like a toy than a car, with its canvas sides, hoops for a canvas roof over the top, and an equally strange container, a jerrican, strapped to its back along with a fifth wheel. The vehicle, as I now know, was a jeep and the man beside it a Canadian soldier. He came over to us to ask questions, but we did not understand his language, so we went on. Next I discovered with equal astonishment a soldier cooking potatoes on a Coleman stove—not a field kitchen in sight. Later we learned more about these aliens: that they actually liked to eat big acorns, and that they whistled after the girls, strange behavior compared with the soldiers we had known hitherto. That day I was also struck by the flimsy Sten guns or Bren guns the soldiers were carrying. Later I understood that while such weapons and tools individually were inferior in quality to their German counterparts, they could be produced faster and in far greater numbers than their enemies could manufacture their weapons. So astonishing were all these sights that I simply did not seem to register a few dead bodies lying near us on the tramway track, unlike several of my siblings, who were more impressed by them than I was.

We turned back to go home, but Chris was eager to see what had happened to the villa Mansion across the road, and I went with him. Unlike Rina and Jacqui, he knew that the Germans had placed an anti-aircraft gun on a flat portion of its roof as a defense against strafing. Now, just like the day before, its front door, above a flight of steps, still stood temptingly open. As I was about to run up those steps Chris stopped me. Something had aroused his suspicions: the scene was too inviting. So we went up one after the other at the very edge of the steps rather than in the middle. Later on we learned that the steps had been booby-trapped, just as Chris thought. As nothing had been left in the house itself, nor on its roof, we did not linger there.

Later that day Chris and I went to look at a bunker he knew about on the military domain in the hope of finding "souvenirs." While I was fascinated by its construction and the view through its firing slot, it contained nothing but a length of electric wire, which Chris took to rig an alarm for our pigsty. I did not feel like returning home yet, so I went through the proving grounds to the fen where we always went swimming. There among the bushes and the reeds I stumbled on the scene of a firefight. Not a bush, not a tree, not a reed had apparently escaped unharmed. A stupefying, cloying scent from the sap of so many bleeding plants hung over the scene. Then I saw the imprint of one or several bodies imprinted as if stamped in the crushed reeds, many rust-brown with bloodstains; a German helmet had rolled a few feet away. This scene, no doubt combined with the bodies I had seen earlier and the devastation wrought by the shelling, all of a sudden overwhelmed me. I sat down and I grieved. Revulsion and then anger seized me. What reason could be so compelling as to justify the sudden destruction of countless young people of all shapes and nationalities and the wealth of their unrealized talents? Were not ideologies responsible for this, ideologies in general, of every stripe, including nationalism and even religion, ideologies that drove people to murder each other under the banner of their intolerance? Was not all ideology poison, and were its political purveyors any better than mass criminals? At that moment something crystallized in my mind, and I realized that war, violence, and aggressive antagonism could never be justified and should never be condoned. Certainly my reasoning was still immature, as one might expect of a fifteen-year-old. Yet, while I would amplify and deepen my position with more sophisticated considerations in the years that followed, I have never altered the essential conviction I reached that day. That day I turned into a pacifist through and through, wary of politics and of most politicians, and I have remained one ever since. After sitting there for a long while, I left and did not even take the helmet as souvenir. And of course I told nobody.

Meanwhile Guido had been in the village and watched some men pulling the boots off the feet of a fallen soldier. The looters of Gooreind were at work again. By now these men were notorious in villages all around because they had managed to loot the barracks of the artillery range in Brasschaat a few miles south of Gooreind, just as the Germans were leaving there and before the Canadians arrived on October 4, two full weeks before we were liberated. As children we were struck only with the audacity of all this pillaging, not the desperation that lay behind it. These people were no longer just a few semi-professional poachers or smugglers. The men who used to work at the barracks of the artillery range had been laid-off for quite a while now, and when the factory burned, its laborers also lost their jobs. All these unemployed people were hard up and tried to make ends meet any way they could.

Looting however, was only one aspect of the power vacuum that had sprung up overnight. Another was the sudden activity of uncontrolled vigilante groups, mostly made up of young men who claimed to be members of the Resistance. Until just a few days earlier the Resistance in the region had apparently encompassed only two or three small organized groups. From at least 1942 onward small networks of people had developed to shelter Jewish people and downed Allied aviators and to transport them to safety far away in Spain or Switzerland. They also helped unwilling forced laborers to flee underground. The network nearest to Gooreind, called Fidelio, functioned as an autonomous branch of what was known as the White Brigade. In and around Antwerp among other organizations of this kind there was a somewhat larger and perhaps older group that formed part of a countrywide organized "Secret Army" led by former army officers. Its members were "Leopoldists," adherents of King Leopold, and our aunt Maria de Moor was in fact their local "president." This group, her eldest son among them, had guided the Allies to safely reach the city and had prevented German forces from dynamiting or otherwise destroying anything in the whole wide harbor area, especially its crucial locks. Also operating in Antwerp, but not in Gooreind, was a communist-inspired Front for Independence. Finally, there were the vigilante groups. These consisted for the most part of youths who had joined one or another Resistance group, such as the White Brigade, only a few weeks or even days before liberation. In Gooreind they had shot at some of the retreating Germans, and in the exchange of gunfire a local young man had been killed. As a result his comrades claimed the mantle of authority. But they did not or could not prevent the arrival of vigilante groups from surrounding villages that had been liberated earlier. Soon the "Whites" began to pursue and to arrest presumed collaborators locally known as "Blacks." Assassination lists were also circulating among such groups.

The day after we were liberated Mother sent Bea to find Father. She first walked carefully to Brasschaat, navigating roads still littered with tree limbs and rubbish; yellow military ribbons indicated safe passages through minefields. A decapitated German soldier still lay along the road. Then on to Antwerp. Bea found Father at the house of our aunt Maria Brusseleers. His story was as follows: When he realized on September 4 that he could no longer return home, he first went to the house of his sister, our aunt Maria de Moor, the one who played a leading role in the local cell of the Leopoldist Resistance army. Her three oldest sons were in the process of volunteering for a Belgian brigade then being organized by the British army, and the British commander of the Antwerp garrison with his staff were quartered in her very large house. She pinned a big Belgian cockade on her brother's jacket and took him in. Here Father was safe for the moment, although Aunt Maria soon learned that some vigilantes were out to arrest him. Was this because he was known as a lifelong friend of a senior poet from West Flanders who had been a prominent collaborator? Was it because he attended the pilgrimage to the Yser Tower in 1941, a monument to peace—despite his allocution there, an allegory about resistance to the occupier? Or was it simply because he was a well-known Flemish Catholic personality? No one knew, but meanwhile Father continued to walk about freely, even accompanying the British commander on some of his rounds around the city. Still, the risk that someone would recognize him increased every day, until he prudently moved out of his sister's house and found shelter with Uncle Pierre and Aunt Maria Brusseleers, who were staunch Belgian patriots but whose residence was not a hub of Resistance activities. He stayed inside all day and only ventured out at dusk in a nondescript overcoat and large hat. That is where Bea found him. He was overjoyed to see her, but she returned with the message that it was still too dangerous for him to return to Wiezelo because of the prevailing anarchy there.

Meanwhile at home, on the very first day of liberation I came across a vigilante hidden among the trees near the house, along the ditch between us and the sisters'. Clad in what may have been tattered remnants of a uniform, he accosted me to tell me in bogus, easy-to-understand German that he was a soldier in need of food trying clandestinely to make it all the way back to Germany. I entreated him to surrender but he would not, so I went inside the house to ask Mother what to do and returned with the message that this was a folly, but that if he wanted to flee he should follow the ditch to the proving grounds and then cross those; he might perhaps find some food in the fork of an oak tree at the limit of our land and those grounds. A little later he apparently tried the same trick with Chris and then with Bea, who merely provided him with some bread and water. Failing to entrap anyone in the family, the vigilante left and we never heard or saw anything about him or his story ever again. He was not the only person to hide in ditches. One of these was a Dutch fascist who was found by Frans, denounced, beaten, and jailed.

A few days later a car arrived sporting a large Belgian flag wound around the carrier on top of it and filled with White Brigade vigilantes, looking for Father. The children were banished to the kitchen and sentries were posted at the corners of the house, all dressed differently from one another, with here and there something reminiscent of a uniform. It would have been hilarious if they had not all been armed. Was it by chance that they found Mother seated in the great hall with a heap of letters strewn all around her on the floor in envelopes prominently bearing U.S. stamps, emblazoned with images of the Golden Gate Bridge? They were old letters from her brother Theo, sent around 1937, but they gave the impression that here was a U.S.A.-loving household. That much I saw before I was hustled into the kitchen. I was told that after the letter episode the vigilantes triumphantly discovered German books in Father's library. Mother pointed to those in English, but these were outnumbered by those in German. Mother then drew their attention to the far greater number of books in French and Dutch, and on the book front the vigilantes had to admit defeat. Making a renewed effort they opened a drawer, only to find a set of ribbons in the Belgian colors. Next Mother showed them letters from various patriotic personalities in Antwerp—whereupon they abandoned the effort. I cannot vouch for what I did not see, but it is clear from some of my siblings' powerful but conflicting memories that this vigilante irruption considerably affected them. In any case the intrusion was not repeated, for the following day one of our de Moor cousins, with a group of his Leopoldist comrades, arrived to guard our entrance gate and turn away any unwanted visitors. A little later, though, a Resistance interrogator arrived with an intercepted letter from a friend of Veva and asked her politely, in the presence of Mother, about the identities of the people alluded to in the sentence "We wonder what will happen to some of our friends." Veva did not know and said so.

The people of Gooreind also did not suffer kindly the intrusion of vigilantes from elsewhere. When the first group of outside vigilantes arrived, they caught some girls who had befriended German or Vlasov soldiers or had begged food from them, and the vigilantes shamed the girls publicly by forcibly shaving their hair as had happened in the villages liberated before ours. Here, however, this type of brutality generated immediate opposition, and the intruders were thrown out by the Gooreind "Resistance" itself, whose attitude was that these were "our girls" and "we take care of our own."

But within days after our liberation the public mood was already turning. No longer was any member of the Resistance automatically a hero, no longer was any accused collaborator a blackguard, and no longer was a person either "White" or "Black"; in the popular parlance, one might be "a black crow with white wings." The resulting situation could only be described as a power vacuum teetering on the brink of anarchy, as the various "Resistance" groups confronted and vied with each other— luckily without using their weapons.

Much had happened during the delay between the liberation of most of the country and that of our region. Belgium was under British military occupation and ruled by a major-general, George Erskine. But this was indirect rule. Prince Charles, the ardent anglophile brother of the king, was now regent. A government led by the few ministers who had fled to London in 1940, supplemented by a few local politicians, governed by decree. The former parliament was completely bypassed for fear that it would vote the government out of office. A separate organization of military courts dealt with the repression of collaborators by means of courts martial. The new government concerned itself principally with the installation of the regent, attempts to disarm the Resistance movements and their vigilante offshoots, the draconian monetary reform known as the Gutt Decrees, and in December the creation of a welfare state. But the government lamentably failed to improve the shortages of food, coal, and textiles. To the contrary, its actions inadvertently fed the black market, which now blossomed as never before.

The Gutt Decrees, which were issued on October 6, had the most immediate impact on us at Wiezelo. They declared valueless all banknotes for a value higher than 20 francs (worth then 40 cents) and replaced them with new notes up to a total value of 2000 francs per "citizen." At the same time all bank accounts were blocked for years, including all income from bonds and shares. Only investments in real estate seem to have been spared. To our household the decrees were a major blow, because most of my family's monthly income stemmed from returns on investment. As my parents' blocked holdings were only gradually freed years later, they were forced to sell one piece of real estate after another to stay afloat, so that a few years later they had sold the title to the farm and about half of the estate at Wiezelo as well. For the immediate future the problem was cash flow, and the sale of property satisfied our most urgent and concrete needs, while effects of the longer-range issues would manifest themselves only later on. In a nutshell, we went from "truly wealthy" before the war to "merely affluent" during the war and to "in straightened circumstances" in the wake of the Gutt Decrees. We all learned quickly what was worth spending money on, such as education, and what was not, such as leisure or comfort. I never forgot that lesson.

A week or two later Father returned home. Was the lesson of his experience in Antwerp that "blood is thicker than water"? But no, family was not just a matter of thicker blood. Certainly family solidarity trumped everything else during the occupation, just as it did now, but with one unspoken condition. All the adults involved judged that every other adult in the family had behaved in an honorable and trustworthy fashion and continued to do so. Even where their opinions differed, my family recognized in each other a set of underlying principles that they could respect. But not all families felt that way about each other, and hence family ties did not always prevail elsewhere.

War Again

Liberation had not freed us from the war at all because immediately after that we found ourselves in the trajectory of the longer-range weapons with which the Germans were now bombarding Antwerp. They were called V-1 and V-2, the *V* standing for *Vergeltung* (retaliation). V-1s were known in England as Doodlebugs. The forerunners of cruise missiles, they looked like a long bomb as they clumsily flew through the sky, and their engines made a noise like a sewing machine. When they flew low, they were nearing their targets, and when one heard the engine stutter or shut off, one dove for a ditch or hoped for the best. The first V-1 fell already on October 4 but landed short of the city. From October 13, 1944, until March 30, 1945, a V-1 was fired at Antwerp every ninety minutes, day and night. The goal was to destroy the harbor facilities that were vital for the further conduct of the war. If all the V-1s had fallen on Antwerp, the city would have been utterly devastated, but three-quarters of them were shot down in the countryside north of the city from around Gooreind southward or fell short there. Besides

Antwerp, the harbors of London and Southampton were also long-distance targets for Doodlebugs, while Liège in eastern Belgium was a target during the Battle of the Bulge. Half of all V-1s and a majority of all V-2 rockets ever fired, however, were aimed at Antwerp.

Hence we saw many of them and became quite used to them. When we were in Antwerp I simply stopped in my tracks whenever I heard the engine fall out, and I waited. Once one of them fell a hundred feet or so in front of me on a block of houses bordering the Meir, and I watched them collapse in a great cloud of dust. I did not run to the scene to watch or to help because we had been told not to do so: we would only be in the way of rescuers. My most memorable of all the V-1s passed low over me, this time in Gooreind along the Bredabaan, and landed as I dived in the ditch. It did not explode but broke up on landing and burst open. Instead of explosives it was packed with miniature copies of the propaganda magazine *Signal*, renowned for its color photographs.

On November 13 a V-1 struck the nave of Gooreind's church and left a gaping hole in the wall behind the pulpit. A day or so later the pulpit disappeared, so Pastor De Wit henceforth preached from a make-shift platform on Sundays. Some time later his Sunday sermon began in a most remarkable way. His first words to his flock, it is said, were "Enough is enough." He went on to confirm that old James, a well-known elder in Gooreind, had died that week, as every parishioner knew already, and he continued: "But what was my surprise when I noticed during the burial service that his coffin had been fashioned out of boards from my pulpit!" He concluded that truly pillaging was never justified and loot should be returned to its owners. That event was the culmination of the audacity of Gooreind's looters. Above all, though, it underscored how many people still remained in dire straits before the impending revival of the harbor that was soon to lead to full employment and the return of some prosperity.

V-2s were much more dangerous than V-1s. The first true ballistic missiles ever made, V-2s were larger, almost invisible, and inaudible because they traveled faster than sound, so their rumbling could be heard only after their explosion. At night observers might see one coming from an upward flash of light in the sky above their launch site hundreds of miles away, but in practice even that information was useless. There simply was no defense against them. Fortunately, there were far fewer

V-2s than V-1s, and they were even less accurate. Nevertheless, no fewer than 1,300 V-2s hit the city of Antwerp. The worst single military loss occurred on November 17, the last day before the first maritime convoy reached the port. A V-2 hit Teniers Square, a major road crossing not far from the central railway station, at the moment when a British unit and some American troops were crossing it. It left 126 dead and 309 wounded. No wonder the city earned the nickname Sudden Death among the troops.

That reputation of great danger, however, was a boon for Gooreind. The harbor needed all available labor, especially longshoremen. Not only were the latter, along with miners, the best-paid laborers in the country, but during the V-1 and V-2 bombardment they received hefty supplements for the extra risks involved in working in a target zone for V bombs. In Gooreind former longshoremen longed to return to their old jobs, and many of the unemployed were eager to follow them. After all, more V-1s were shot down around Gooreind than exploded in Antwerp, and so the compensation, colorfully called *bibbergeld* (trembling money), was an extra bonus. Not only that. Once the first convoys of ships entered the harbor from November 18 onward, its management was taken over by the U.S. armed forces, and their long-shoremen supervised the loading and unloading of freight by the local workmen. Those soldiers were professionals of the trade, like the local men, and both sides honored the traditional practice that goods "which fell between ship and quay," that is, goods damaged during unloading, were considered officially lost, albeit not for everyone. Accidents of this nature were frequent, if only because of the frantic pace of unloading, and they produced a bonanza, so that during the winter many people in Gooreind acquired new boots, clothes, winter coats, jerricans, tools, and the like. All in all, then, the V bombardment turned into a prosperous period for this segment of the local workforce and gave birth to a thriving black market.

Good for longshoremen perhaps, but not for others. The worst disaster occurred on December 16, when my dear daredevil cousin Jacqui, along with over five hundred other people, was killed by a V-2 in the cinema Rex near the main railroad station in Antwerp. The very same day the Germans launched their last offensive of the war in the southeast of Belgium. This was the Von Rundstedt offensive, better known as the Battle of the Bulge, its aim being to drive a wedge between the American and the British troops and to capture Antwerp. As a result of Jacqui's death and also of the new military situation, my parents immediately wrote a letter to those of their children at boarding schools and warned us not to return home at Christmas for security reasons. A day or two later Mother traveled to Bruges and told us there about Jacqui's death and about the looming military threat. Perhaps she stressed that threat so much that it overshadowed everything else, but the news about Jacqui really sank in about a day later. And so Guido and I stayed at school over Christmas.

Then on New Year's Eve 1944 a V-2 fell a hundred feet at most from our home at Wiezelo. As I was not there, I let Bea tell the account.

On December 31, 1944, it was very cold (-5° F, it was said, but that is probably exaggerated). We [the older children] were practically sitting in the hearth to beat the cold and separated from the rest of the hall by folding screens. The shutters over the windows were all closed, and it was almost pitch-dark. That explains why no one among us was wounded. The "little girls" and Nico were in bed. I think it must have been around nine o'clock in the evening when that missile fell at the time that we were only sitting sadly in the hearth. Annie and I had agreed to do no washing-up that evening until we had used all the dishes, and there were just enough dishes from the good set for New Year's Day.

The missile fell, and we did not hear it: neither its arrival, nor its explosion. But it was as if the whole house collapsed. Even the outside doors, lifted out of their hinges, gaped wide open before they completely tumbled over. The staircase was full of glass and other bits of debris. Father followed me upstairs, and as we arrived there, Nico was already shouting that he was unhurt. Suze and Veerle also. Marleen, who slept in the room next to mine, did not move. When I finally got her arm I thought that she was dead. But she slept. Because of the cold she had pulled all the blankets over her head. Her arm was a little scratched. It was a true miracle: no one was injured. People from Gooreind arrived fairly quickly to gawk and to be of help. I believe that all of us then went to sleep on the floor in the hall.

The next day, January 1, 1945, Father sent Annie with the children (I think Rina was with them) to Sister Maria Beata [head of the Holy Sepulchre school in Turnhout where all the older girls had been to boarding school]. She found a place for them to stay. I stayed behind with Father, and the people of Gooreind boarded up the house as best they could. And all the dirty dishes were broken!!

Clearly our house was now uninhabitable without windows or doors and with its flat roof corrugated by the blast into a huge wave, while the ceilings upstairs were nearly all caved in. Living among strangers, most of the children were now refugees without parents, with only twenty-three-year-old Annie in charge. My parents could not accompany them, for if they left the house, even for a single day, it would certainly be looted, Gooreind being what it was. Today the Red Cross or a similar organization would care for the children, but at the time there was no such ready assistance. As long as friends or acquaintances were available, they were expected to help. Within days Sister Maria Beata, or the owners of the house that were lodging my siblings in their attic, found a lawyer willing to let them squat in 't Sluiske (the small sluice). That was the name of his dilapidated single-story summer cabin, a dwelling without electricity or running water in Oud Turnhout somewhat east of the town. So they all moved and camped there. Oud Turnhout turned out to be one of the most remote corners of Belgium. The children had almost no money apart from what my older sisters earned by doing odd sewing jobs linked to the black market through the intermediary of Chris. He was still a weekday boarder at St. Victor in Turnhout, while on weekends and during vacations he traded in that market, thanks to a classmate whose parents ran a laundry service that turned out to be a hub of local black market trade. His activities also brought some money in the till.

Besides potatoes, which Annie obtained on credit from the farmer next door, as well as some milk for the small children, there was little else to eat, and during that bitter winter they had only inferior coal dust—actually a sort of peat—to heat the kitchen stove and warm themselves. To make matters worse, English soldiers, camped nearby, soon began to pester the older girls, despite Chris's efforts to prevent it. Matters came to a head one night when Annie heard a group of them trying to break in through a window. Right away she sent a small child off for help to the farmer next door, while all the others together tried to keep the soldiers out of the window. Upon hearing the news, the farmer set his watchdogs loose, and they drove the intruders off before they succeeded in entering the house.

Meanwhile Guido and I were at school, for shortly after Father's return, the abbey school had reopened its doors, "new" money had somehow been found, and we had been sent back to resume our education while keeping out of harm's way. Once there, we had no true inkling of what was happening to our siblings. It is ironic that, as I wrote in a letter to my parents on February 22 of that year, Guido and I produced four comic sketches for a visiting group of about 120 orphaned children from Antwerp evacuated to Bruges and accompanied by senior Girl Guides who knew my sisters well. Remembering the trouble I had at first had with the Bruges dialect, these were produced in the broadest Antwerp slang, to the obvious delight of the youthful audience.

We learned of our own siblings' difficulties only when we went to visit them at Oud Turnhout for Easter leave on March 31, a day after the last V-1 fell on Antwerp. As the fifteen-year-old senior I was in charge, with Guido, one year younger, in tow. Because the Allies used so much rolling stock to pursue the war in Germany, traveling was difficult, and trains were overloaded and late. We reached Antwerp only in the late afternoon, at which point we boarded the tram for Turnhout, which was also late. When we arrived there, it was dusk. My instructions were to go east from the end of the line in a town neither of us had ever visited before, arrive at its cemetery, cross it, and continue along a farm road, where we would then somehow recognize the cabin. By the time we arrived at the cemetery, though, it was pitch dark; a blackout was still mandatory, and there was no moon. Moreover, this was the kind of cemetery abounding in monuments that threw menacing shadows everywhere. I was not too certain of where I was going, and Guido was becoming a little panicky. But we emerged on a farm road of sorts into a flat landscape where nothing was visible for more than a few yards in any direction. So I started walking and resolved to ask my way at the first dwelling I found. After a little while a deep shadow on the nearby horizon seemed promising. But as soon as I left the road a posse of guard dogs began to bark as if the end of the world had come. So we returned to the road to try another house a little farther away. But every time we began to approach a home there were more dogs. Finally I saw a chink of light not too far away, and we ran for it: dogs or no dogs. There were none, the door opened as I knocked, and we almost stumbled over our siblings huddled around the stove. We were home.

The next morning we discovered the camping conditions at the cottage. At the rear of the house ran a brook, regulated by a little sluice. The brook provided our water, and on it lay a raft made of empty jerricans. It was now warm enough for hardy children to play in and around the water, and that was all the younger children did day after day. Most of the time this included me, although once Chris took me along to visit a military "cemetery": a dumping ground for disabled tanks. I recall climbing into a tank and wondering at the cramped conditions inside. The older girls ran the establishment, and Chris was often coming and going on business. A day or so later our parents came over from Wiezelo on rickety bicycles with worn-out tires to bring vegetables, linen, and probably some money. When they left they discovered to their displeasure that in a misguided effort to improve their equipage Chris had carefully painted the lettering *Michelin* on every single tire.

Two months or so after our return to school, at a moment when I was moodily loafing about a playing field, a single British fighter plane swooped in very low and waggled its wings over me, to signal that the war in Europe was over. It was May 8. Some weeks later the repairs at Wiezelo had progressed to the point that the house was habitable again, and the Vansina refugees returned from a half-year of squatting at Oud Turnhout, having lost a school year, but without further harm. As to the considerable cost of the whole incident, Father was heard to opine that V bombs must have been invented to enrich glaziers.

Back to Normal

In the late fall of 1944, when Guido and I were sent back to school—now once again housed at the abbey of St. Andrews—we found that every effort had been made to reestablish the usual rhythms of the boarding school in the familiar surroundings of yore, exactly as had been customary before 1942 and without retaining anything from the experiences of its years in exile. It was as if that interruption had never happened. The main difficulty in achieving this state of prewar normalcy was the return to the strict discipline that had obtained before the years in the wilderness, a regrettable goal in the eyes of quite a fraction of the pupils. But the weight of tradition prevailed, and everyone gradually resumed the expected stance of passive obedience. Starting in February 1945, when the danger of further war rapidly receded, the school authorities began to reintroduce the extracurricular activities that had been brusquely abandoned in the spring of 1940. Not only were we now playing extramural hockey and soccer, but to my delight a few tennis courts were opened in spring where we learned the rudiments of the game. I also liked a series of evening sessions on classical music appreciation ranging from Beethoven to Debussy. Preparations were made as well to resume the teaching of piano or violin during the following year and to revive the prewar practice of school excursions.

But when I returned to the abbey school that fall, I was not the child I was when I had last left the school in Drongen. In the interim I had witnessed scenes and tasted fears that fell beyond the usual compass of childhood. At fifteen, moreover, I was also an adolescent and now as awkward as any of them. Judging by some of my letters to my parents in the early spring, I could act the responsible adult ("Guido does not work—he does not heed my reproaches" or "I hope both of you are healed and take some rest now"), the child ("Are there still V's? and please tell me in your answer a bit more about the damage inside the house and the situation of my room"; "Tell Nico in secret that he should clean our house under the thornbushes"), and the melancholy gangling teenager ("Something else. I grew 3 centimeters in two months and gained 1 kilogram"). But in my letters I see nothing of the brooding moods typically associated with adolescence.

The atmosphere of the classroom certainly favored that last avatar. The grade I had entered, the penultimate one of the humaniora, was labeled "Poesis" and was supposed to arouse the poetic and literary sensibilities of the pupils. In Dutch and in French we read sixteenth- and seventeenth-century poetry and drama and practiced writing it. By that literary standard moodiness and melancholy were clearly an interesting stance to take, while reacting with childish enthusiasm was obviously despicable. We stayed at the abbey over Christmas and New Year, but I remember nothing at all about it. My letters show that I remained quite interested in what happened at home but only once, in February, was there a cri de coeur when I wrote: "I hope that the war will soon be over, that the V-1 and similar stuff will soon cease, that I will be able to return home soon, and that all will be well." What I do remember most vividly from that school year is the unexpected renewal of my former loathing of this milieu, not because of the return of the old discipline but because it seemed to me that the back-to-normal movement had revived all the old pretensions of my fellow students about belonging to an elite, practically as a birthright. That made me morose at times, and increasingly so as the year wore on.

And yet much of what went on at school was quite stimulating. We studied all the usual fields, with the minor addition of some geology and a few really rudimentary notions of physics. But I found some topics quite challenging, and no longer just in fields I had always liked, such as geography, where an almost year-long spatial examination of the economy of modern Italy enthralled me. Oddly enough for someone as weak in the subject as I was, I became enamored with three-dimensional geometry, as taught by the prefect Dom Feuillen, and was surprised by my reaction. A bear of a man, Dom Feuillen would wander from left to right in front of the class as he expounded, with little bits of chalk in his hands, and when he noticed that someone was not paying attention he had this trick of flicking a bit of chalk quite accurately at the culprit, more for effect than with any sense of objurgation, and we did admire his skill at dispatching such missiles. What he really taught me was that mathematics could be interesting and imaginative and that even I might "get it." I also liked the play *King Oedipus* by Sophocles, which we studied nearly all year long in Greek. In doing so I learned to appreciate what seemed to be the greater versatility and vividness of that language over Latin. In the latter language we were plodding through the historian Tacitus for a long while, but then we turned to the more entertaining late Latin of Saint Augustine. These kinds of experiences explain a passage in one of my letters: "The work here becomes easier and more interesting by the day, although it is naturally not that easy with regard to mathematics"; and "as you can see we hear all sorts of interesting talks."

Among these talks was one that I was especially sorry to miss. "Last Sunday," I wrote, on January 28 of that year, "a certain P Gérard spoke about the Congo (he lived there for twenty years); unfortunately I was unable to attend it. A group of boys interested in the Congo has formed a club and they will collect more information in order to become more knowledgeable about the Congo. Don't worry, I am not leaving for

Matadi yet; sadly enough I cannot even be part of that group." No inkling there that the writer might be a budding Africanist, surely.

Life at St. Andrews continued to unfold placidly without any significant disturbances all the way to the end of the school year on July 18. Meanwhile, what of life beyond the bounds of St. Andrews? At one point before the end of the war there was talk of a British base in a village nearby, and twice a single German raider dropped a few bombs in a field near Bruges while we lived in a cocoon at school. At our school there was no discussion of military operations whatsoever, no mention even of major events, let alone popular disturbances in Belgium, and only a desultory official acknowledgment on May 8 that the war in Europe had ended. In June, as a special treat, we even managed to visit some of the watering places on the coast, without any awareness that a fresh wave of anarchic attacks on suspected collaborators had shaken the area only a fortnight earlier. At St. Andrews World War II had been firmly put in the past: it was history before it had even ended. Externally, at least, I too put the war behind me. Final exams came and absorbed all my attention, anyway. As usual I barely passed in mathematics and did well or very well elsewhere. Still, I was disappointed in my performance and felt that I would remain "second place" forever, whatever the field of study. I did earn a first prize in Dutch. But was I not the only pupil in class whose maternal language was Dutch? In that mood, on July 19 I left the cocoon of St. Andrews to head for home.

Yet elsewhere in the country, and especially in Antwerp, the effects of war continued to dominate the landscape, even after the Battle of the Bulge and the end of the V bombardment, until all the fighting was over. I only saw the war's new impact there when I was finally allowed to come home for a few days in early June. The city was still the major entry port for all Allied military forces. It was contentedly buzzing with full employment at the harbor, and American culture was all the rage. On a Sunday I caught my first sight of GIs, strapping young men dressed in their best uniforms, as they briskly paraded on the Meir to the sound of Sousa marches or the wildly popular "Anchors Aweigh." On the promenades at the Scheldt one saw Liberty and Victory ships moored everywhere. These vessels were neither elegant nor exceptionally well made; indeed, their propellers were prone to fall off at times—a propensity that gave sober meaning to the cautionary placards hanging from their sterns: "Beware of propellers." But they could be constructed at a shipyard in record time, and this ease of manufacture resulted in a plethora of such watercraft in the Antwerp harbor. Curiously, it is in connection with these ships that I first met the name of Kenosha, Wisconsin—the state where I was eventually to settle—because some of them had been launched at a shipyard there, on the shores of Lake Michigan. A few miles out of Antwerp, across the Scheldt, the Americans had built a giant camp called Top Hat to lodge their troops as they arrived at or departed from Europe for the Far East or for home. The use of the harbor for almost all Allied imports was an unprecedented bonanza for most working people, and they attributed it all to the Americans. These workers disliked the attitude of the British, with their seeming presumption to indirect rule, but they adored the United States and its popular culture, to the point that more than a few of them even dreamed of making the city a perpetual American enclave in Europe.

Closure

A day or two after my return home in July Mother called me to her little office for a talk. She started by observing that I did not seem to like the atmosphere at the school at all, then expressed great satisfaction at my results, and proceeded to suggest that perhaps I did not care much for St. Andrews because I was bored, and that I was bored because I was ahead of the bulk of the class. Did I really want to return there? She then informed me that there was an institution in Belgium called the Central Jury, where one could take a set of exams in September that covered all six years of secondary education at once. Perhaps I should try that? If I succeeded, I could immediately attend the university, and if I failed I would only be a little late in returning to school. I do not recall whether she added as an afterthought that success would save the household a good deal of money given the high cost of the abbey school, but I perceived that point as well. I assented immediately to her plan without giving much thought to the future beyond the desirable fact that I would be free of the school. Clearly, distaste for its elitism overrode its attractions. It was both a sudden and a radical decision, the first of several similar ones I was to make in the future.

To this day I still do not understand how Mother could even conceive such a project: my grades were not that good, and I had not actually complained much about the climate at school. A review of my letters from St. Andrews produces only the occasional remark to suggest that I was suffering from a lack of intellectual challenge. "This trimester, however," I once wrote, "the subject-matter is exceptionally easy, something about which I am naturally very happy." Did my mother read too much into such sentences? Today I am convinced that the ruinous impact of the Gutt Decrees, combined with the cost of the recent repairs of Wiezelo, had something to do with it. Anyway, within days she found tutors for the two areas in which she thought I would need them, trigonometry and Greek epic, and the project took off. The first tutor was a young engineer in Brasschaat who lived in a small but cozy little villa. Dry as cinders he was when introducing sines, cosines, or tangents, but in no time at all he managed to raise my interest in and enthusiasm for trigonometry. The other tutor, also young, was blind, as is poetically apposite for one who teaches Homer. Twice a week I would meet him at the Melkmarkt to read the Odyssey in the little "Florentine" room off the courtyard in the back. The setting was quite romantic as we sailed all summer long with our hero from distant Troy to Penelope's halls and dwelled on obsolete forms or features borrowed from pre-Greek languages.

Meanwhile the aftermath of the war unfolded. A new maid suddenly appeared in our household. She was Maria Ostinova, a Ukrainian, who had been working as forced labor in Germany. She had fled as soon as the Allies arrived there, for fear of being returned to the USSR, and reached Belgium clandestinely, where somehow she met and fell in love with a certain Victor. But this Victor could not hide her, so she came to our household and stayed with us until all danger had passed. For indeed, by early summer a Soviet mission appeared at the main barracks of the proving grounds to repatriate its nationals who had fallen into German hands and secretly immigrated here. As Maria and many others feared, the Soviets considered it treasonable to surrender to the enemy or submit to forced labor. Unless someone had performed exceptional acts of sabotage, any prisoner of war or any forced laborer could expect to be deported to Siberia or worse. We were convinced that this had probably been the fate of the three central Asians from whom we never heard a word after they had left us.

Ever since April or May most Belgian former prisoners of war, forced labor recruits, and survivors of concentration camps were finding their way back into the country. Others, however, including most Jews, were never seen again and had presumably perished. Nearly everyone who returned had stories of hardships and horrors to tell. Some came back with tales of betrayal by persons they knew, and many among them sought revenge. Early in May the point was reached where this mounting resentment broke out in a new wave of vigilante attacks against alleged collaborators that resulted in some lynchings, and in thousands of fresh arrests. Irrational fears of hidden enemies fueled the unrest, which was further propelled by overall stress related to the continuing shortages of bread, clothes, and other basic necessities.

The following episode illustrates the severity of the anxieties as well as the shortages. When I returned from school I had grown so much that I needed new clothes. But such things could not be found. It so happened that our aunt Torty, who for many years had been managing programs of social assistance, received a large consignment of used clothes from the U.S., and I was outfitted with some of the leftovers from this delivery. My kit included light blue checked trousers of the golfing persuasion, which the locals immediately labeled "Rubens' pants"; an oversize off-white pullover, redolent of yachting, which they soon dubbed "the white elephant"; and an incorruptible sea-green colored lady's coat. The first time I wore the outfit to Antwerp I had barely alighted from the tram and crossed the square before I was halted by a policeman convinced that he had caught an escaped prisoner of war in disguise and perhaps—who knows?—on a sinister mission. However, my identity papers were in order, and I was too young to fit the profile. Reluctantly, he let me go.

The tensions induced by the revelations of those freed from captivity had only begun to ebb slowly late in July, when the authorities in Antwerp released a documentary movie about Auschwitz to a local cinema and urged everyone, including all the older children, to watch it free of charge. Along with everyone else I went, and the horror of the film left me speechless. Two aspects of it struck me as the very essence of evil: first, a segment showing prisoners loading bodies in striped pajamas on wheelbarrows as so much cordwood and trundling them to a crematorium of sorts, and second, the realization that the whole movie had been put together from amateur footage filmed by guards—people who, far from being ashamed of their deeds, were presumably recording them to boast later about their valiant occupation. Like many others, I was numbed by these images for days, and there was no dismissing this as mere propaganda. The evidence was too real, too undeniable, and it etched itself into my and everyone else's consciousness forever.

A few weeks later, again in Antwerp, I learned about Hiroshima, in this case from a newspaper while standing on a street corner appropriately beneath a monument bearing a huge crucifix. I understood the extent of the devastation that the atom bomb had caused, less so the deadliness of its radiation, and nothing at all about the physics involved. But what I understood was awful enough: humanity had finally found the tool of ultimate destruction. And on this terrifying thought the war really ended.

September came, and with it the week of exams for the Central Jury. First there were days of written tests. Remarkable among them were two documents to be translated: a Greek text about the surface of the moon and a Dutch one to be rendered in French that dealt with commercial fishing. One of the silliest pieces of writing I have ever seen, it ran more or less like this: "In the morning the fishermen go out to sea. They catch A-Z fish and then they return to port," in which A-Z represent some twenty names of different kinds of fish. The Dutch composition was on a theme of one's choice, and I wrote an impassionate plea for the need to cultivate tolerance and love for all people in order to defeat hatred, fear, and violence, with special emphasis on the evilness of ideologies. It must have sounded utopian and juvenile, but at least it was timely. Several days of writing were followed by a day-and-a-half-long marathon of orals covering most of the subjects studied in high school. Mathematics was the only tricky part here. The problems in set theory and trigonometry went without a hitch, and I surprised myself in geometry, but I only solved the algebraic equations because someone watching on the sidelines whispered the answer from there. At the end of it one of the examiners, a well-known cleric and writer, unexpectedly asked me to transmit his compliments to Father. A week or so later the results were proclaimed. I had succeeded rather against the odds.

So I returned posthaste to school, where Dom Feuillen began by berating me for being so late. "You will have a hard time catching up in class," he said, before I told him my news. Upon hearing it, he pointed to some of the consequences of this success I had not thought about. Not only was I missing the finishing touches to the humanistic education bestowed on the rhetoricians, as the students of the last year of the humaniora were called, but my decision had precluded any careful consideration of a possible religious vocation. Indeed there was no sign of any vocation at all. As we shall see, he was certainly right on that point.

When I now look at my education up to that point, certain gaps are obvious, some of which were never completely filled. Partly due to conditions in wartime, and partly due to the curriculum itself, I had not taken any serious course in physics and none at all in chemistry or biology. Thus I had never heard a word about Darwin's theory of evolution. Indeed it would have been surprising if any Catholic school at the time had mentioned such a heresy. Furthermore, even in an education oriented toward the humanities there were some strange lacunae. My education had failed even to acquaint me with the names of Theodor Fontane, Heinrich Heine, Joseph Roth, Thomas Mann, Gustav Mahler, or any other German-Jewish author or composer, and the Gestapo's raid on Father's library in Bruges emptied it of such writers as well. Because I had skipped that last year, I had received no instruction whatsoever in philosophy. Less obvious was my almost total ignorance about the Enlightenment in the eighteenth century. Although the lack of that last year of high school is to blame in part, no Benedictine abbey school was going to teach Voltaire, Rousseau, or the Encyclopedists in depth, and certainly not one where most of the monks were ready to dismiss the whole of the French Revolution as a terrible mistake. The result was that decades later one of my colleagues would describe me as essentially a creature of the seventeenth century with some nineteenth-century plumage.

On the positive side, I had acquired a strong foundation in the European humanities, with considerable proficiency in Dutch and French literature as well as a good deal of German literature, and I was familiar with the standard Latin and Greek authors taught at that level. I also had some comparative literature, mostly Russian. But no English—no

Shakespeare, for instance. Thanks mainly to Father's library, I could find my way about in Western history and Western art history. I also had some experience of classical music. And I was keenly interested in the world beyond Europe and its customs. That, for better or for worse, was the baggage I took with me to university.

7

In Search of a Vocation

October 1945 to July 1951

The war was over, and so was my childhood. One year after liberation the family at Wiezelo was changing radically. The tight unit we had been in war began to disperse as the older children started to strike out on their own, each focusing outward, eager to move away. In that autumn of 1945 only Annie had a career while Veva stayed at home for the time being to help with the household. Nearly all the others in this group were in their last years of schooling and expected to emerge in the foreseeable future, diplomas in hand, and find their own way in the wider world. Already the residential core of the family had shrunk to just my parents, the three youngest girls, and Nico. That core dissolved a year later when all four were sent to boarding schools.

As family ties loosened I entered a phase of adolescence when my world began to revolve more and more around myself. I had my "own heart and soul," I informed Mother in a letter from this period and no longer shared those of "the whole household." Still, I continued to seek my parents' approval, and in a spirit of filial duty I embarked on the course they had set for me—without actually putting either heart or soul into the task. For the next few years my most absorbing issue was my own future, and my most pressing task was to find a vocation. So much did this topic absorb me during this period that I had no time at all for the affairs of the country. I did not even truly understand them and therefore perceived them as little more than tedious background noise.

Aftermaths

In the spring of 1945 the Soviet juggernaut had not rolled over the advancing Allied troops as some had feared. Instead everyone was well aware that the United States and the USSR were sliding into a standoff. That situation left many insecure enough during the following years to start learning Russian, my mother among them. Remembering no doubt the Vlasov soldiers, the Central Asian fugitives, and Maria Ostinova, she realized the need to acquire at least some rudimentary Russian — and anyway she liked languages. So she bought herself a secondhand Berlitz method textbook and a dictionary and took to study the language in her limited free time. It took a long time, but she kept at it and eventually became fluent enough to read Tolstoy's *Resurrection* (another secondhand book!) in the original, albeit I think with a translation facing the text.

The Allied occupation formally ended on July 14, 1945, and Belgium recovered its independence, although it was obviously no longer free to choose its foreign alliances. In particular there was no going back to the policy of strict neutrality Leopold III had imposed during the inter-bellum years. Instead Belgium was now part of Benelux, a union between Belgium, the Netherlands, and Luxemburg and soon about to join NATO when the alliance was founded in 1949.

The country itself was seemingly moving forward to its past. By autumn 1945 the two major parties, the Catholics and the socialists, had reestablished themselves and were very busy regaining their grip on most institutions of civil society — trade unions, pension funds, health benefit societies, life insurance schemes, sport clubs, brass bands, youth associations, and even leisure clubs — so as, once again, to nearly completely fuse social and political life in the three main Catholic, socialist, and conservative/liberal prewar ideological pillars. Except for those Catholic associations organized or supervised by the church, the others had all become autonomous from their political parties during the war. Now each party hastened to reinstate its constituency before the government could even be allowed to hold elections. They succeeded, and elections followed in February 1946. As foreseen they resulted in a duopoly of Catholics and socialists who jointly gathered over 70 percent of the vote. The strongest faction of each party had prevented various breakaway socialist and Catholic groups from emerging on their own, and they limited the communist vote to a bare 12.8 percent, a far cry from the communist breakthrough that many were expecting. The liberal party with 9.6 percent of the vote just managed to survive. Acting in concert, the leaders of the three main parties had also eliminated any threat of a resurging Flemish party by equating the whole of the Flemish movement with the minority of collaborators. In 1946 any overt expression of Flemish aspirations was still considered evidence of past collaboration, and hence there were no such expressions. In later years those aspirations could find an outlet only within the framework of the Catholic party. No politician at the time realized the dire consequences that the wholesale rejection of the Flemish movement was to entail in the then distant future.

The political landscape that emerged in 1946 remained unchanged until the mid-1950s. It included a major innovation — namely, that the unquestioned faith in the unbridled capitalism of earlier times had waned in favor of social compromise. The social pact that embodied this had been elaborated during the war and was already signed in December 1944. It created a welfare state mediated by the familiar pillars and hence the parties, although the major economic holding companies still continued to play a disproportionate role in the Belgian economy until the 1950s. At first the economy revived, and rationing began to be lifted in 1945, but then growth faltered so that rationing could still not be completely eliminated, although it became very gradually more and more restricted until only bread and coal were rationed by January 1950. By then Belgium's tapped-out and run-down coal mines and steel industries had become such a prominent economic and political headache that the country now began to trail its neighbors throughout the whole following decade.

After 1946 there remained two major strictly political issues: the return of the king and the handling of the repression — that is, the arrest and punishment of all alleged collaborators during the war. Nearly the whole political establishment wanted Leopold III to abdicate, essentially because it deemed him to be too autocratic, but a large majority of the population wanted his return. Talks between the government and the king started just after the end of the war in May 1945 and broke down completely. Then the leftist ministers began to paint him as an arch-collaborator who had dared discuss the future of the country with Hitler. They refused any sort of popular plebiscite about the question whether the king should be allowed to return home and resume his rule until 1950, when they could stonewall no longer. The yes vote won an overall majority of 57 percent but failed to obtain this in the industrialized

In Search of a Vocation

parts of Wallony and even in Brussels (only 48 percent). Given the opposition of most politicians and a near insurrection of Walloon blue-collar labor, the 72 percent majority of the yes vote in Flanders was disregarded altogether, and the king was obliged to abdicate by August. But the monarchy itself was saved, and his son Baudouin succeeded him in September 1951. The royal question did not directly affect me or the rest of the family except that it was the first time I voted.

The other major issue was the repression, which was conducted in military courts by prosecutors, called auditors. Given the large numbers of detainees, most of these courts were created from scratch. As we saw already, the system was forestalled at first by Resistance vigilantes who arbitrarily arrested and interrogated an estimated 70,000 persons in a few days—and they bypassed it again with complete impunity in May and June 1945, even though by then the courts had been operating well over six months. Vigilante groups also publicly lynched or stealthily murdered a presumably small but still unknown number of alleged collaborators. According to the statistics cited by the historian Vincent Dujardin, the military courts opened an astonishing total of 728,866 files (562,346 without duplicates) between September 1944 and December 1949. That is many more than in France or the Netherlands—although in France there had been many more extrajudicial executions. On a per capita basis more people were convicted in Flanders (0.73 percent) than in Brussels (0.56 percent) or in Wallony (0.52 percent). All the convicted lost their right to vote for as long as they lived, although this decision was reversed in most cases after 1949. Hence these convictions all had a long-lasting effect on the numbers of voters in the future. Considering that the accused persons were adults, that the vast majority among them were men, and that women gained the right to vote in 1949, the number of condemnations, not per person but per future potential voter, is important. It more than triples the figures given, so that by taking their families into account close to 3 percent of all adult voters in Flanders were condemned, without considering many who had been questioned or even jailed and later freed without charge.

In practice there were two categories of collaborators: economic and other collaborators. The legislation concerning the first kind was ambiguous. When the government ministers left Belgium in 1940, they mandated A. Galopin, the CEO of the largest financial holding company in the country, to take charge of economic policy and keep the economy ticking so as to avoid massive unemployment. The captains of industry obliged, and the highest magistrates and permanent officials in all the ministerial departments kept their own services functioning as well. Hence, even those who collaborated on a grand scale, by producing steel or coal, pouring concrete for fortifications, or producing army uniforms, for instance, were not prosecuted, nor were most blue-collar workers who went to work voluntarily in Germany. Among the small number of people who were indicted on charges of economic collaboration, most had run small businesses, not even always linked to the German war effort, but their owners were disliked for various reasons in their communities. Moreover in 1945 the state's revenue authority was given the authority to arbitrarily levy whatever fine was thought appropriate on "windfall profits" from any small business whose owner displeased them for one reason or another.

That is what happened to my uncle Joe Verellen. He was well known as a Belgian patriot, and as soon as Brasschaat, where they lived, was liberated, his two oldest sons had volunteered to serve in the Belgian Brigade of the British Army. But during the liberation itself uncle Joe prevented the lynching by a small mob of a severely wounded German soldier and sheltered him in his house. Asked why he had done so, he replied that this man was "also some mother's child." Was this perhaps why he was assessed a fine of twenty million (new) Belgian Francs as "windfall profits"? Was it because his foreman, who lived on his premises, had been a member of a Flemish fascist party? Was it envy or maliciousness by competitors? Or a mix of the above? We will never know. In any case he was unable to raise this huge sum of money. Uncle Joe happened to be fluent in Spanish as a result of his travels in Mexico and in the Dominican Republic. Facing ruin and also fearing an imminent war with the USSR, he decided to emigrate to Argentina, so his whole family immediately began to learn Spanish. As soon as he managed to sell his main asset, his house, to the director of a major bank, he converted his whole fortune into jewelry in Antwerp, mainly in diamonds, and they left the country. During their travels to Tandil in Argentina his wife, my godmother, displayed all these jewels on her person and crossed every border by pretending that all this glitter was just fake costume jewelry.

Political collaborators included those who had enrolled in foreign armed forces like the SS; administrators appointed during the war by fascists such as the head of the gendarmerie, wartime burgomasters, and nearly anyone appointed to a position at a university; and politicians such as members of a fascist party, propagandists for the abolition of the Belgian state, or recruiters for the German armed forces. Whatever their justifications, they were all obviously guilty by the standards of any military tribunal representing the state of Belgium. But the repression went much further than that. In practice anyone who had anything to do with the Flemish movement during the war or even with public expressions of Flemish culture at that time was tarred with the same brush as the relatively small minority of genuine collaborators. That included nearly all the well-known Flemish poets, writers, composers, musicians, architects, and artists.

Thankfully our immediate family escaped the repression unscathed. Veva was questioned by two uniformed members of the prosecutor's staff at the rural police station in Gooreind. They wanted to know why she had rallied the VADV (*arbeidsdienst*) rather than go into hiding when she was drafted to forced labor. They accepted her reply that she believed that to assist compatriots who were victims of the war, such as the victims of the bombardment of Mortsel, was better than any alternative. They then questioned her about Father, and she enumerated his repeated refusals to collaborate. She was then asked to sign the record of her testimony without allowing her to read it. When she replied that she first wanted to read it, one of the men slapped her so hard that she flew against a door. That brought the local policeman into the room, who warned the interrogators that he would not tolerate any ill-treatment in his station. They then tried to force her to sign by bending her hand backward, but she still managed to read the document before she signed and thereby agreed that the record did reflect her testimony. After that incident the military courts left both her and Father alone.

To illustrate the murkiest side of the repression I only cite a single case of someone whom we all knew well: the abbot of the Benedictine abbey of Steenbrugge, Dom Modestus Van Assche. Soon after liberation he was arrested and jailed in Bruges, accused of having betrayed a member of the Resistance who had hidden weapons and ammunition in the abbey as well as two of his Benedictine brothers involved in this.

On this occasion Dom Modestus was freed through the intervention of a socialist government minister and former Resistance leader who knew him well. A month or so later, however, he was jailed again, this time on the basis of a disputed accusation made by an untrustworthy secret agent of the SS, who had himself been punished by his SS superiors for blackmail. A little later, and without any judicial reason at all, the abbot was transferred to a prison at Forest near Brussels where he was so seriously ill-treated that he almost died. He then was hastily transferred to St. Johns hospital in Bruges where he subsequently died, so his case never came to trial. I can hardly imagine that an abbot, as committed as Dom Modestus was to the ideals of Benedictine peace and to his community, would betray his own monks. It is, alas, all too easy to imagine that the charges were concocted by the kind of rabid haters of the Flemish movement who in 1946 stealthily blew up the very Yser tower Dom Modestus had blessed at its inauguration in 1930.

Today it is still unclear who was responsible for the rejection of the whole Flemish movement as traitorous. Some historians claim it was part of a communist plot carried out through vigilante groups. Others point the finger at French-speaking elites in Flanders, who were prominent as prosecutors in the military courts. Still others implicate various political figures. But what the contemporary political establishment as well as some later historians overlooked is that this policy of repression resulted in the permanent alienation of a significant proportion of the electorate from any Belgian identity both in Wallony and in Flanders, far higher than the percentage of voters accused of collaboration in court, and proportionately more so in Flanders than elsewhere. True, the Flemish secessionist party was now crushed, but the rejection of the whole Flemish movement, irrespective of the party they favored, would eventually lead to the demise of Belgium itself as a unitary state.

At the time the dynamics unfolded as follows. Nearly every arrested person had relatives or friends who became just as alienated by that arrest as the arrested person. A new network of mutual solidarity sprang up among these embittered relatives of jailed Flemings. These families reached out to assist each other, often with the help of sympathizing intermediaries. One of these was a Benedictine father I knew who was nicknamed "the flying corpse" because he was emaciated and nearly always on the road hitchhiking from town to town to comfort the stricken. In doing so, he created new relationships, unwittingly or not, between different families or strengthened existing ones while at the same time spreading news about the activities of their foes. As an immediate result of the repression a sizeable proportion of the electorate in Flanders went underground until 1954, when a new secessionist party was launched. But a much larger proportion of voters felt alienated. That group only increased over time, first after 1949 when women acquired the vote, and then after 1950 when the results in Flanders of the referendum about the king were summarily shoved aside. After that most Flemings continued to vote for various parties in every election, but in their minds they voted not as Belgians, but as Flemings.

Fiasco, 1945–1947

When the Central Jury was over, I discovered that while I was old enough to attend the Flemish branch of the University of Louvain, I was not old enough to choose a career. Father decided that I would become a physician, because medicine was what the three older sons of his sister Maria de Moor were studying, and she herself was married to a physician. The most astonishing aspect of the situation, however, was my incredible lack of foresight. During the whole summer I had simply never thought about who precisely I wanted to be nor what I wanted to become. I was completely unprepared and merely accepted his decision, albeit without any enthusiasm. This acceptance was about to plunge me very quickly into the two most miserable years of my life.

Mother accompanied me to Louvain a few weeks after the start of the academic year. After finding a boarding house for me and a student eating house—where French fries and sausages were featured at nearly every meal—she left enough money for me to enroll and even to buy the appropriate student cap. I found Louvain to be a compact medieval city like Bruges, though one with few old buildings. It was a typical European university town, where most downtown streets were lined with academic buildings of various sizes and from various centuries, alive with students briskly flitting to and fro as they went from one activity to another. The next day I began to attend classes, and when Saturday morning came I followed all the other lemmings in a general exodus home for the weekend, as was customary at all Belgian universities.

At the time of my enrollment Belgian universities admitted anyone with a high school diploma, and despite the large number of Catholic high schools there was only one Catholic university. Hence one might expect a large number of students at Louvain. Actually the surprise was rather that there were not more of them, especially among Flemings and among women. Although nearly all the female students lived in dormitories, only a minority of the young men did. There they were supervised and advised by mentors acting in loco parentis. Most male students rented rooms in town and so were completely left to their own devices. Before the war all was well because only a self-defined elite sent its children to university, and there were far fewer students than after 1945. Now, however, the number of students far exceeded the capacity of the system. Most of the curriculum for the candidacy degree, the first in the university sequence, consisted of public lectures delivered to large audiences, classes of five hundred or more being quite common, a wholly novel situation for me. Learning was mostly by rote, and there were no examinations except for finals, which were all oral and all scheduled at the same time during the first days of July. The failure rate, especially in the first years of study, known as the *candidatures*, was appalling. Failures exceeded successful outcomes by far, even if one includes those students who scraped through during a second session of oral examinations in September organized for those who had failed in July. A small proportion of the students failed in September then enrolled again in the following year for the same course, but no one was allowed to enroll a third time for the same course of studies.

When I first enrolled the only remedy invented to cope with this high rate of failure was a set of written midyear straw tests in February designed to inform students of how well they were doing. But the examinations at the end of the year did not take these tests into any account and still covered the material for the entire year. There was no formal orientation, nor was there any support for the majority of students living outside of the dormitories. Supposedly that gap was filled by student fraternities or circles, corresponding more or less to different regions of the country or to different disciplines. The largest among them, those of medicine and of law, counted hundreds of members and hence were completely useless except for carousing at night and singing militant songs of a bygone era in the streets, and so were practically all of the regional ones. Unlike the situation before the war, political militancy among students was a rarity, and most students were wholly alienated from politics. Anyway, in practice I found myself utterly alone, for I was far too young compared to other students and hence of no interest to them at all.

The curriculum for the first year of medicine included only four subjects: chemistry, physics, botany, and logic. What mattered most were the formal public lectures, although there were also laboratories in chemistry, physics, and botany. I found it all quite strange, for I had never encountered chemistry, botany, or logic in high school, there were no textbooks for these subjects, and I had missed the first lectures, which in chemistry at least turned out to be especially crucial. Hitherto I also had never attended any laboratory. Among those the chemistry lab was the most memorable. It took place in a factory-sized room filled with zinc-covered benches and gas lines. There were about one hundred work stations and practically no supervision by the single harassed laboratory assistant. The equipment was antiquated, and the first thing one was instructed to do was to blow glass tubes into vessels and retorts over Bunsen burners. After that I was too impatient to carefully follow instructions and usually failed to produce the outcomes expected for each experiment. But in one case I drew general attention by growing a crystal to a phenomenal size, thanks, I suspect, to unwarranted impurities.

I now had a lot of free time compared to my life in high school, and it did not take me long to find out that I was not interested in any of the disciplines taught nor in a career in medicine. I was not yet mature enough to work out what to do, nor how to make good use of this free time, either to complement my lecture notes or to pursue other interests or hobbies, and I was too young to make friends with other students. The result was absolute boredom soon accompanied by an ever-increasing despondency. Even today most of my recollections about this period are a jumble of half-forgotten, nearly botched tasks, outright failure, or feelings of hopelessness. In that situation and with that disposition, I was not surprised that I failed to make the grade in July 1946.

Yet among the events of that school year an accidental meeting proved to be significant in the long run. After botany class one day I met an acquaintance of someone at the abbey school, and he convinced me to read an introduction to Mendelian genetics. That interested me so much that I took extensive notes. It so happened that a little later the professor organized the yearly straw test, and lo and behold the question was about Mendel. I was in class but had not intended writing much, so I only had some odd bits of paper with me. But this question inspired me, and I used every last scrap of paper I had to answer it. A week later I was again in the audience among the hundreds of other students when the professor discussed the results of the test. It sounded as if every answer had been a dismal failure, and mine was probably so bad that he did not even mention it until the very end when he suddenly called my name and told me to stand up, whereupon he waved tatters of paper about to show why it was a disgrace to submit such a rag for a test. Nevertheless my scribbles, he continued, turned out to be the only full and correct answer to the question. From then on he knew at least who I was, followed my lamentable progress, and eventually recommended me to Professor Jozef De Smet, a historian. This anecdote also suggests that if I really had been interested in the subjects I studied, with some guidance I might well have succeeded.

Back home for the holidays I was soon in better spirits and cheerfully left on a hiking trip with Bea. Hiking was fast becoming a passion with me. It all began when a few of us children had first gone on a daylong hike in early January 1946. It was a brisk morning with a sun frozen red low on the horizon as we set off on a steady march to our goal a few villages away. I just loved it and started to hike whenever possible. This vacation, though, was special because we had never been on longer tours. Now the recent invention of youth hostels made it possible to travel quite cheaply. Bea had planned an affordable trip well before the holidays, and we embarked on an excursion that took us all around the Grand Duchy of Luxemburg. Every day we hiked from place to place through the hilly countryside, stayed at youth hostels, subsisted most of the time on oatmeal and bread, and sat by campfires in the evenings to sing, swap stories, and listen to tales of seasoned trekkers in a variety of languages. We also learned a good deal about local conditions and customs and much about the foreign countries from which some of the other travelers came. Such hikes taught us that the slower you go and the more byways you follow, the more you learn. No one dreamed at that time of hiking as preparation for fieldwork or schooling for budding ethnographers. But it certainly was.

After that interlude, however, I found myself back in Louvain to prepare for the examinations in September. I had returned merely out of a sense of filial duty as I wrote to Mother in late August: "I hope that I will succeed for you [my parents], because to me it is completely irrelevant." Then I added that my vocation was to be some sort of artist, or a writer, or perhaps a violin player, but not a doctor. It was a typical immature letter for an adolescent, and my parents completely disregarded it, all the more so because they were artists themselves and knew what that implied. When I failed my exams again a few weeks later they merely sent me back to try the same courses again.

A month or two later I decided to take matters in my own hands by running away to join the French foreign legion. I had saved some lunch money and took the train to the last Belgian town before the border of Luxemburg. I planned to cross the border on foot (I had no passport), then hike to the French border, cross it, and then to the gendarmerie in the nearest town of Lorraine to sign up for the legion. As I had very little money, I imagined that I would feed on the fruit of the quetsch plum trees that lined many roads in Luxemburg. But when I alighted from the train in the twilight, the plan began to sound flawed to me: why cross borders illegally twice rather than once? So I decided to take a twenty-five-mile hike to a town on the Belgian border with France. The moon was shining as I walked through the night, and I began to reflect that this course of action was perhaps a bit rough on my parents, and was it not probable that a convinced pacifist would not fit in the foreign legion anyway? I entered the town just before dawn with the realization that this had been a mistake and that I should return home. So I just continued my hike but now bearing northward for perhaps another fourteen miles or so to reach a station on the main railway line where I found that I could just afford a train ticket as far as Antwerp with the remainder of my money. When I eventually reached home after another hike late in the afternoon, there was no upheaval at all. I still wonder if anyone, except for my parents, had even noticed that I was missing. Father's official reaction to my behavior was that if I hated these studies so much, I could always look for a clerical job in some office. Actually, though, my parents tried a delay tactic. I was to return to Louvain and do my very best to succeed this time. The matter would then be reconsidered after that school year. Meanwhile I was allowed to study the violin, and as an afterthought Mother also suggested that I pursue some sport for relaxation.

I took violin lessons with a tutor. I chose to attend gymnastics classes, and I also enrolled in elementary Russian. By year's end I had made only modest progress on the violin. Still I persevered and continued to devote considerable amounts of time every day to its practice. Russian, however, was a complete flop, more so through the tutor's fault at lecturing than through mine. His only qualification for teaching was that he was a tsarist émigré, and his instruction consisted in only teaching grammar and that only by rote. He lined up endless declensions, with timely paradigms such as "the tsar's house" and verbal templates like the perennial "I love" or a surprising "the devil knows" without any practice in either speaking or reading. So I dropped out at the end of the year. Gymnastics, on the other hand, I really enjoyed, and I was good at it. It turned out that I showed promise for high and long jumps with springboard and for spectacular feats on the trampoline. Hence I would continue gym training for two more years and only reluctantly abandoned it after that.

I do not believe that my parents encouraged me to pursue hobbies that year in order to find out where my eventual talents might lie, but by year's end it was evident that I was not to be a performer. Nevertheless I loved classical music and attended concerts or recitals whenever I could afford it. I showed promise for acrobatics, but there were no careers in that direction. Reading literature was not considered a hobby in our family, even though it was one. I read a great deal and saved whatever I could from my food allowance to acquire cheap secondhand copies of masterworks and so build myself a collection of books about poetry, prose, and theater, all in addition to works borrowed from my father's library in those fields or in art history. Yet before the school year was over I became utterly convinced that any fiction, however enthralling, could not match the appeal of true stories "that really happened," as evidenced by historical fiction and biography.

At long last summer and examination season dawned again. This time I had really worked hard to succeed even though my heart was not in it. However, I failed again, albeit by a small margin—a result that left me both disappointed and mortified. I did not understand it at the time, but a lack of support by others, a lack of preparation for the disciplines in this field, a lack of appeal in terms of vocation, a lack of maturity, the large size of classes, and the difference between my own age and that of my fellow students all combined to make success extremely unlikely. At first I could only dwell on the negative side of the experience: two lost years and the almost complete absence of comrades or friends to replace the social network that I had abandoned when I left the abbey school. I would only become aware of the positive side many years later: the value of failure as a safeguard against self-conceit, the benefit of disaster in building character, the need for and the limits of self-reliance, the crucial importance of personal inclinations for the success of one's undertakings. What is more, in my first two years of higher education I actually acquired the basics of the physical and natural sciences that had not been taught at the abbey school.

On a New Tack

This second failure finally convinced my parents that we really were on the wrong tack, so they decided that I should study law instead. Mother tried to convince me that once I had done so I could become a rural justice of the peace, earn enough to live on, and have a good amount of free time to pursue hobbies. By this time I was more skeptical of maternal advice, and I was not buying her argument. For my own part I was drawn toward the study of history. As it happened, at the Belgian universities there was, at that time, a single core curriculum for the first two years of study that led to the degree of candidate in all disciplines in the humanities or in law. Besides that, there were only a few other courses specific to law and a few others to history. Therefore I could combine both.

I accepted my parents' plan without giving up mine, and in September I enrolled in law and history. To prepare myself I began to read several historical works in a literary vein including for the first time Leo Tolstoy's unsurpassed historical novel *War and Peace*. I compared this account to one by Adolphe Thiers, *Histoire du consulat et de l'empire*, which presented itself as a work of history, but I had no idea how to evaluate their competing claims. On Father's recommendation I also read A. Brugière, duc de Barante, *Histoire des ducs de Bourgogne*. Barante was the foremost French historian of the Romantic period, celebrated for the literary excellence of this book and especially its lavish descriptions of pageantry at the Burgundian court. But as I would later learn his inspired writings were wholly unacceptable to academic historians such as his contemporary Leopold Ranke, who strove to establish an historiography founded on precise and specific evidence.

The core curriculum in the humanities and in law consisted for the most part of standard semester-long courses in the fields of history, literature, and the Catholic creed, without the inclusion of even a single course in social science. There was one elective per year. In the first year we had a set of four lecture courses covering the history of Europe from ancient times to the present and one introducing us to historical critique and the rules of evidence. We also studied classical Latin authors, Dutch literature, and Catholic metaphysics. For my elective I chose ancient art history. I found most classes to be even larger than those in the sciences, yet I now felt quite comfortable with the situation: we had textbooks or their equivalent for all the courses; much of their contents, apart from historical critique, was already familiar to me; and I had now reached the age of most other students. The additional requirements for law school included only two more courses, one on comparative literature, with emphasis on French, and one on ethics, both given for classes of the same size and under the same conditions. The additional requirements for the history degree included a course in human geography—a subject I had always liked—and an introduction to the historian's craft. The whole program amounted to about fifteen hours in lectures a week, thus leaving many hours for other pursuits.

Although I devoted some of that leisure time to violin practice and gymnastics, I still managed to squander time in the fall for some silly ventures such as taking part in a bicycle race in the city of Ghent against the team from the university there, a race that ended in a memorable pile-up. After New Year 1948, however, I had no more time for such capers, and not only because of the straw tests in February—all of which I passed. By then I had also joined the Historical Circle, the formal association of history students, of which I became an enthusiastic and active member.

This change began with that year-long introduction to the historian's craft. When I found the lecture room it turned out to be a spacious, airy, book-lined seminar room in the university library. I also discovered to my considerable surprise and delight that the class was small. It included only nine persons of which I was the only young layman. Six others were unmarried young women, one was a nun, and the ninth member was Father Devos, a member of the Redemptorist Order. Our instructor was Professor De Smet, officially assistant to the senior but ailing Professor Canon Albert De Meyer. De Smet was a diocesan priest in his thirties, of a mild but also no-nonsense disposition who, apart from teaching, also acted as a mentor in a large dormitory for men. He was a specialist of the Middle Ages and an expert in the historical method, which explains why he taught the introduction to historical critique in the set of core courses. He had heard about me from his colleague who was my botany professor. Professor De Smet became my unofficial tutor that year and would later be my major professor for both the MA and PhD dissertations.

In addition to the unusual setting and the unusual class size, this course was also of a different cut than the other ones. De Smet was determined to make historians out of us, and do it hands-on. He began by instructing us in the rudiments of the profession: how to find information in the library through the use of a variety of reference works; how to compare their information for its credibility and value; how to use such sources to construct meaningful bibliographies; how to record proper bibliographical references on note cards; how to frame an issue for research; how to differentiate between syntheses, monographs, book reviews, and text editions; and how to evaluate writings in each of these categories technically, according to their presentation, their handling of evidence, and more. He set us weekly exercises and thoroughly discussed the results in class. He was an out-and-away positivist like all the other historians of the department at the time, but perhaps even more so than the others because he taught the rules of evidence and believed perhaps most passionately in their logic. He certainly instilled this positivist attitude in us along with a certain disdain for flowery literary narrative that always seemed to hide a lack of hard evidence. As for historical novels, even the best ones were definitely not history.

By January these rudiments had been imparted, and each one of us was given an issue to research and on which to report. Mine was to find out how far Viking raiders in the tenth century had ascended the Dyle River that flows through Louvain and where exactly they had been defeated by Arnulf, the Holy Roman Emperor. It was fun to figure out where the river ceased to be navigable for Viking boats at that time and how the volume of its flow had varied over the centuries, and it was an eye-opener to learn about its long history of embankments since then. By year's end my paper was forced to conclude that the river was so different today from what it probably was at the time that one could not say exactly how far the raiders ascended it, nor where they were defeated by the emperor.

Just as much as my technical education began with this course, my social and sentimental education began late in October with our induction as First Years in the Historical Circle. One after the other we entered a darkened room to swear faith to August Potthast, the author of a multivolume reference work of sources for the Middle Ages, as we faced a skull illuminated by the flickering light of a candle. Then the electric lights came on, and we were introduced by the *praeses* (president) of the Circle to our fellow students of the more advanced classes. There were few of them because the field had attracted only two or three students per year since the war. Hence it included only four laymen at this time, of which two were in the class just senior to ours. They were Lode Wils, who was specializing in contemporary political history, and Jos Van den Nieuwenhuizen, who specialized in medieval church history. Like me they both came from Antwerp, but Jos followed much of the same curriculum I did, and as a result I saw him far more often than Lode. Moreover the latter was so reserved or shy as to be nearly secretive, whereas Jos was far more assertive and outspoken, albeit in an equally unobtrusive way. Despite our different personalities, Jos and I got along famously from the start, and by the end of the school year we were fast friends.

Only a few weeks later all of us were drafted to prepare for the annual Christmas party organized by our Circle for students and faculty in history and to be held on the afternoon of December 22 in a large upstairs room of the most central restaurant in town. The program for such festivities always consisted in the presentation of poetry and prose readings for Christmas interspersed with carols and a musical intermezzo or two or a light-hearted sketch followed by cozy tea with cakes. All of us First Years joined fellow students as members of a choir led by Father Devos, who was choirmaster in his convent, to sing the carols, some of which were well known and others truly arcane medieval pieces. We all met several times a week for rehearsals at the house of the First Year girl in our class whose family was from Louvain. Then came the last-minute rush for supplies and to fix little details, so that the last afternoon before the big event found all the girls busy decorating the reception room and its Christmas tree, while I ran around as their gofer and otherwise folded colored paper into pleasing shapes alongside two of them. The real results of all this activity were that by the time of the party our Circle had become a real community for us all, and I had fallen under the spell of the paper folders. I had now reached the stage when boys are easily infatuated, and the girls would be only the first of many to follow. Luckily for me the girls of my class were all far more emotionally mature than I was, and this succession of crushes amused them.

Apart from the carols my own contribution was to be a rendering of "Silent Night, Holy Night" on the violin. But as I lifted the bow to start, the master of ceremonies decided that the carol should sound subdued, and he darted over to fit the violin's bridge with a mute clip, an object I had never even seen until then. However, this clip did not remain in place, and disaster struck. While playing I tried to rescue it with the bow, with dire results that unnerved me to the point that I ran through the piece in record time to the accompaniment of guffaws all around. At that moment I learned the full meaning of the word *shame*. This rout, combined with an increasing lack of time necessary for practice, made me switch from the violin to the recorder soon after that party. I quickly mastered that instrument on my own, and by the next Christmas party I played a faultless piece with piano accompaniment and so made up for my earlier failure. Thereafter I continued playing the standard repertoire for recorder during many years until I left Belgium.

After the February straw tests, the Circle rarely met officially, but in practice its junior members of the two candidatures saw each other all the time in and out of class, and I remained the gofer when one was needed. This created all sorts of contacts and common experiences that continued to strengthen bonds between us. The most obvious instance among these was the growing friendship between Jos and myself. The most dramatic example of it, however, occurred the day when Mitonet

Rubbens, a girl in the Second Year, called on me for help. She was moving, and she wanted to get a cast iron stove weighing about two hundred pounds on the truck. I managed to lift the monster and put it there. But it was so heavy that in doing this its rim cut deeply through the fleshy parts of my wrist from the bones on one side right to the other. What now? We were not aware at all about emergency services, but she knew someone who was either an advanced student in medicine or a brand-new physician, and she got me to his place. There he stitched me up without benefit of any anesthetic because that was still a precious commodity, and he had none around. With distractions like these, May came around all too soon, and with it the traditional celebration of the "swan's song," a last outing of our Circle. We hiked to a pond in the woods, known as the Sweet Waters, to take leave of our *praeses* and others who were graduating and about to leave student life. Not long after that, examination time arrived. I took the exams for a history degree in early July and passed with distinction. What a contrast with the despair a year earlier! Now I felt as happy as a lark on cloud nine!

To judge by the outcome, the direction I had taken was evidently the right one, and so my parents did not object that their choice, law, was only to follow in September. When I passed those exams with distinction as well, however, they were so pleased that they gave me a book about European art history without any oral comment but with the inscription: "From Father and Mother for the distinctions. September 1948." That was truly an extraordinary gesture on their part because they never repeated it, not even on the occasion of my MA or PhD degrees. In a typical unspoken way, it thus concluded our discussion regarding my vocation.

Meanwhile, even before September, I was allowed to accompany Bea on a short hiking tour in Switzerland. Having obtained a final degree in business economics, she meticulously worked out a tight budget for the trip and secured the necessary money. The plan was to take the train to Zurich and then hike along a set of picturesque lakes in middle Switzerland before heading for Basel and return home by train from there. This was our first trip in a really foreign country far away (the Netherlands and Luxemburg did not count), hence we left with high expectations flavored with the tiniest pinch of trepidation. The first days went just as planned. We traveled along the shores of the lovely

Zurich lake, enjoyed the landscapes, climbed a low local mountain for the view, and then turned southward to the next complex of lakes. We had reached the first of those when we had to deviate from the plan. First a youth hostel was closed, but we were lucky to find refuge in a local cottage where the kind-hearted lady treated us to good food in return for stories from Belgium. When we left the next morning she even gave us some chocolate, a product that was still extremely rare at home. At the next youth hostel the following day we stumbled on a troop of girl guides whose summer camp had come to an end. They were packing when we appeared, and they were curious about our origins and our plans. Something about us must have struck their fancy, because on their departure they gave us as many of their unused items as we could carry, including such essentials as oatmeal or packaged soups as well as some delicacies like slabs of chocolate of all kinds. For us this was a huge amount of food, and it allowed us to stretch out our trip much longer than planned, so we changed our itinerary accordingly. We crossed the Alps, visited the Italian lakes, and then returned to our original route. One evening on the way back, as we were sitting on a bench in a city park, Bea told me that she had chosen her future. This trip was her last fling before entering a convent a month later. That news, that sudden irruption of reality into this make-believe fairyland around us just now, hit me hard. Bea would no longer be around—the family was breaking up. So what did the future hold for me?

Staying on Course

Autumn came, and I was back in Louvain embarking on the curriculum of the second year from new lodgings I shared with Jos high up in the attic of a house. Our flat was on a level with the pediment of a church on the other side of the street featuring a sacred drama in sculptured form, a scene we often watched seated at our window with our bare feet in the gutter while discussing everything under the sun. That year's core curriculum included only two literature courses—one classical Latin, one Dutch—and a course on experimental psychology, but there were four law courses, including a rigorous survey of Roman law. The program for history consisted in a geography course, a course about the history of Belgium that included several lectures about the Belgian Congo, a continuation of De Smet's introduction to history, and his exercises in medieval Latin. As my elective I chose a course on Byzantine history, and I also attended a set of lectures on eighteenth-century classical music.

The great revelation that year was medieval Latin poetry. Here lay hidden a world of beauty, completely unknown even to experts on the literatures of the Romance and Germanic languages that followed the Latin language and were profoundly inspired by it. To understand my enthusiasm it suffices to look at a well-known and unsurpassed masterpiece: the *Dies irae*, a poem about the Last Judgment that is best known as the words to a hymn that forms part of the Roman Catholic Requiem mass. The public usually dismisses this poem as just the inspiration for many musical compositions ranging from a Gregorian chant much copied by later composers to Verdi's torrential rendition and thereby misses what makes it a masterpiece. Those "words" are actually verses arranged in strophes. The first lines of the poem provide an example:

Dies irae, dies illa	[Day of rage, the day
solvet saeclum et favilla	the world dissolves in ashes.
teste David cum Sybilla.	according to David and the Sybil.]

These lines illustrate not only the poem's meter (expressed in voice stress rather than vowel length) and its complex rhyming scheme, but also the incredible power achieved through an economy of language as paired images in each verse (dissolves/ashes, David = biblical / Sybil = classical) encompass whole destinies. It is that sort of combination that tends to be typical for the best medieval Latin verse.

As the new *praeses* of the Historical Circle that year, Jos was intent on organizing worthy activities, starting with a splendid Christmas party and following up in the spring with interesting outings. I as his roommate was naturally called upon for advice and assistance. Hence the Circle captured most of my attention, although I also managed to learn how to execute proper Cossack dances from a Russian émigré student who lived in the house. We were briefly diverted from these useful pursuits when our professor of Belgian history called on his class to participate in a "spontaneous" demonstration in Brussels to protest against the arrest of Cardinal Mindszenty in Hungary. It sounded like fun, and buses were provided for the purpose, so I went. We marched to the houses of Parliament brandishing signs and shouting in front of their tall railings. I do not know what came over me apart from the sheer challenge it presented, but I managed to climb on top of one of the two-story-tall pillars between the spear-pointed railings to shout "Mindszenty" from up there. But not for long. The police charged at and chased every one else away, leaving me stranded atop my perch. Unable to get at me they then called the firemen and left. That provided an interval to scramble down the pillar, vault over the railings onto the sidewalk, and slip away. Just a daredevil lark—except that the next morning's newspapers had a picture of me as professional agitator atop my pillar. Luckily enough no one in the family recognized me. Still, that experience ended my political career on the same day it was launched.

By the time of the Christmas party all was ready for an impeccable formal traditional celebration but with a twist. Jos agreed to add an informal part to the festivities, and I plumbed new depths of imagination as I wrote a short satiric musical spoof in verse. Titled *Beatrice and Innocence Murdered*, it was inspired by the legend of Dr. Faustus. The plot runs as follows: A learned professor has written a work in four volumes but unfortunately lacks any evidence for his conclusions. Clio, the heathen muse of history who is the archivist in hell, comes to his rescue and gives him the evidence in return for his delivery to her of Beatrice, a comely co-ed, who through an accident in the celestial card catalog was born six centuries too late. In her distress Beatrice calls on her intended lover, Dante. Assisted by Jeanne d'Arc, the latter descends into hell and delivers her. Juvenile stuff, certainly, but also fun for all concerned. We all had a great time rehearsing this sketch, but I do not remember how the usually stately audience of professors reacted to it. Still it is probably not by chance that De Smet exploited both my admiration for medieval Latin poetry and my weakness for satire to assign me, as a sort of honor's paper for that year, the task of translating and annotating a satire in verse with all the trimmings of a text edition, including an introductory discussion and three different sorts of footnotes.

After Christmas the school year unfolded without further memorable events until Jos decided one day in spring 1949 to take the Circle on a visit to the well-known park of the Congo Museum in Tervuren only about eight miles away. But he wanted to explore beforehand whether it would also be worthwhile to visit the museum. So one day he and I walked out there and met Albert Maesen, the conservator for ethnology.

As a young and enthusiastic art historian and cultural anthropologist of Africa with missionary instincts, Maesen was not merely content to show us around the galleries, but in addition he brought us upstairs to the apartments of his section, where he opened one closet after another to show us row upon row of statues illustrating one point or another of the many points he made. I had never visited the museum and had never seen any African art before. Because African canons were so different from the classical one, most of the sculptures, with their oversized heads and sexual organs, disconcerted me and seemed unattractive, but the masks were more familiar and reminded me of expressionist work. It was an interesting visit, and our second visit to the park and the museum with the Circle was a great success. Then I forgot all about African art as my attention was soon drawn to other issues, like the conclusion of my paper for De Smet and the preparation for the forthcoming exams. Those went very well; I finished with "great distinction"; and along with all my classmates I earned the degree of "candidate," the equivalent of a bachelor's degree. This allowed me to pursue a "license" in history, a higher degree equivalent to a master of arts. So the following year I embarked on the curriculum for the license with the rest of my cohort except for two of the young women in my class who married and abandoned their studies as was then the custom for nearly all women.

During the summer, Jos managed to book a small canal boat in the Netherlands for a holiday along its waterways and to fill it with half a dozen members of our Circle, mostly young women accompanied by a brother or an admirer. We all enjoyed ourselves hugely as we went sightseeing, swimming, and visiting all sorts of places, including Hoorn and Enkhuizen, two historical towns closely linked to the Dutch East India Company that were not easy to reach overland. I knew that to be so because by then I had hiked several times through the Netherlands, mainly with Veva, but we had never made it to destinations like these. The trip further cemented a mutual comradeship between us that was to last throughout our license years.

The program for the license required a thesis based on original research and course work over two years without any testing before the end of the second year. Then final oral exams took place in all these subjects, not unlike the written preliminary examinations before the doctorate at American universities. The rationale of the program was dictated by the goals the Belgian universities pursued in training historians. Only a tiny minority of students strove to obtain a doctorate and to pursue careers in research or as university teachers. The rest aimed to become teachers in secondary education, as the national parliament foresaw when it had prescribed this curriculum, a course of studies that was followed at all universities with only minor variations among them. An obligatory minor in geography was included with the same goal, the ability to teach geography. In addition four more courses in education as well as supervised practical teaching in a real high school were required to obtain a certificate called *aggregation*, a diploma that was essential for high school teachers.

To satisfy the need to train teachers the program included six thematic courses as follows: histories of economics, of Belgian institutions, of philosophy, and of law; geography; and art history. These courses satisfied the background requirements for teachers while at the same time they fulfilled the needs of history courses in the disciplines involved. But to fulfill the program's second goal, namely to train professional researchers, it also included five technical research courses: public archives and archiving, paleography, a study of charters, so-called auxiliary sciences, and a seminar on historical method. By today's standards the research component of the program was remarkably restricted. It focused entirely on medieval or early modern history and ignored the techniques and theories needed to cope with economic, social, or cultural (as distinct from intellectual) history. Nor did it include any training in quantitative history, and occasional magisterial snide comments about social history as "mere cheesecake" made clear that its omission was not accidental. But as fledgling scholars at the time we did not even dream of questioning the program set out for us.

In addition to the formal program, however, we also met eminent scholars such as Fernand Braudel, leader of the celebrated French Annales school, who lectured us about the history of the Mediterranean. On another occasion one of our professors took us to a meeting of the historians of the Low Countries at Muiden in the Netherlands, where we heard the likes of Peter Geyl discuss whether or not successive subjective interpretations lead to greater historical certainty, and Jan Romein, a contemporary historian, who extrapolated from the past to predict a coming "Age of Asia." Last we were given a whole semester of lectures on the Carolingian Empire by the foremost medievalist of the age, François-Louis Ganshof, professor at Ghent, who also was the only one among these leading lights to share the positivist attitudes of our professors.

Actually, the heart of our training as professional historians was the research seminar in historical method held in the by-now-familiar seminar room. All the license students met there under the supervision of De Meyer as the senior professor and De Smet as his junior. Every week one of the students, starting with the most advanced, presented the current state of his or her research. Our presentations were then assessed by our peers, according to the logic of the rules of evidence. Finally De Meyer evaluated the presentation and its critique. But the seminar was not the only occasion when points of historical critique were taught. When appropriate the subject was raised in all other courses as well. Actually it was that relentless hammering on a strict application of the rules of evidence in assessing data that turned us into professional historians, more so than learning about archives, charters, or ancient scripts.

One issue in particular that stemmed from applying the rules of evidence was the relationship between religious belief and historical credibility. We were told several times that while being historians we should suspend our beliefs "in brackets," as the expression went, to return to it after reaching conclusions. In a technical course about the lives of saints (*vitae*) as sources of history, the professor pointed out that miracles should not be dismissed out of hand as impossible, because we do not absolutely know the limits of what is naturally possible, a point he illustrated by citing "genuine" miracles at the pilgrim site of Lourdes, that is, miracles certified as such by a physician. The unspoken but perfectly understood conclusion, however, was that this reasoning also applied to all the biblical miracles. Still, as De Smet once confided to me, to be steeped in the rules of evidence could sometimes be quite hard on one's beliefs. I could not follow him there, for at the time I myself found it easy to separate my own impeccable and completely positivist Catholic convictions from an equally positivist critical attitude toward sources. In any case the documents with which I was working did not involve any test of religious beliefs, and hence I did not have to face the issue.

Not long after New Year 1950 De Smet called me to propose a rather esoteric MA topic: How useful to historians were medieval Latin dirges composed in honor of rulers or celebrated scholars and performed at their funerals? The issue involved the kind of Latin poetry I liked, the rules of evidence with which I felt comfortable, and an unusual degree of originality as well, since these were oral sources that had been written down from memory sometimes long after the funeral. This was oral history at a time when oral history was not really considered scientific. So I set to work, becoming familiar over the next year with various libraries, copied texts, collected microfilms, and translated Latin, and I learned how to build and present a long argument. I gathered most of the raw data after classes ended in the early summer of 1950. At that time I was ensconced in our old house in the Markgravestraat and used the rich library of the city in its seventeenth-century quarters on the square of St. Carolus. Those surroundings were very familiar and quite satisfying. It culminated in an MA entitled in translation *The Historical Value of Latin Dirges for Deceased Contemporaries (799–1313)*. Little did I imagine that a mere two years later this exercise was to open my mind to oral traditions as evidence for the history of the Kuba in the Belgian Congo.

This research for the MA also made me realize the unavoidable need for at least a passive knowledge of several languages if only because De Smet would not accept ignorance of a language as a valid excuse for overlooking any item in the bibliography. He suggested sitting in on a course of Italian, with the comment that given knowledge of Latin and French, acquiring Italian would be easy, and so it proved to be. English, given a knowledge of Dutch and French was supposedly equally easy— except that it was not. I met English first in dubbed films, but the bill-board for the film *Brief Encounter* taught me how unreliable that approach was. The billboard showed a woman reading a letter, and I translated the title as "Meeting by Correspondence": *brief* meaning "letter" in Dutch and *encounter* resembling the French for "meeting," *rencontre*. To reach the correct solution I should have linked *brief* to French *bref*. That experience taught me to be wary of English. As it happened, however, the bibliography for my thesis included only two articles in English: one about themes in Greek and Latin epitaphs and the other about Anglo-Latin satirical poets. In both cases I was able to understand the drift of the English through my background in Latin and Greek. So the need to learn English was postponed.

Following the trip on the Dutch canals, I truly blossomed in an environment of easy comradeship that now pervaded the Historical Circle. And during those two years while I was pursuing my degree, I seemed to soak up whatever interested me just as easily as blotting paper does ink. Thus for the official Christmas party of 1949 I produced *Miracle Plays for Christmas in the Middle Ages*, having done all the necessary research during the fall trimester as well as the preparations for the production myself. The performance featured several of my fellow students reciting extracts in verse from various plays, including even some unpublished ones. Although the project had required a considerable investment in time, the effort had not interfered with my usual scholarly obligations.

As Jos was to take final exams in the spring of 1950, he handed the direction of the Circle over to me with the agreement of its members, but that school year I took only a few new initiatives. The main activity was an excursion by bus to the ruins of several celebrated medieval abbeys where I first saw the kind of results one can expect from archaeological excavations. On the return journey to Louvain we also visited a particularly sumptuous eighteenth-century castle that also housed a few African art objects among other curiosities. That summer I took a vacation from Louvain and the Circle, went sailing in northern Holland for a week or so, and then spent most of my time working on the MA. The next fall, back in Louvain, I changed lodgings for a pleasant room on the ground floor in a quiet peripheral street, not far from those of two classmates, and concentrated on my studies while preparing the next and final Christmas party of the Circle, a party that by now was almost wholly standardized.

The main event for me during that last semester was an instructive interlude that had nothing to do with the university or with studying. One day in early spring a shed adjacent to the home of a painter on my street, close to my lodgings, caught fire. A little knot of spectators including the anxious owner of the shed passively watched the fire grow as they waited for the firemen. The owner was wringing his hands because his shed illegally contained three fifty-gallon metal drums of highly flammable chemicals used for paints, and he feared they might explode.

Learning this I ran inside the burning shed, found the drums, managed to tip one over and rolled it out, fully expecting some of the men outside to help me, but they did not dare. So I dived back in for a second drum as smoke began to billow around me. This drum was warming up, but I still managed to roll it out. Back again I went for number three, coughing and without seeing much, while the ceiling above my head was now catching fire. This drum's metal was so hot that my hands were blistering, but somehow I managed to get it out as well. Only then did the spectators roll the drums out of sight, just before the arrival of the firemen, and all was well except for the burns on my hands. The embarrassed painter took me inside, found some cream and a dressing, and to thank me gave me the smallest measure of sherry I have ever drunk. The whole episode taught me the meaning of the saying "to pull the chestnuts out of the fire"! It also showed that I was still foolhardy, ready to take risks without assessing them first and hence still immature.

As the second semester progressed everyone in my class was becoming more anxious about the final exams, and because they formed a majority of the Circle's members, I organized only a few afternoon walking tours that spring. Anyway, by then the interests and activities of my classmates were changing. Late that spring we first organized a costumed dance among ourselves in Antwerp that I duly attended as Taras Bulba, the Cossack, and that turned out to be only a prelude to several formal balls to which many of us had been invited, which signaled our passage from student-like ways into genuine adulthood.

An Unforeseen Turn:
Vocation Found?

In early or mid-June 1951, I was visiting Jos during a study break in the preparations for my final exams when he told me that the Museum at Tervuren was advertising a position for an ethnologist to pursue two or three years of research on an African population in the Congo for a certain Institut pour la Recherche Scientifique en Afrique Centrale/ Instituut voor Wetenschappelijk Onderzoek in Centraal Afrika (Institute for Scientific Research in Central Africa) usually referred to by its acronym IRSAC. Was I interested? He had also just proudly informed me that our careers teaching high school would last umpteen years and be crowned by a pension of such-and-such amount, all of which sounded quite depressing. Postponing that fate by applying for the position described in the advertisement attracted me far more. True, it was not in the field of history and I was not qualified for it, but then, indeed, who was? Cultural anthropology or ethnology as it was known to us at the time was not a recognized discipline at any Belgian university, and Frans Olbrechts, the museum's director, was the only one who taught a course about the subject at Ghent University. But the word *research* was magnetic, and the advertisement wafted an exotic whiff of adventure as well, and so why not give it a shot?

So I called Tervuren, an interview was set up, and I returned to my preparations for the final exams but added some reading for this interview as well. I succeeded in laying my hands on a secondhand copy of the handbook *Ethnologie* written by Frans Olbrechts and studied it along with the rest. Each chapter was followed by a short bibliography, and I learned those references by heart. Besides this I also browsed through a hefty cultural history of Africa in German by a certain Leo Frobenius that I found in Father's library. Thus equipped, I took the interview during the week of my finals. I was pleased because in my answers I managed to refer in passing to a number of books that Olbrechts recommended in his bibliographies and also because the luxurious surroundings of the impressive office in which the interview took place had not intimidated me.

Then it was back to Louvain posthaste to prepare for my finals. On the very evening before the test results were announced at the university I received word from Tervuren that they had selected me for the research position, and I apparently accepted on the spot. I broke the news to my parents by postcard, mailed that same evening. The next morning I was granted the license in history "with great distinction." Reflecting on it now, I am aware that just like the many other rites of passage that punctuated my progress through life hitherto, both the final exams and the job interview taken on their own were two expected and appropriate rites of passage to induct me into responsible adulthood. The oddity of the situation merely was that these events occurred in inverse order.

Nevertheless here I was again, kicking over the traces as I had done about the abbey school—this time in protest against Belgian society and its preordained paths. Once again Mother was all for the idea, and Father did not object. The decision was sudden, but the turn of events was perhaps not wholly unexpected. If not, why would Jos draw my attention to the advertisement? I also suspect that long ago De Smet had already detected my reluctance to fit into that readymade, one-size-fits-all mold. As to Congo, at the time the region held no special attraction for me. In practice Congo, including Ruanda-Urundi, was the only Belgian colony and therefore the only region on offer. As it happened, in 1951 the colonial administration and all its agencies were still vigorously recruiting personnel both to fill the gaps left by four years of interrupted communications between Belgium and its colony caused by the war and to hire additional personnel to execute an ambitious ten-year development plan that had been adopted two years earlier. Indeed, Chris, having obtained his diploma in agronomy, was one of those recruits and had just left us for Congo that February. Had I been Dutch I would probably have gone to New Guinea. Be that as it may, at that particular moment what attracted me was the prospect of research on the cultural history of a foreign people. It did not matter where in the world I did the research. So Congo it was.

I deluded myself in thinking that the appointment to this institute for research in Central Africa would just be a welcome interlude before the onset of a routine career. Actually, it turned my life around. It proved to be a complete rupture with the past, and I paid for it, once again, with the loss of my social network of coevals and comrades. But I had finally stumbled on that long-sought vocation, and this tale of growing up in Belgium during turbulent times concludes with that decision. From that time onward my life entered a different setting, and my experiences became part of another tale, one that I have narrated elsewhere. It is called *Living with Africa*.

Epilogue

It soon became evident after my arrival at the Tervuren museum that whatever Olbrechts's opinion was when he hired me, I was woefully unprepared to leave for Africa barely a month or so later. I had not had any training in anthropology or any of the other social sciences, nor did I know much about the ethnography of Congo. Therefore, by early September IRSAC decided to send me first to University College, London, to complete my training, as Olbrechts put it. I was expected to take the final examinations for the bachelor's degree in anthropology at the end of that school year. It certainly was a challenge to absorb a three-year program in social anthropology and master the English language in that time. But I made it with flying colors, and perhaps Olbrechts never realized how little I knew when I first applied for the position. Meanwhile, already in February 1952 a letter informed me that my assignment was to study the Kuba people in Congo. These people were renowned for their arts, and that was probably the reason IRSAC and Olbrechts chose to send me there. However, on my return from England, my first task was to write a short synthesis of everything already known about the Kuba and their neighbors for a volume of the Ethnographic Survey of Africa. At this point my training in history came in handy to help me uncover far more unpublished materials in Tervuren's own papers than had been expected. Only after completion of that short monograph did I finally leave for Congo in December 1952. Thanks to some outstanding teachers who had tutored me in London and in Tervuren, I was by then sufficiently competent in a technical sense for the required task and knowledgeable enough about the state of academic knowledge concerning Kuba society, culture, and language.

Only now do I realize that however woefully unprepared I was in the technical sense when I arrived in Tervuren, I was much better prepared than I knew, by past experience and perhaps by temperament, to undertake fieldwork. To begin with, I had been forced to adapt on three different occasions to a different culture: to Bruges, to St. Andrews, and to London. I had also abandoned social networks beyond the family: when we moved from Antwerp, when I left St. Andrews, and when I left Louvain. So to adapt to a new setting, that of the Kuba, was by now a matter of degree, not of kind. Once ensconced there and living on my own, I also found out that I did not miss other Belgians or other white-skinned people, unlike most other colonials who complained that they were overwhelmed by loneliness in the absence of "peers" to whom they could talk. I was never lonely and quickly made new acquaintances among the Bushong, as the local Kuba call themselves.

The German occupation, and my experience at the abbey school, reinforced by some of the lessons implicit in the stories Dom Lou told, allowed me to recognize almost instantly the condescending or dismissive essence of colonialism and also some of its effects on the Kuba. I thus realized from the start that I would be told only what they wished to tell me. In Belgium, and especially in my family, I was used to withholding information from those who did not need to know, and so I expected the same from the Kuba. As it happened, silence among them just as within my own family was an important way of expressing one's feelings. When I settled among them I had therefore already learned never to push or trick someone into revealing anything they did not want to tell, but to wait patiently until I was trusted enough to be told.

In practical terms I had been familiar with danger ever since the war and its strafing aircraft or mortar shells. I had learned to recognize danger when I saw it, to assess it quickly but without panicking, if possible to react to it—as when I dived into ditches or rolled out the drums of chemicals in the shed on fire—and then to hope for the best: scared, yes; incapacitated, no. My wartime experiences helped me several times in the field to cope with predators, wild storms, even a raging river, and later on with the danger posed by armed men as well. Gooreind had also familiarized me with living in rural circumstances and taught me to be comfortable with wilderness. Hence I adapted almost automatically to the challenges of living in small villages, including the exigencies of a lifestyle ruled by agriculture in a way that most urbanites would envy. In addition, my practice of taking long hikes served me extremely well in these new surroundings.

Experience during the war had inured me to a monotonous diet and a shortage of clothing, shoes, and many other items, while life in Gooreind had taught me to manage without electricity or even running water—experience that stood me in good stead for my fieldwork in rural Africa. But the war had also taught me that I could survive for a while by relying on the abundance of a single food, and since I was completely ignorant about malnutrition, I ended up once at a hospital with a remarkable lack of most vitamins. That was not the only drawback of my past experience. Until I went to Africa I had never had the opportunity of learning how to drive, and after only a week of hasty instruction on high mountain roads in eastern Congo, it took several accidents and several years before I started to trust the mechanics of the jeep I was driving and to become a more reliable driver. Also, while I had some experience with wounds and influenza, I had no idea how to cope with diseases. I tended to endure tropical diseases as if they were just a cold that would pass in time, and, of course, they did not. Hence fieldwork was often handicapped by poor health and sometimes interrupted by medical matters.

Boarding the ship in Antwerp for the Congo was the threshold to my adult life. In crossing that threshold, I carried with me not only technical knowledge and general know-how, but also a few essential ideas and convictions about the nature of the world and of its people. These conceptions have remained crucial to me throughout my career, although they continued to evolve as a result of further experiences and studies between then and now. First the notion of civilization: I had imbibed the notion of civilization as a state of grace bequeathed to us from Graeco-Roman times and enriched over the ages to reach its acme in France or Britain, but I had also seen how many French-speaking people used it to denigrate anything Flemish, and I knew that peoples, such as the Chinese, had civilizations of their own. So I equated civilization with culture: Every people had their culture, and while culture was not really primordial, all cultures were old and changed only very slowly over time. Moreover, to me every culture tended to coincide with a particular ethnic group or "nation," but nations were not states. The latter I still thought of as convenient administrative structures that formed part of an overall international order and only corresponded approximately to the distribution of ethnicities or nations. I was also aware that individual identity necessarily included a multiplicity of allegiances to different entities all nestled into each other like Russian dolls.

Influenced again by my upbringing, I was convinced that language, "the soul of the people" in the Flemish movement, lay at the core of culture, and therefore that anyone studying a foreign culture needed sufficient knowledge of language to communicate with people directly. I had been lucky enough to be tutored by two eminent linguists in descriptive linguistics and introduced to the type of language spoken by the Kuba, so that I was ready to study it without being bogged down by the sort of misapprehensions that most Flemings carried at the time about "better" languages, "purer" languages, and "differing innate predispositions to learn foreign languages."

In my mind religion and art were both essential parts of culture, and I expected to find them everywhere. But my experience so far with religion, mainly with Catholicism, and also with art soon proved to be a formidable handicap in that my expectations led me completely astray. I practically equated religion with an established church and its practice, a special institution with its own leaders, dogma, nearly immutable ritual, sacrifice, prayer, and a body of ethics. When I did not find such a complex I was baffled: how was it possible for a people not to have a religion at the core of their culture? It took me far too long to realize that it was my conception of religion that was wrong. I had to rethink the fundamental meaning of religion before I could truly recognize its expressions among the Kuba. As far as art was concerned, the issue was less serious. The absence of any art for art's sake I had encountered before, but I was stymied for a while by the apparent absence among such an artistic people of the very notion of art, until I eventually found that they thought of art as "pattern" and of its appreciation as the physical sensation of a pleasant feeling or taste.

I tended to equate the social theories I had learned in London with ideologies, and so my rejection of ideology translated into a distrust for theory, especially when it became dogmatic. In keeping with the positivist spirit of Louvain, I preferred by far conclusions drawn from empirical and experimental data over general theory. In particular, I automatically rejected any determinism, whether social or environmental, because as a historian I had been steeped in the overriding importance of contingency. My familiarity with the rules of evidence made me quite wary of functionalism because it seemed to be so often based on imaginary factors linked only to presumed outcomes by mere correlation. Hence I could not accept the doctrine that functions could be discovered only by participant observation, that is, by the direct testimony of the researcher, while the testimonies of the people involved were worthless, because by definition they were always misguided. Was this not the acme of arrogance and intolerance? What people said should at least be as important as what others concluded by observing them.

Finally, my MA thesis had made me well aware of the historical value of oral tradition according to the existing rules of evidence, and I was familiar with living traditions from the tales current in our own family, especially on Mother's side. So when a Bushong person drew my attention to such a tradition only a few months after my arrival, I suddenly realized that oral traditions were a valid key to study Kuba history as long as the rules of evidence were applied to them, and that to better understand the Kuba one needed to look beyond a static snapshot of their society to its development over time. I followed this up, and hence after barely six months or so in the field I became a historian again, albeit a historian of Africa, a rarity in academe at the time. Another six months after that I first met the fascinating girl I wed less than a year later. Claudine was a Francophone Belgian, born and for the most part raised in the then Belgian colony of Ruanda-Urundi, and for her, living in Africa among Africans was home. That marriage clinched my vocation as an Africanist.

Ever since I have been a historian of Africa. After fieldwork among the Kuba I wrote a PhD in history about oral tradition and Kuba history, and I stayed on as a researcher for IRSAC until the fall of 1960. By then my approach to oral traditions was acquiring a certain notoriety, and I was invited to the University of Wisconsin–Madison. I spent most of my professional career there as a teacher and a researcher, although I have also taught from time to time at other institutions, gone out to do research, and served as a member of the small core bureau of the committee that directed the publication of UNESCO's General History of

Africa. That bureau met frequently to commission, evaluate, and edit every single draft chapter of its eight volumes before submitting them for approval by the whole committee. Over the course of time many Africanists have come to know my work through my contributions to historical method, studies on the early history of various parts of Central Africa, papers concerning the history of a group of African languages known as Bantu, essays in historiography, as well as contributions to textbooks and other didactic materials. Few among them, even among the students I taught, realize how deeply my research and my teaching has been indebted to experience gained and lessons learned during the turbulent times of my youth. And yet the impact of those years has been profound and lasting.

Suggestions for Further Reading

Any autobiography is always rooted in reminiscences and sometimes, as is the case here, reminiscences that seem to date back more than three-quarters of a century ago. Yes, "seem" because what we remember actually are not the events themselves but our most recent evocation of the events, and that is almost always much younger indeed. That is one aspect of the intricacies posed by reminiscences as historical evidence. For more see the works by Elizabeth F. Loftus and especially her first book, *Memory: Surprising New Insights into How We Remember and Why We Forget* (2nd ed., New York: Ardsley, 1988), and her recent *Eyewitness Testimony* (Cambridge, MA: Harvard University Press, 1996). From long practice of oral history I have also been aware of these pitfalls and address some of them in *Oral Tradition as History* (Madison: University of Wisconsin Press, 1985).

Here I have attempted to remedy the deficiencies of oral history as much as possible. The greatest single weakness of these data is their chronology. Even a relative chronology of the sort "I remember that A happened before B" is never completely reliable as I found out, once again, when checking my own memories for this book. So I relied only on written documents to date reminiscences. Secondly, memories can be altered over time for many reasons whenever they are evoked, and it is good to keep this in mind because reminiscences are evocations. Indeed the mind can also create wholly false memories; yet, on the other hand, some reminiscences remain strikingly faithful to the events they describe. There are various ways by which to evaluate the reliability of such reminiscences, and I have used these as best I can. I have also double-checked them where I could do so. In this context a large number of their relevant reminiscences were written down recently and severally by my siblings (especially Veva, Chris, and Guido), and they have been quite valuable, at least insofar as they seem to be independent, as confirmations or rejections of my own memories. When reminiscences other than mine are included they are specifically attributed to their sources in the text, and they are included because they are especially revealing about the period.

For similar reasons a small number of writings such as the odd school report and a few letters have been equally useful.

Some readers may wish to learn a little more than I have included about the historical contexts of this biography and about some of the events it relates. A solid first introduction to Belgium and an elementary one to the cities of Antwerp, Bruges, Brussels, and Louvain can be found in the relevant articles in the *Encyclopaedia Britannica* in the 1971 and 1974 editions. Beyond that I recommend Renée Fox's *In the Belgian Chateau: The Spirit and Culture of a European Society in an Age of Change* (Chicago: I. R. Dee, 1994) as a highly readable introduction to Belgian society as she encountered it several decades after the war.

With regard to Belgian history the only recent book-length general study for this period available in English is Martin Conway, *The Sorrows of Belgium: Liberation and Political Reconstruction, 1944–1947* (Oxford: Oxford University Press, 2012). It is essentially a history of politics and is overly biased toward Brussels and the francophone part of the country, not only and perhaps unavoidably by virtue of his main theme but also, and certainly avoidably, because the study is based on a lopsided collection of source materials. Conway also has an obvious pro-British bias in general, while his evaluation of military history tends to be wholly uncritical. Still, the book remains a good starting point and includes a sound summary of the war years as well as a detailed discussion of the first crucial years thereafter. Next one should consult Michel Dumoulin et al., *Nouvelle histoire de Belgique*, volume 2 (Brussels: Éditions Complexe, 2006). This volume includes three separate tomes of which two are relevant. Emmanuel Gérard, *La démocratie rêvée, bridée et bafouée (1918–1939)*, is the most widely informed and the least biased of the two; Mark Van den Wijngaert and Vincent Dujardin wrote *La Belgique sans Roi (1940–1950)*, a text that consists of two parts. The first, by Van den Wijngaert, deals with the war, and its quality is on a par with Gérard's book, while the second part, by Dujardin about the postwar period, is far weaker, and its interpretations are often heavily partisan. So it is fortunate that the Dujardin volume almost completely overlaps with the Conway volume. On economic history one can consult André Mommen, *The Belgian Economy in the Twentieth Century* (London: Routledge, 1994), and on the relations between Belgium and its colony, Guy Van Themsche, *Belgium and the Congo, 1885–1980* (Cambridge: Cambridge University Press, 2012). For the Congolese in Belgium see Zana Aziza Etambala, *In het land van de Banoko: De geschiedenis van de Kongolese/Zaïrese aanwezigheid in België van 1885 tot heden* (Louvain: Catholic University, 1993, 85–86 for the available statistics), and Anne Cornet, "Les Congolais en Belgique au XIXe et XXe siècles," in *Histoire des étrangers et de l'immigration en Belgique de la préhistoire à nos jours*, ed. Anne Morelli (Brussels: Couleurs Livre, 2004, 375–400).

Belgium's military history during World War II begins with the eighteen-day-long campaign of 1940. The account by Major L. F. Ellis, *The War in France and Flanders, 1939–1940* (London: HMSO, 1954), is easily accessible, but like nearly all military histories it tends to justify after the fact what happened and to be celebratory rather than critical. The history of the whole campaign is still bitterly disputed, as even the merest glance at the Wikipedia articles "Campagne des dix-huit jours" and "Achtiendaagse veldtocht" (The Eighteen Day Campaign) shows. Among the more recent accounts are Henry Barnard, *Panorama d'une défaite* (Gembloux: Duculot, 1984), Bruno Comer, *Mei '40: De onbegrijpelijke nederlaag* (Louvain: Davidsfonds, 2010), and Karl-Heinz Frieser, *Le mythe de la guerre-éclair: La campagne de l'Ouest de 1940* (Paris: Belin, 2003, 130–41). For the air war in Belgium, Richard Overy, *The Bombing War: Europe 1939–1945* (London: Allen Lane, 2013), is a superb study. One can consult further references to the bombardments of every town or city on the Internet via Google. On the campaign of 1944 and the Battle of the Scheldt, see Stephen Badsey, *Arnhem 1944: Operation "Market Garden"* (London: Praeger, 2003), a recent overview by a military historian that is perhaps still not critical enough yet; Cornelius Ryan, *A Bridge Too Far* (New York: Simon and Schuster, 1974), another book about the same battle, is the best-known account and was turned into a movie. The Battle of the Scheldt is also recounted in C. P. Stacey, *Official History of the Canadian Army in the Second World War: The Victory Campaign* (Ottawa: Queen's Printer, 1960), again an uncritical celebratory account. Overall that battle claimed the lives of between twenty-three and twenty-five thousand combatants and an unknown but considerable number of civilians. However, relatively few of these deaths and casualties occurred on the eastern fringes of the advance to Woensdrecht, including in Gooreind.

There exist many histories about the Flemish movement. For its earlier history see Shephard B. Clough, *A History of the Flemish Movement in Belgium: A Study in Nationalism* (New York: Richard R. Smith, 1930), and its social context at the time, Carl J. Strikwerda, *A House Divided: Catholics, Socialists, and Flemish Nationalists in Nineteenth-Century Belgium* (Lanham, MD: Rowman and Littlefield, 1997); for the period considered here, Lode Wils gives a short overview in his *Histoire des nations belges* (Ottignies: Quorum, 1996). Those who read Dutch should consult his three-volume *Honderd Jaar Vlaamse Beweging* (Louvain: Davidsfonds, 1977, 1985, 1989), especially the last volume because it includes a discussion of the war and the following repression. For Wils (3:247–53) the repression was carried out according to a well-thought-out communist plan, but others dispute this. Theo Hermans, Louis Vos, and Lode Wils, *The Flemish Movement: A Documentary History, 1780–1990* (London: Athlone, 1992), complements the other titles cited. For the liberation, Wilfried Pauwels, *De Bevrijdingsdagen van 1944: Honderd dagen tussen anarchie en burgeroorlog* (Antwerp, 1994), documents an atmosphere "between anarchy and civil war."

With regard to Flemish literature the only relevant book in English is the superficial Vernon Mallison, *Modern Belgian Literature, 1830–1960* (London: Heinemann, 1966), although René Felix Lissens wrote a short introduction in English as "Belgian Literature: Flemish" in *Encyclopaedia Britannica* (1971 ed., 3:416–18). His major work is the textbook *De Vlaamse letterkunde van 1780 tot heden* (4th ed., Amsterdam: Elsevier, 1967). For more detail the standard reference work is Frank Baur, Anton Van Duinkerken, J. Van Mierlo, and G. S. Overdiep, *Geschiedenis van de letterkunde der Nederlanden*, 7 volumes (s-Hertogenbosch: Malmberg, 1939), where one finds entries for all the writers mentioned here including Hendrik Conscience, Guido Gezelle, and Ernest Van der Hallen.

Within this literature a fictional biography of the celebrated Flemish writer Hugo Claus entitled *The Sorrow of Belgium* (New York: Pantheon, 1990) is particularly relevant to *Through the Day, through the Night* because it covers almost the same time span and is based in part on the author's experience of his own youth. But *Sorrow* is a fictional creation: it deliberately selects and blends or separates events from different places or times and redistributes these over several personages as required by its esthetic endeavors. Hence its very literary excellence prevents it from illustrating history in a reliable way.

Concerning Dirk Vansina one should consult Joos Florquin, *Ten Huize van . . . Ontmoetingen met Vlaamse kunstenaars en andere vooraanstaanden* (At the home of . . . Interviews with Flemish artists and other prominent people), volume 4 (Louvain: Davidsfonds, 1968, 68–122), and the TV documentary of which this is a partial transcription. The documentary also reproduces some of his main paintings. His major writings have been reprinted in his six-volume *Scheppend Werk en Essays* (Creative works and essays) (Gooreind/Antwerp: De zilverberk, 1961–65). See also his *Verschaeve Getuigt* (Bruges: De zeemeeuw [1953], 702–805) for the period of World War II. For a complete bibliography, consult *Digitale bibliotheek voor de Nederlandse letteren* (DBNL). Rajesh Heynickx, *Pelgrimkunst: Religie en Moderniteit, 1910–1940* (Louvain: KADOC/expo 2, 2008), sketches Dirk Vansina's place in the Pelgrim movement.

An excellent illustrated introduction to the city of Antwerp is A. de Belder, *Illustrated Antwerp* (Edegem: Kunstuitgeverij, 1990s). There are several editions, and the commentaries are in several languages; for images of sites described in this biography see pages 82–83, 100, 104, 105, 111–18, and H. Cock city plan (1657) inside the back cover of the 4th edition; today the standard history is Gustaaf Asaert et al., *Het grote geschiedenisboek van Antwerpen* (The great history book of Antwerp) (Antwerp: Stadsarchief Antwerpen, 2010), written under supervision of the city's archival service; an illustrated brochure edited by W. Cassiers, *Antwerp, Flanders, Belgium* (Antwerp: City of Antwerp, 1977), is especially useful for its illustration of the city plan by Virgilius Bononiensis (1565) showing the houses that stood here just before the new house (1567) was built, but it also contains photographs of the commodity exchanges and the façade of St. Carolus mentioned in the biography; about the entrance to the house in the Markgravestraat see Bart Goovaerts, Ovide Maas, Jan Prenen, and Jules Van Paesschen, *Antwerpse Poortjes* (Antwerp: De Vlijt, 1980, 96–98). For a history of Antwerp's

Jewish population read Lieven Saerens, *Vreemdelingen in een wereldstad: Een geschiedenis van Antwerpen en zijn joodse bevolking (1880–1944)* (Foreigners in a metropolis: A history of Antwerp and its Jewish population) (Tielt: Lannoo, 2000), and his "De jodenvervolging in België in cijfers" (Figures about the persecution of Jews in Belgium), *Bijdragen tot de eigentijdse geschiedenis* 17 (2006): 200–225.

Concerning Bruges, the photo album edited by Georges Sion, *Bruges* (Brussels: Ch. Dessart, 1957), is useful while Barbara G. Lane, *Hans Memling: Master Painter in Fifteenth-Century Bruges* (London: Harvey Miller, 2009), evokes the city in its heyday. The relevant history of St. Andrews Abbey is recorded in Christian Papeians de Morchoven, *Met Abt Theodore Neve van uitdaging tot uitdaging* (With Abbot Théodore Neve from challenge to challenge) (Tielt: St. Andries Ziekenhuis, 2002). The same author also published *1942–1992: 50 ans* (n.p., n.d. [1992]), a commemorative brochure about the travels of the school during the war years. It is at St. Andrews that Dom Pierre-Célestin Lou Tseng-Tsiang wrote *Souvenirs et pensées* (Bruges: Desclée, 1945; published in English as *Ways of Confucius and of Christ* [London: Burns Oates, 1948]) and gave me a copy of these reminiscences signed in Chinese and French. As to Louvain and its university, Valentin Denis, *Catholic University of Louvain, 1425–1958* (Louvain: Catholic University of Louvain, 1958), and Mark Derez, *Leuven: Town and Gown* (Louvain: Louvain University Press, 2001), are excellent introductions to the university, the first written at the time when I studied there and the second after the major transformations of the late twentieth century. With regard to Gooreind, I recommend Marcel Leunen's *Wuustwezel-Gooreind: Historisch Fotoboek* (Hoogstraten: Kempische boekhandel, 1984).

For an account of my career after I arrived at Tervuren see my *Living with Africa* (Madison: University of Wisconsin Press, 1994); about my first fieldwork see "History in the Field," in *Anthropologists in the Field*, ed. G. Jongmans and P. C. W. Gutkind (Amsterdam: Assen, Van Gorcum, 1967, 102–15); and about one of my later spells of fieldwork see "Venture into Tio Country," in *In Pursuit of History: Fieldwork in Africa*, ed. Carolyn Keyes Adenaike and Jan Vansina (Portsmouth, NH: Heinemann, 1996, 113–26); my activities at the University of Wisconsin are on record in an interview with Mrs. Laura Smail as part of her UW Madison Oral History Project, 1986–1987.

Index

German military occupation, 108, 114, 123–24, 148, 171, 227; administration, 95–96, 108, 116, 148–49; deportations, 117–18, 134, 140–42; requisitions, 111, 118, 120, 122, 142, 143, 172, 187

German soldiers, 95, 108–9, 120, 137–38, 148, 170–76; casualties, 173, 174, 175, 176, 200; at the front, 150, 167, 171–72; resisting Nazism, 108, 139–40

German-speaking cantons, 7

Germany, 22; and Belgium's food supply, 99; bombed by allies, 135, 147; forced labor in, 117–18, 127, 134, 137–38, 191–92; holds Leopold III captive, 145, 147; invades its neighbors, 83, 91, 104, 107; power peaks, ebbs, 117–18, 136, 140, 185; war effort, 127, 140, 200

Gestapo, 109, 145, 194

Geyl, Peter (historian), 219

Gezelle, Guido (poet), 87

Ghent, 142, 143, 144, 145, 210; state university at, 40, 139, 220, 223

Gooreind, 75, 79, 107, 133, 141, 201; and aunt Maria's villa, 89, 149, 170; bombarded, 168–69, 180–84; described, 72–75, 127–19; and fieldwork, 227–28; isolated, 151; liberated, 166, 173–79; poaching, 130; vigilantes, 175, 176–78; wartime looters, 149–50, 170, 175, 181. See also Meezennestje; Wiezelo

Grammens, Florimond (protester), 55–56

Great Britain, 83, 120, 228. See also British armed forces; England

Great Depression, 6, 8, 9, 10, 18, 32, 54–55

Greek (ancient language), 102, 106, 188, 191, 193, 194

Guicciardini, Lodovico (historian), 9

Gutt Decrees, 179, 191

Hans (German officer), 108–9, 139

Haydn, Franz Josef (composer), 14

Hedin, Sven (writer), 148

Heine, Heinrich (poet), 194

Herman, Claudine (Jan's wife), 230

Hiroshima, Japan, 193

historians, 9, 206, 209–10, 219, 220, 221, 230

Historical Circle, 210, 212–14, 216, 217–18, 222, 223

historical method, 210–11, 220, 231

history, 28–29, 48; different subjects of, 29, 195, 210, 215–16, 219, 231; oral, 221, 230–31; studying, 209–12, 214–22

Hitler, Adolf, 55, 57–58, 80, 149, 198; conspiracy against, 140, 148

Holland. See Netherlands

Homer (epic poet), 191

hunger, 98–99, 104–5, 109–12, 131

Huysmans, Camille (statesman), 4

ideology, 174–75, 229

intolerance, 175

IRSAC (Institute for Scientific Research in Central Africa), 223, 226, 230

Italian language, 118, 221

Italians, 77, 133

Italy, 22, 136, 188

Izegem, 119–23, 126, 135, 142–43

Japan, 58, 102

Jerome, Jerome K. (writer), 103

Jesuits, Society of Jesus, 41, 49, 51, 166–67

Jewish religion, 8

Jews, 6, 145, 194; persecution of, 57, 117, 134, 140–42, 192–93

Vansina, Guido (Jan's brother), 21, 25; liberation, 170, 175; at play, 15, 39, 115, 131–32; at school, 105, 113, 114, 135, 183, 185–86; trip to/from school, 81–82, 119, 123–25, 129

Vansina, Hortense (Torty; Jan's aunt), 18, 25, 26, 192

Vansina, Maria Magdalena (Marleen; Jan's sister), 21, 25, 109, 148, 167, 170, 183

Vansina, Maria-Theresa (Mietje; Jan's sister), 13, 21, 25, 129, 137–38

Vansina, Pharaildis (Veerle; Jan's sister), 21, 25, 26, 111, 183

Vansina, Suzanna (Suze; Jan's sister), 25, 92, 183, 212

Vansina, Victor Désiré (Bonpapa; Jan's grandfather), 25, 26, 31, 36

Verdi, Giuseppe (composer), 216

Verellen, Joseph (Joe; Jan's uncle), 25, 27, 32, 133–34, 200

Verellen, Suzanne (painter; Jan's mother), 4, 22–23, 25; as mother, passim

Verellen, Théophile (Theo; Jan's uncle), 17, 25, 27, 178

Verellen, Théophile (Jan's grandfather), 25, 26–27

Verne, Jules (writer), 148

Versailles, Treaty of, 106

Vlasov, Andrey (Russian general), 149

Vlasov forces, 149–50, 167, 168, 170, 178, 197

V missiles, 132, 180–82, 185, 186, 187, 189

VNV (Vlaams National Verbond; a Flemish party), 7, 55

Volk (journal), 139

Voltaire (writer), 194

Von Rundstedt, Gerd (field marshal), 182

Waffen SS, 138, 141, 171–72; alumnus, 107–8, 118; general, 148; informer, 202

Wagner, Richard (composer), 77

Wallony, 8, 84, 99, 199; language, 8

Weber, Anita (Jan's godmother), 25, 27, 200

welfare state, 18, 179, 198

West Flanders (province), 84, 88, 139, 177

West Flemish dialect, 85–86, 87

White Brigade (Resistance organization), 176

White Fathers (missionary order), 36, 49

Wiezelo (house and estate): damaged by V-2, 183–84, 186; exceptional events, 158, 161–62, 163–64, 172; liberation of, 176, 194–95, 197; in peace time, 75–85, 218; return to, 125, 132–33, 141–42; wartime daily life, 144, 146–53, 170

Willemot, Jacques (Jan's schoolmate), 122–23

Willy (German soldier; batman for Hans), 108–9

Wils, Lode (student; later professor), 212

Wisconsin, University of, 230

Woensdrecht, Netherlands: battle for, 166

World War I, 23–24, 80–81, 92, 119; history of, 48, 148. *See also* Yser Tower

Wuustwezel, 26–27, 72, 74, 80, 83, 129

Xavier, Dom (teacher), 122–23

Yokohama, Japan, 58

Ypres, 121

Yser Tower: dynamited, 202; pilgrimage to it, 24, 115, 139, 177